Gaviotas

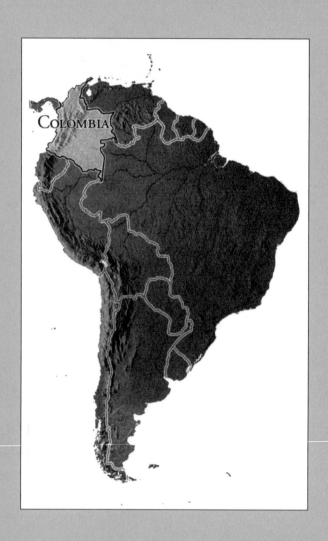

A VILLAGE

TO REINVENT

THE WORLD

Alan Weisman

CHELSEA GREEN PUBLISHING COMPANY
WHITE RIVER JUNCTION, VERMONT

Portions of this book have appeared earlier, in different form, in the *Los Angeles Times Magazine*, the *New York Times Magazine*, and on National Public Radio.

Lines quoted from *El Saucelito*, copyright © 1995 by Jorge Eliécer Landaeta, are by permission of the composer.

Permission by the authors for use of material from the following is gratefully acknowledged:

Bernal, Gonzalo L. *La Sonrisa de Los Bosques*. Obra inédita, 1995.

Zethelius, Magnus, and Michael J. Balick. "Modern Medicine and Shamanistic Ritual: A Case of Positive Synergistic Response in the Treatment of a Snakebite." *Journal of Ethnopharmacology* (Lausanne) 5 (1982): 181–85.

Calligraphy by Bonnie Spiegel.
Text design by Ann Aspell.

Printed in the United States of America on recycled paper.
First printing, this edition, July 2008
10 9 8 7 6 5 4 3 2 1   08 09 10 11 12 13 14 15

The Library of Congress cataloged the original edition with the following Cataloging-in-Publication data:

Weisman, Alan.
    Gaviotas : a village to reinvent the world / Alan Weisman.
        p.   cm.
    Includes bibliographical references.
    ISBN paper 1-890132-28-4 cloth 0-930031-95-4
    [10th Anniversary Edition ISBN: 978-1-60358-056-4]
    1. Columbia—Environmental conditions.   2. Human ecology—Columbia.
    3. Columbia—Description and travel.   I. Title.
    GE160.C7W45   1998
        338.9861—dc21   97-48395

Our Commitment to Green Publishing
Chelsea Green sees publishing as a tool for cultural change and ecological stewardship. We strive to align our book manufacturing practices with our editorial mission and to reduce the impact of our business enterprise on the environment. We print our books and catalogs on chlorine-free recycled paper, using soy-based inks whenever possible. Chelsea Green in a member of the Green Press Initiative (www.greenpressinitiative.org), a nonprofit coalition of publishers, manufacturers, and authors working to protect the world's endangered forests and conserve natural resources. *Gaviotas* was printed on 60# Joy White, a 30-percent postconsumer-waste recycled paper supplied by Thomson-Shore.

Chelsea Green Publishing Company
PO Box 428
White River Junction, Vermont 05001
(802) 295-6300
www.chelseagreen.com

for Beckie

Contents

~

~

In 1994, a team of independent journalists was funded by the Corporation for Public Broadcasting, the Ford Foundation, and the John D. and Catherine T. MacArthur Foundation to produce a series for National Public Radio, which would document humanity's search for solutions to the greatest environmental and social problems threatening the world. One member of that team, Alan Weisman, took his quest to an unlikely spot: war-torn, drug-ravaged Colombia. Twenty-five years earlier, he'd been told, a group of Colombian visionaries had decided that if they could fashion self-sustaining peace and prosperity in the most difficult place on earth, it could be done anywhere. Then they had set out to try.

For sixteen hours, Weisman traveled by jeep past roadblocks manned by army, paramilitary, and guerrilla forces to reach what those visionaries had forged in the harshest setting they could find: the extraordinary community called Gaviotas.

~

Support for this book was generously provided by:

The Burr Oak Fund of the Tides Foundation
Kristie Graham of the Amazon Foundation
The Macon and Regina Cowles Foundation
The Westport Fund
Homelands Research Group

OVERTURE

Years before Belisario Betancur became president of Colombia and proceeded to startle his fractured nation by risking a fledgling peace with Marxist insurgents who, at that time, ruled more territory than the government; before he filled the halls of state with works and recitals by Colombia's greatest painters, musicians, and poets, and invited the public in to see and hear; before he had the wizards from Gaviotas outfit his presidential mansion with their artful devices that coaxed the sun's bountiful energy through Bogotá's dour skies—long before all that, he heard a story that he never forgot.

It was the kind of thing, he explained thirty-five years later to Paolo Lugari, the founder of Gaviotas, that jerked everything else into perspective. "It still does. Listen."

"I will, *Presidente*. And then I have one for you."

This was March, 1996: They were in Betancur's northeast Bogotá apartment, sipping chamomile tea. Outside, a cold rain pummeled the 9,000-foot skirts of the Andes. The roundfaced, silver-haired former president, now 73, sat in his leather chair, wrapped in a thick blue sweater and red wool scarf. Lugari, bearded and burly, evidently oblivious to the chill, wore his usual lightweight tropical suit. In his large hands, the china cup and saucer looked frail as eggshells.

"The year," Betancur began, "was 1962. I was a senator then."

A senator: Back then, the very notion had seemed miraculous. Belisario Betancur was one of twenty-three children born to nearly illiterate peasants. When he was eight, he'd found an illustrated volume of ancient history on his village school's bookshelves. Intrigued by the quaint pictures, he learned to read it. Soon he was scouring encyclopedias for more about the Peloponnesian wars, about Carthage, about the Roman emperor Hadrian, about anything Greek or Latin.

At his teachers' urging, his stunned parents eventually sent him to a seminary in Medellín, where he spent the next five years conversing solely in those classical languages—even on weekends, when Spanish was permitted, because he was routinely being punished for some breach of cloister decorum. His masters ultimately concluded that, however brilliant, he was too impetuous for the priesthood; the rector who expelled him arranged for his placement in a university. There he studied law and architecture, but ended up a journalist.

It was not an auspicious time. In 1948, Colombia had fallen into a horrific civil war; over the following decade, an epoch known today simply as *La Violencia*, hundreds of thousands died. There was little of comfort to report, but during those years Betancur discovered something of which most of his compatriots seemed barely aware: To the east of the Andes, which bisect Colombia like a great diagonal sash, lay half the country, virtually uninhabited save for scattered bands of nomadic Indians.

The destiny that led him over the mountains took the form of a pilot who invited him to see exotic places seldom mentioned in the press. He went, and then returned as often as he could. What he found was Colombia's Amazon forest and, further north, *los llanos:* a vast savanna, drained by the Río Orinoco, that stretched clear to Venezuela. Both were so huge and untouched that Betancur was soon convinced that, one way or another, the key to his country's future was there. Years later, in 1982, as a candidate for the presidency he would fly over the *llanos*, spot the community known as Gaviotas, land, and conclude that he'd been correct.

It took the first and only military dictatorship in Colombia's history, which began in 1953 and lasted four years, to finally snuff *La Violencia*. In its aftermath, Belisario Betancur, one of a scarred generation of survivors who had dreamed for an anguished decade of setting their country straight, entered politics.

"So there I was, a senator in a country trying to resurrect itself, having dinner in Washington, D.C., one evening at the Inter-American Development Bank."

At that time, 1962, the Inter-American Development Bank was a fresh offshoot of the World Bank, which had burst like a huge weed from the rubble of World War II and begun to broadcast its seed everywhere. The directors of the new multinational monetary funds were charged with cobbling together a battle-fatigued planet, by moving money into distant places where frequently the locals never before knew they needed it. Sooner or later, Betancur realized, these could include regions such as Colombia's Amazon forest and the *llanos*. His country needed development, he believed, but who would decide what kind? On his last visit to the *llanos*, a Guahibo Indian shaman had peered into a cloud of ritual tobacco smoke and correctly divined the precise arrival time of Betancur's overdue bush pilot. What did bankers at international lending institutions understand about such people and places?

That night over dinner, Bank president Felipe Herrera, a Chilean economist, told of a tiny Indian village on the high altiplano near Bolivia's Lake Titicaca, where he'd gone on a feasibility study for a proposed hydroelectric dam. Upon completing the site visit, his team realized they hadn't used their entire travel budget. Since the village lacked everything, they assembled the local chiefs and explained that they had some money left. In gratitude for hospitality and assistance, they'd like to give it to the community as a gift. "What project would you like us to fund here in the name of the Bank?"

The Indian elders excused themselves and went off to discuss this offer. In just five minutes they returned. "We know what we want to do with the money."

"Excellent. Whatever you want."

"We need new musical instruments for our band."

"Maybe," replied the Bank team spokesman, "you didn't understand. What you need are improvements like electricity. Running water. Sewers. Telephone and telegraph."

But the Indians had understood perfectly. "In our village," the eldest explained, "everyone plays a musical instrument. On Sundays after mass, we all gather for *la retreta*, a concert in the church patio. First we make music together. After that, we can talk about problems in our community and how to resolve them. But our instruments are old and falling apart. Without music, so will we."

"And now," said Betancur, offering Lugari a silver dish of fried plantain slices, "let's hear yours."

"*Señor Presidente*," said Paolo Lugari, shaking his head, "you're not going to believe this."

Juanita Eslava hadn't known whether to believe it either. The forest was enchanted, she'd essentially been told, by no less than Dr. Gustavo Yepes, director of the faculty of music at Bogotá's prestigious Universidad de Los Andes. Juanita, grand-niece of a famous Colombian poet-composer, Luis Carlos González, and granddaughter of a popular singer, was training at Los Andes to become a lyric soprano. She was on her way to a rehearsal for a 1996 European choral tour when she saw a notice on the bulletin board stating that a place called Gaviotas was looking for a few daring musicians.

"I don't know," she said, when Dr. Yepes explained that it was to help start an orchestra in a tropical paradise. "I'd have to miss Europe."

"Europe will be there next year. It's not going anywhere. When are you going to get another chance to do anything like this?"

That was hard to say, because Juanita had never heard of anything like this. For that matter, who had? Seriously, *los llanos?* Europe seemed closer.

She had at least heard of Gaviotas. That was unavoidable for any Los Andes student, because the road that climbed through the skirts of the cordillera toward campus wound right past the office that the Gaviotans maintained in Bogotá. It was impossible to miss: an assemblage of brick and glass cubes, surrounded by colorful bursts of oddly graceful machinery rising above the eucalyptus. These included several windmills mounted on glossy yellow masts of varying heights, whose blades were not the typical narrow triangles but aluminum skewers, tipped with paddles shaped like cross-sections of an airplane wing. Alongside these stood a collection of bright red canisters of different sizes, assorted pipes and levers painted royal blue, and a bank of silvery rectangular surfaces. To passersby, the impression was technological yet pleasing and sculptural, like the promise of an appealing future waiting just beyond the encroaching urban bedlam below.

Engineering students at Los Andes knew about the silver rectangles, which had begun to appear around Bogotá during the mid-1980s, while Belisario Betancur was president of Colombia. Conventional wisdom said that solar panels wouldn't work in a city that was overcast more than half the year, but Gaviotas had come up with coatings for their models that gathered the energy even of diffused sunlight. Besides the presidential palace where Betancur formerly resided, their solar collectors were now atop condominiums, apartments, convents, orphanages, and on the brick edifices of Bogotá's 30,000-inhabitant Ciudad Tunal, the largest public housing complex in the world to use only solar energy to heat its water. The nation's biggest hospital had not only converted their water heating system but had also installed solar "kettles" designed by Gaviotas technicians, capable of wresting temperatures sufficiently scalding from Bogotá's scant sunshine to purify water for drinking and sterilizing instruments.

But Dr. Yepes didn't even mention solar collectors to Juanita. He was talking about music. And trees.

Gaviotas wasn't just some high-tech research firm designing newfangled gadgetry, he assured her. Gaviotas was actually a place—a wondrous place in the middle of the practically treeless tropical plains of eastern Colombia, except it was now in the middle of a forest. An incredible forest of its own making. And now Gaviotas would soon be making music as well.

"Música llanera?" Juanita asked. If so, what did this have to do with her? The traditional country music of the Colombian *llanos*, with its harps, four-string *cuatros*, and twangy *bandolas,* was a long way from the Italian arias she sang.

Overture

Gustavo Yepes explained. One evening a few years earlier, he had been introduced to Paolo Lugari after a choral performance of Bach's sacred music. That night, Lugari had pumped Yepes's hand and boomed in his basso profundo, "Tell me, Gustavo: How do composers' creative passions, which are born of random, nonlineal emotion, deal with the structure of music, which is mathematical and therefore lineal?"

It was a strange, remarkable question, but Yepes had heard that this was a strange, remarkable person. "I imagine it's much the same," he replied, "as what happens at Gaviotas. People who dare to build a utopia use the same materials available to anyone, but they find surprising ways to combine them. That's exactly what composers do with the twelve tones of the scale. Like you, they're dreamers. In a dream you aren't limited by what is assumed to be permissible or possible."

"Gaviotas isn't a utopia," Lugari interrupted. "Utopia literally means 'no place'. In Greek, the prefix 'u' signifies no. We call Gaviotas a *topia*, because it's real. We've moved from fantasy to reality. From *utopia* to *topia*. Someday you need to come see it."

That day, Yepes told Juanita, had unexpectedly arrived in October, 1995. Paolo Lugari had called to say that some German journalists had chartered a plane out to the *llanos* to see Gaviotas. There was an extra seat, and he especially wanted Yepes to accompany them.

"Why me?"

"You'll see."

What he saw—and heard—belied Lugari's protestations; to Yepes, Gaviotas seemed not only proof that utopia on earth was possible, but that it was arguably more practical than what currently passed for conventional society. Five hundred kilometers away from his increasingly frightening city, Yepes had found himself in a tranquil village, shaded by the gallery forest of a tributary of the Río Orinoco and filled with flowers and dazzling, melodious birds. The people of Gaviotas collectively exuded a quality so novel that Yepes wasn't sure he'd seen it before—but once encountered, it was unmistakable: They were happy. They rose before dawn, worked hard and productively, ate simply but well, and were peaceful. The machinery they used dominated neither them nor their landscape: it was mostly of their own design or adaptation, and mostly quiet. "May I retire here?" Yepes had asked Lugari, after watching children playing on a see-saw that was also a water pump, which tapped kid power to replenish a reservoir for the Gaviotas school.

"Don't wait to retire. Come sooner. You're exactly what we need."

They were walking down a red dirt path that led past a grove of mango trees, an outdoor basketball court, polygonal modular living quarters, and a community meeting hall with a parabolic swoosh of roof, contoured from shining metal to deflect the equatorial heat. Just south of town, the path widened into a road, with a tall pine forest rising on either side. They exchanged waves with six men and a woman dressed in caps, colored neckerchiefs, tee shirts and tool belts, who rode past on thick-tired bicycles. Lugari steered Yepes into the forest as he began to explain. "For the past quarter-century—ever since Gaviotas began," he said, "I've been studying the history and literature of utopic communities."

"I thought you said this wasn't utopia."

"Neither were any of those other places. They were attempts." Lately, Lugari had been reading about the famed experiment of 17th century Paraguay, when Jesuit priests arrived to evangelize the New World. Until then, colonizers throughout most of the Americas had considered indigenous peoples either expendable savages or exploitable slaves. But the Jesuits who ended up far from the trade routes, in the distant region where the borders of Brazil, Argentina, and Paraguay now converge, saw the resident Guaraní Indians as a kind of *tabula rasa:* untainted *Homo sapiens* in their natural state, potentially perfectable. Being missionaries, of course, meant having certain preconceptions about perfection, and these Jesuits soon set about replacing the natives' language, god, and means of sustenance. Their missions, aptly named "reductions," were consummately paternalistic but nevertheless benevolent, self-sustaining communities that prospered for more than a century, until the Jesuits fell into disfavor with Spain and Portugal and were expelled from colonial Latin America.

Paolo Lugari was not interested in evangelism—Gaviotas didn't even have a church. What enthralled him about that historic Paraguayan experiment was the music. "Everyone," he told Yepes, "was taught to sing or to play a musical instrument. Music was the loom that wove the community together. Music was in school, at meals, even at work: Musicians accompanied laborers right into the corn and *yerba mate* fields. They'd take turns, some playing, some harvesting. It was a society that lived in constant harmony—literally. It's what we intend to do, right here in this forest. That's why I asked you to come."

But Yepes wasn't listening—or rather, he *was* listening, but not to Lugari's words. He stopped and held up his palm. "Quiet for a moment," he said. Silence, except for the drumming of a woodpecker and a rustle of breeze in the pine boughs. Then: "Keep talking," he whispered.

"What?"

"Did you hear it?"

"Hear what?"

"Talk."

They were in a thicket enclosed by forty-foot Caribbean pines and a leafy tangle of decidous trees and shrubs. Even at tropical noon, the forest air was delectably cool. Amidst the profuse foliage of the understory, it was hard to discern that the pines were actually growing in evenly spaced rows. Thirteen years earlier, this woodland—now the biggest reforestation in Colombia, more extensive than all the government's forestry projects combined—had been mainly empty savanna, devoid of anything but low, nutrient-poor grasses. By 1995, the number of trees Gaviotas had planted was approaching six million.

Yepes was taut with excitement. "Paolo. Just say something. Anything."

Shrugging, Lugari started to explain how, when he and the early Gaviotans first came out here from Bogotá in the early 1970s, they had tested hundreds of crops, but nothing thrived in these highly acidic, leached tropical soils, whose natural levels of aluminum bordered on toxicity. Then, a Venezuelan agronomist seated next to him at a conference in Caracas suggested trying tropical pine seedlings obtainable from Honduras.

The trees grew. The Gaviotans debated among themselves whether it was wise to cultivate an exotic species. Some argued that the issue was political, not environmental, since the same pines also grow in Panama, which was once part of Colombia. Had the United States not stolen the isthmus and installed a puppet government in order to dig their canal, these would still be native Colombian trees.

The controversy, along with the matter of what to do with pines since they weren't edible, was settled by a succession of random occurrences, the kind of unpredictability that the Gaviotans had come to love as they tinkered with improving reality. Who could have guessed that Caribbean pines would prove to be sterile in the *llanos*, posing no invasive competition to local flora? Who could have known that their bark resin, a natural protection against the tropics' array of hungry insects, would flow so copiously here that it could be harvested like maple syrup—more, really, like milk from cows, because tapping the thick amber liquid seemed to stimulate production without hurting the trees? Or that here pines would mature nearly a decade faster than forestry texts predicted? Or that until a few months ago, Colombia had been importing millions of dollars' worth of resins annually for paint, varnishes, turpentine, cosmetics, perfume, medicines, rosin for violin bows—until, that is, Gaviotas inaugurated a forest products industry that involved leaving trees in place, not mowing them down?

"And, most wonderful of all, Gustavo, who could've—"

"Wait."

"I was just getting to the most important part."

"Did you say violin bows?"

"Right. That's one of the reasons I wanted you to come here. But not just rosin. We realize that when we have to thin the forest we can use the surplus wood to start a musical instrument factory, and—"

"Do you have any idea how perfect a place this is to make music?"

"Exactly. That's why we wanted you to come here."

"No," Yepes insisted. "You don't know what I mean. Listen."

So Lugari did, and that's how, three months later, Juanita Eslava found herself not in Paris, but in the middle of a forest under a full moon at midnight, in what most of her compatriots considered the middle of nowhere, preparing to sing an aria by Respighi. According to what Yepes had told her, yet another random stroke of luck had inexplicably imbued the Gaviotas forest with magnificent acoustics. "We were standing in the woods," he recalled, "and suddenly I realized that I could hear distant voices, as though they were amplified. I clapped my hands. Then I yelled. I made Lugari whisper. There's incredible resonance in there. We don't know why. Maybe the forest canopy vibrates. Maybe it has to do with the physics of unorganized spaces. Paolo wants an engineering student to write a thesis about the effect. I just want to build a bandshell to focus it."

Like a pair of excited kids, right there Yepes and Lugari had started planning an outdoor amphitheater-in-the-pines, with some form of retractable roof for rain, like the one on the Gaviotas administration building. "Probably need to encase the whole thing in mosquito netting, too," Paolo had added. They envisioned concerts of classical symphonic instruments and also a resident *llanos* orchestra, comprised of entire sections of Orinocan *cuatros*, *bandolas*, and harps made from renewable Gaviotas pine.

Juanita wasn't so sure about these ambitious schemes: Rather than forty *bandolas* plucking Beethoven's Sixth, she preferred the idea of combining violins and cellos with folk instruments to create a sonorous new mix of timbres. She was impressed, though, at how serious the Gaviotans were about their musical future. During the 1970s and 1980s, when many of its famous technological innovations were being developed, Gaviotas entered agreements with Juanita's university and several others to bring scientists and engineers here to research their graduate theses. Under the most recent accord with the Universidad de Los Andes, however, Gaviotas had requested painters, sculptors, and musicians. "There's no such thing as sustainable technology or economic development without sustainable *human* development to match," Lugari had told her when she arrived. "Over twenty-five years, Gaviotas has accomplished much, but we need so much more."

Juanita's mission was to establish a classical music program in the Gaviotas school: the first step toward building an orchestra. She was also to get to know, and record, resident Gaviotas *llanero* musicians. And, finally, she was to tramp around the woods until she found the spot where her voice projected best, so the Gaviotans would know exactly where to build their theater—if, in fact, this business about its alleged acoustic properties were true, and not simply Yepes' imagination having been seduced by the spell of the place.

So there stood Juanita Eslava, her long dark braid glinting under lemony moonlight in a forest that her distinguished professor swore had magical properties, ready to find out. For some reason, she had delayed this moment until now. Maybe it was because Gaviotas had turned out to be such an island of blessed tranquility in the midst of her roiling nation. During her first month here she had learned as much as she taught, from listening to *músicos* who could echo the gallop of horses on their *bandolas* and the sweetness of the trade winds on their harps. Every morning, she awakened to a delirious symphony of nesting tanagers, cotingas, and oropendolas outside her window. The Gaviotas schoolchildren she taught to sing were the healthiest humans she'd ever met, happy and unafraid as the monkeys cavorting overhead. Everything was so sublime that maybe she was scared to spoil it by putting something she suspected was implausible to the test. But on this night of a full moon, a group of her new friends finally had dragged her off to sing in the trees. They spaced themselves at varying intervals: ten, twenty, fifty meters away from where she stood. Then they waited.

Juanita struck a tuning fork against her knee, hummed the pitch, closed her eyes, and inhaled deeply. All around her was lush, fragrant evidence of an indisputable miracle, a portent that the place might very well be enchanted. In the moist, sheltered understory of the Gaviotas pines, an indigenous tropical forest was regenerating. A team of frankly amazed biologists from Colombia's Universidad Nacional already had recorded 240 species probably not seen in the *llanos* for millennia, except in fragments of terrain alongside the streambeds. Another unpredicted stroke of fortune had rendered moot the concerns about introducing a monoculture of *Pinus caribaea* into the *llanos*—it was as though the savanna's thin green ribbons of riparian forest had overflowed their banks and were spreading across the plain.

Some trees, such as the slender purple jacaranda Juanita was leaning against, already towered higher than the pines. With thousands more hectares available for planting, the Gaviotans had decided to let the native species slowly choke out the *Pinus caribaea* over decades and return the *llanos* to what many ecologists believe was their primeval state: an extension of the Amazon. Already, the populations of deer, anteaters, and capybaras were growing.

When she opened her eyes and began to sing, an angel's aria from Respighi's *Lauda Per La Natività Del Signore* emerged.

> *Pastor, voice che vegghiate*
>   Shepherds, you who watch over
> *sovra la greggia en quista regione;*
>   your flocks as they graze here;
> *i vostr'occhi levate*
>   lift your eyes

By the calendar, this was just before the March equinox, but Juanita had spontaneously decided to invoke Respighi's celebration of the Nativity. Her voice, hesitant at first, began to billow through the forest like a silver mist, expanding as it swirled from tree to tree. Nightjars, owls, and lapwings joined in, cooing in plaintive dissonance that resolved into haunting harmony as she continued:

ch'io son l'Agnol de l'eternal magione.
> for I am the Angel of the eternal mansion.

Ambasciaria ve fone
> I bring you a message,

ed a voie vangelizzo gaudio fino
> and news of pure joy

Celestial music rose into the branches. The forest canopy gathered and magnified her clear tones, showering them down around her friends like gently falling pine needles. When she finally ended, they gathered around and embraced her, several nearly in tears. Luisa Fernanda Ospina, the bacteriologist in charge of quality control at the resin factory, stared in awe at the trees rising moonward. "This place is proof that God exists," she declared.

Gonzalo Bernal nodded. During the 1970s and early 1980s, he had directed the Gaviotas school; now, in the 1990s, he was community coordinator. "Now I know for certain that we live in paradise," he whispered. "We can hear angels."

"So now Gaviotas will become a choir of angels. When I went there the first time," Belisario Betancur reminded Lugari, "I merely saw prophets. But I have a weakness for prophets like you who preach in a desert. It was like I'd heard a message. I immediately wanted to convert all Colombia into a Gaviotas."

He leaned back and gazed at a pair of framed sketches above the gray velvet couch opposite his chair, landscapes of the Colombian Andes. "Imagine," he sighed, "if this were all Gaviotas."

The sketches, signed and dedicated to him, were studies for oil paintings by the Colombian master Alejandro Obregón, one of which now hung at the United Nations, the other in the Vatican. Over the bookcases were more works by Colombian artists, gifts for the presidential palace that were later removed by Betancur's successors. The most famous of these, a painting that became the symbol of his presidency, occupied the space over the mantel. It showed a plump white dove with a fig leaf in its beak, portrayed by the renowned Colombian painter and sculptor Fernando Botero.

In the 1980s, its likeness had been borne aloft by exhilarated throngs marching through the streets of Bogotá, Cali, Medellín, and Cartagena. Botero's dove adorned posters for concerts, banners for theater festivals, children's clothing; it became the embodiment of the hope engendered by Betancur's peace initiative. While in office, he had proposed an unprecedented amnesty to thousands of Marxist rebels who had formed guerrilla armies a few years after the 1957 truce that ended *La Violencia* supposedly brought peace to the land. This new uprising, which had killed many thousands, was still underway and was now the longest-running armed insurgency in Latin America. Under Betancur's plan, guerrillas could trade their weapons for the chance to create their own political party and battle legitimately within the civil system. The largest insurgent army agreed to participate, and, in 1984, scores of guerrilla soldiers laid down their arms. Subsequently, the party they and their sympathizers founded, the Patriotic Union, won elections nationwide for mayoral seats, town councils, and for Colombia's national congress.

Within a decade, the majority of those victors—some two thousand, plus two presidential candidates—had been assassinated. The perpetrators, who sometimes issued gleeful press releases, were right-wing paramilitary death squads.

The guerrillas, of course, retaliated. Soon, their attacks and ambushes surpassed former levels, as did kidnappings for enormous ransoms to finance their subversion. In a monstrous reprise of *La Violencia*, massacres of civilians whose villages were supposedly aligned with one side or the other became almost weekly events. These atrocities were blamed on both right-wing paramilitaries and left-wing guerrillas, but rarely solved. Both extremes had become so deeply corrupted by the bounty of the narcotics trade that, after a while, it barely seemed to matter which was which.

Faster even than the Gaviotas pines, cattle ranches of drug lords had advanced across the *llanos,* in cadence with the march of coca cultivation in the Amazonian provinces to the south. By 1996, the current presidential administration was so tainted by a scandal involving drug spoils that several prominent members of the president's party and campaign staff—including Fernando Botero's own son, the ex-Minister of Defense—were in jail. When a massive Botero sculpture of the peace dove was wrecked by a bomb that killed dozens in a Medellín park one Sunday, the grieving artist directed that it be left in pieces as a monument to the shambles his country had become.

Approaching the end of the century, Colombians frequently had come to wonder aloud whether their nation could actually survive. "These things take time," Belisario Betancur would remind people. "I never thought that the process we began would be completed during just one presidential term. Over three or four decades, peace was systematically destroyed in our country. It was like an *ovillo*, a ball of wool that had been unraveling for years. To pretend that one could roll it up in four years would have been an illusion. But we had to start somewhere."

During Betancur's time in office, the *llanos* became the haven to which he retreated so often that his own party leaders complained, because there were no votes out there. "Not many votes, but so much Colombia," he'd reply. The boundless landscape restored his spirit, and Gaviotas—where his plane often touched down unannounced—was where he could happily stand in line for meals like everyone else, surrounded by people who, since they lived contentedly without any government themselves, embraced him and not his office.

"The history you are writing reads like poetry," Betancur said, as he and Lugari embraced at the door. "And now you're setting it to music, too."

"You will join us for the first concert," Lugari replied. "It will be in your honor."

The old ex-president beamed at the thought of returning to Gaviotas.

Overture

"This," he once told Gabriel García Márquez when he sent him there, "is what Colombia needs."

"This," he'd repeated, as President Felipe González of Spain and his family boarded a plane bound for Gaviotas' grass airstrip, "is what Latin America needs."

And when a group from the Club of Rome visited Gaviotas in 1984, Club founder Aurelio Peccei declared to Betancur, "This is what the world needs."

Part I ∼ THE SAVANNA

WHAT IMPRESSED AURELIO PECCEI AS EXACTLY WHAT THE WORLD needs lies about sixteen hours east of Bogotá by jeep—depending on mud and the number of army or guerrilla roadblocks encountered—along a frequently impassable road that at first zigzags and loops high above the city, then plunges over the Andes and vanishes, often quite literally, in the direction of the distant Río Orinoco, Colombia's border with Venezuela. When he made the trip there in 1984, flying in a Twin-Otter turboprop, Peccei was already near death. Nevertheless, he endured bruising currents over the cordillera and hot thermals uncoiling from the *llanos* in order to see Gaviotas. So crumpled from arthritis that he had to be massaged for an hour each morning just to rise from bed, he insisted on mounting a bicycle and joining the Gaviotans as they pedaled between home, dining hall, hydroponic farm, and factory. Ten days later, Aurelio Peccei died, content that he'd been blessed with a glimpse of authentic hope—hope in the face of events, already swiftly unfolding, that had been predicted more than a decade earlier by a famous report commissioned by his Club of Rome.

That 1972 document, titled *The Limits to Growth*, had warned the Club's international membership of industrialists, scientists, and statesmen that unless global society somehow learned collective restraint in matters both consumptive and reproductive, within a century human beings would overwhelm the boundaries of viable existence. The report to the Club of Rome was lauded by environmentalists but scorned in various other circles as Malthusian panic-mongering. By 1992, the report's authors acknowledged in their book *Beyond the Limits* that they had erred— but not as detractors had claimed. Their subsequent calculations and computer projections indicated that, during the two intervening decades, civilization had already surged beyond sustainable limits. Especially in the tropics, there was evidence that warnings of impending scarcity had actually stimulated a rush to grab the goods while they still existed. Dur-

The Savanna

ing the final decade of the twentieth century, consequences of this heedlessness were already apparent worldwide, as entire agrarian societies forsook exhausted lands and converged on cities that had begun to spread like stains across the continents.

At mid-century in Colombia—that tormented nation where, improbably, Peccei found such promise—two-thirds of the population had been rural, a third urban. By the 1990s, as in much of the world, those percentages had reversed. The once-graceful capital of Bogotá now heaved against the Andes like surf pounding a cliff, grinding the very bedrock as new arrivals carved footholds on the mountainsides. As the population of Ciudad Bolívar—a colonization on Bogotá's southern flank, optimistically named for the liberator of South America—approached two million, it was declared the world's biggest squatters' settlement.

The fact that similar cauldrons around São Paulo, Lima, Mexico City, Manila, Lagos, *et al.,* claimed the same bleak distinction didn't diminish the implications for Bogotá. The onslaught was even inching up Guadalupe and Monserrat, two guardian peaks that hover above the city. The alabaster Virgin atop Guadalupe now appeared to lift her palms in despair over the rising menace below—violence was fast becoming Bogotá's leading cause of death—and the funicular that ferried pilgrims down from Monserrat's chapel shrine was often greeted by gangs of muggers. After repeated assaults in front of their nearby Bogotá office, the Gaviotans regretfully bolted the gate and posted armed guards (albeit carrying blank ammunition).

In 1966, the year when Paolo Lugari first crossed the mountains and saw the *llanos,* Bogotá's profile was not yet clogged with skyscrapers erected to launder extraordinary sums of narcodollars. Nor were its streets already glutted with so many cheap imported cars that people routinely did business via cellular phones from taxis paralyzed in mid-traffic—an unintended consequence of Colombia's embrace in later years of global free trade. Before the onset of the New World Order's open markets, and of the lurid blemish on Colombia's underside known as narco-economics, Bogotá was known as the "Athens of the Americas" for its twenty-seven universities and thirty-three museums. It was a dignified, provincial city of vine-covered, gabled brick houses, in neighborhoods lined with ficus trees and wax laurels, stretched along the bronze backdrop of the Andes.

Immediately to the west lay six hundred square miles of fertile alluvium deposited by the Río Bogotá and its tributaries, planted in vegetables and dairy pastures. Today, nearly anywhere that this green plateau has not been subsumed by the city, the cultivation of food crops has given way to thousands of plastic-domed greenhouses that rise from the soil like giant blisters. Inside, ornamental flowers are propagated in chemical troughs, misted repeatedly with pesticides to ensure market perfection, then whisked daily from the nearby metropolitan airport to the United States, Europe, and Japan. The Río Bogotá, now a chemical sump from which swimmers have been warned away until the year 2015, winds like a venomous snake through villages of flower workers who sometimes go weeks without running water, so deeply has the aquifer been drawn down to slake the demands of export-quality chrysanthemums and roses.

Only by night, from the vantage of the road that climbs above the remaining red-tiled roofs of the weakened old heart of the city, with Monserrat's pale church shimmering overhead through the gathering fog, is Bogotá still beautiful. Its lights extend a hundred times the breadth of the original settlement, forming a galaxy that fills the altiplano. The plastic bubble greenhouses, beneath which lies buried some of the richest soil in Latin America, glow like indistinct nebulae racing away from the western edge of the known universe.

In the opposite direction, across the moutains, lie the dark *llanos*, a little less empty than when Gaviotas materialized there a quarter-century back, but still with room and possiblities to spare. It was those possibilities that Paolo Lugari had in mind when he made his surprising decision to go there.

Paolo Lugari was born in 1944. He grew up in Popayán, a serene colonial city near the snowy Puracé volcano in southwestern Colombia. He was schooled at home by his father, an Italian attorney, engineer, and geographer who had visited Colombia and found the tropics so irresistible that he married the great-great-granddaughter of a nineteenth-century Colombian president and stayed. Popayán, with its white facades, scrolled ironwork, and cobbled streets, was the ancestral home to several founding families of Colombia, and chairs at the Lugari table were often filled with statesmen and diplomats. As a boy, Paolo was encouraged to absorb their dinnertime discourse; often, Mariano Lugari would interrupt the conversation to satisfy himself that his young son understood what he had just heard.

One evening when Paolo was in his mid-teens, the guests included Father Louis Lebret, a former French naval captain who had taken Dominican orders and now taught in Paris at the Institute of Economics and Humanism. Colombia's military dictatorship had passed, and Lebret had been invited personally by Mariano Lugari to give a seminar on how the new civil government might humanely plan the country's future. While his polyglot father translated, Paolo concentrated as the tall priest posed a Socratic question to the others over the dessert brandy. "How," he asked, "can we define development?"

"By the amount of paved kilometers of road per citizen," suggested Lugari's uncle, Tomás Castrillón, then Colombia's Minister of Public Works. Lebret shook his head.

"By the number of hospital beds per capita," said the Minister of Health. No again.

Equally incorrect, evidently, were the treasury minister, who offered a ratio of gross domestic product divided by the population, and a director of Banco de la República, who proposed calculating the percentage of total wealth that a given society had invested in infrastructure.

"Development," Lebret finally told them, "means making people happy." Eyes snapped toward him. "Before you spend your money on roads and factories, you should first be sure that those are what your citizens really need."

Paolo Lugari passed his university exams without ever attending class. A fervid orator, he won competitions at Bogotá's Universidad Nacional, and, on the strength of a single inspired interview, he netted a scholarship from the United Nations Food and Agriculture Organization to study development in the Far East. In the Philippines, he toured public health projects, sewage treatment centers, and the International Rice Research Institute. Abandoning his official itinerary, he lingered at a generating plant powered by sugar cane wastes, then spent weeks at a water buffalo ranch, fascinated by the versatility of a beast that could serve as draft horse, tractor, beef steer, milk cow, ox—even as a boat, he marveled, as he splashed across rivers buffalo-back.

Returning to Colombia in 1965, he was hired by a commission planning the future of the Chocó, a tropical wilderness that stretched half the length of Colombia's Pacific coast. Someday, he was told, a new canal linking the Atlantic and Pacific would slice across the upper Chocó. The region's deep rivers made a sea-level channel possible, a clear advantage over the chronically sluggish locks of the Panama Canal, two hundred miles to the north.

The Chocó, today one of the world's largest remaining intact virgin rain forests, was inhabited by several jungle-dwelling Indian communities and by descendants of escaped black slaves who had lived there for centuries. Was it necessarily a good idea, Lugari began to wonder, to hack a supertanker canal through their homeland? Exactly which people would be made happy by such development? And what would happen to the jungle itself, when water from two separate seas started flowing right through it? "What will be more important to Colombia one day," he asked in his report, "connecting the oceans or maintaining our biology?"

He had been employed there for some months when his Uncle Tomás, the Minister of Public Works, invited him along on an inspection flight of the nearly barren lands on the other side of the country: the Orinocan *llanos*. Paolo didn't love to fly, but he was curious. Almost the only project

The Savanna

the government had ever undertaken out there had begun ten years earlier, in the mid-1950s, when the military authority briefly attempted to scrape a highway across the huge prairie. At that time, the idea was to open the eastern portion of Colombia to refugees fleeing *La Violencia*, the decade of civil slaughter waged between the nation's two major political parties, the Liberals and the Conservatives. Many survivors, driven from their farms in the rich coffee highlands to the west, had wandered into the roadless *llanos*.

They didn't find much. Unlike the fertile Andean slopes, covered with wildflowers and coffee blossoms, nearly nothing grew on the sun-baked plains except a few low-nutrient grasses and a squat tree called the *chaparro*, which had evolved a multilayered bark to withstand the scorch of prairie fires. The palm groves along the streambeds seethed with malaria-bearing mosquitos. During the eight-month rainy season, anyplace the sod was broken turned to caramel-colored muck.

That included the vaunted new trans-Orinoquia highway, now forsaken, which Paolo Lugari's uncle didn't intend to resurrect. "Not much to look at," he apologized as they winged over the vast, bleached grassland.

But young Lugari didn't even hear him. He was thoroughly rapt, mesmerized by the immense savanna that, from the window of the DC-3, became wonderfully confused with the horizon. *Los llanos*, spiderwebbed with languid tributaries and measuring four times the size of Holland, added up to the most striking landscape he had ever seen. He started having visions.

~

THE ROAD FROM BOGOTÁ TODAY TUNNELS OUT OF THE FOG OF THE Andes, straightens as it passes through the sweltering agricultural center of Villavicencio at the base of the cordillera's eastern slope, and drops into the *llanos*, flat as a leaden green sea. The narrow asphalt strip continues a while longer past irrigated stands of African oil palms and cashew trees, scraggly pastures that hold gaunt Brahma steers and their attendant cattle egrets, an occasional white-washed roadhouse with orange ceramic shingles, and several small airstrips. More than thirty years after Paolo Lugari set out in an open-topped green Land Rover with his younger brother Patricio to find something he'd spotted months earlier from the air, DC-3s still chug through the pale *llanos* skies, transporting cargo and gasoline to jungle outposts and, as the local *llaneros* well know, frequently returning stuffed with coca flour.

The road passes country estates belonging to barons of Colombia's fabulous emerald mines and to some of its newly, flagrantly rich: the *narcotraficantes*. At a long iron bridge, it crosses the Río Meta, the second largest tributary of the Orinoco, which wallows like a huge silver slug in rice fields that have replaced the gallery forest along its banks. A few kilometers farther, just before the crumbling pavement gives out entirely, the trans-Orinoquia trail briefly climbs the Alto de Menegua, a strangely beautiful, karst-like formation of miniature red hills. A bronze totem near the highest point of these eroded outcroppings marks the geographical center of Colombia. Like all pilgrims who follow this rutted track into the *llanos*, the Lugaris paused here when they passed this spot. Although barely a hundred feet above the plain, the rise nevertheless affords an arresting view of interminable savanna and sky.

From this vantage, a jutting monolith on the southwest horizon, silhouetted against orange-tinged nimbus clouds, appears to be a spur of the Andes. In fact, it is at least ten times more ancient. The 80-mile-long, 6,000-foot Serranía de la Macarena is an island remnant of the Precambrian Guyanan Shield—the westernmost fragment of a geologic formation more than a half-billion years old. The Macarena was Colombia's first biological reserve, created in the aftermath of a 1942 Pan-American conference on flora and fauna, during which international scientists gathered in Washington, D.C., despite World War II and strategized about how to preserve it. What compelled them was a series of field surveys, beginning with a Shell Oil exploration in the late 1930s, which suggested that this uplift, rising from the grassy *llanos* and girdled by thick rain forests, might be the most biologically complex spot on earth.

The Savanna

Geologists speculate that South America may have been the first continental chunk to break away from the original planetary land mass, separating from what is now Africa nearly ninety million years ago; thus, its flora and fauna are among the most primitive on earth. Later, North America followed, and where they joined, barely five million years ago, an intense biological interchange commenced. That juncture is present-day Colombia, whose topography couldn't have been more ideal for this encounter had a museum curator designed it. Because it straddles the equator, Colombia has no seasonal temperature changes, but its elevation extremes provide a range of constant climates from torrid to tundra—an optimal ecological niche for practically any form of life that arrived.

As a result, Colombia has more bird species than any other country; it is second in plants and amphibians, and third in reptiles. Only Brazil possibly surpasses it in total number of species, but Brazil is seven times bigger. With more rivers than all of Africa, including the Amazon and the Orinoco; with coastlines on both the Pacific and the Caribbean; and with three distinct Andean ranges separated by broad, rich valleys, Colombia's extravagant natural blessings would be the envy of the world, if the world weren't otherwise distracted by the country's sorrows.

Like a terrestrial Noah's ark, during geologic epochs when much of the rest of South America was inundated, Colombia's Serranía de la Macarena was truly an island, providing a natural refuge for species seeking high ground. Over time, it became a repository of Andean, Amazonian, Guyanan, and Orinocan flora and fauna—thus, the most intense concentration of life forms and endemic species within a country that has, per area, the world's most diverse ecosystem. The Macarena is home to tapirs, spectacled bears, white-lipped and collared peccaries, giant armadillos, ocelots, margays, kinkajous, agoutis, giant otters, fresh-water dolphins, various crocodiles, eight different primates, more than half the world's orchids, and more than a quarter of Colombia's 1,780 known species of birds.

As the Lugaris bumped their way past the Macarena, they saw animals of all kinds spilling through the *llanos*. Brocket deer were running in open savanna. Big, bushy palm anteaters waddled across their path. A puma emerged from a stand of moriche palms along a hidden river, flashed over a stretch of open plain, then disappeared into another streamside thicket. At times they had to slalom the Land Rover around armadillos, porcupines, and several varieties of land tortoises. While awaiting the departure of a pontoon ferry on the Río Meta—there were no bridges then—they witnessed a parade of huge rodents rooting along the muddy river bank, assorted as if by orders of magnitude: two hare-sized pacas, an agouti as large as a spaniel, and a family of three capybaras, the adults easily a hundred pounds apiece. Roseate spoonbills and scarlet ibises flapped up and down the watercourses, caimans napped atop a swamped dugout canoe, and Paolo—mosquito-crazed and sufficiently impressed by a baby anaconda slithering practically underfoot—finally convinced the drunken boatman to let him pilot the ferry.

The ferryman, who had arrived in the *llanos* just after *La Violencia*, offered to sell them bloody hunks of fresh-killed tapir and a young jaguar's spotted hide. The Lugaris declined and forged on through the extended dusk, splashing through the reflections of clouds in puddles the size of ponds, the Land Rover's paint obliterated by a crust of reddish grime and its windshield nearly opaque with insect splatter. The flattened world around them drained down to four or five basic tones—the rust of the soil, the rain-leached chartreuse of the grasslands, the purplish locust hordes that whirled across the *llanos* like small cyclones, and the dull gold talons of the crested caracaras that chased them. The occasional glint of some primary color—a red shirt hanging on a branch outside an Indian's thatch maloca, or the flapping blue poncho of a straw-hatted *llanero* trotting by on a bay colt—was a shock.

Before *La Violencia*, the human inhabitants in this part of the *llanos* were mainly nomadic Guahibo Indians, who, like the *tigres*, roamed the capillary streams of Orinoquia, spear-fishing, hunting with curare darts, and gathering wild cassava and oil-bearing palm beans. Then the government began encouraging refugees to migrate across the mountains, tempting them out to the distant eastern territories with slogans such as

"Land without people for people without land." As white settlers trickled in, pushing cattle in front of their horses, the Guahibo gradually found themselves surrounded by fences.

The concept of land ownership baffled them; for a while, they simply ignored the shiny new strands of wire, slipping through with bows and arrows to harvest some of the docile, meaty ruminants that had arrived along with their new neighbors. About the same time that Paolo Lugari was gamely patching tires every fifty kilometers or so on his first overland journey into Orinoquia, a group of white colonists in Arauca territory to the north wearied of this. They invited sixty or so Indians to a banquet, seated them before a spread of pit-roasted steer and various tubers, and then pulled pistols and machetes. After they burned the bodies, they resumed eating. It had no more occurred to them that killing Indians was wrong than it had occurred to the Guahibo that fenced cattle were somebody's property.

The Guahibo family with whom the Lugaris shared catfish and cassava when the Land Rover mired near their thatched maloca had learned to leave other people's cows alone, but they were now living like cornered animals. The fences across their ancestral hunting routes had a similar disorienting effect on these cyclical nomads as the draining of ancient wetlands has on migratory birds. With their habitat wrapped ever more tightly in barbed wire, the Guahibo's supply of game dwindled. With few agricultural skills and no tradition of dwelling in permanent settlements, malnutrition and parasitic infection seeped into their lives. No longer able to range freely under the limitless *llano* sky, they were down to two bad choices: either build their malocas near streams and sustain the resident malarial mosquitos, or live out on the barren savanna itself, where soils were useless and water had to be carried over long distances.

"You don't have a well?" Paolo asked their hosts. The shallow, hand-dug pit they showed him was as fetid as the water they hauled up from the streams in their woven moriche pails. No doctor ever came here; the closest school was hours to the south, at a convent run by some ancient nuns whom they apparently found frightening. So remote and inaccessible

were these steamy eastern plains from highland cities such as Bogotá and
Medellín, or from Cali's prosperous western valley, that the government
had little influence or control over the lives of either the Indians or the
colonists. Instead, what gradually filled the vacuum of authority and
brought a modicum of order was *la guerrilla.*

Although the Lugari brothers drove halfway across the *llanos* that first trip
without meeting guerrilla soldiers, travelers over the same route in later
years would often encounter their roadblocks and checkpoints. On occasion, the rebels would briefly occupy the bamboo-shaded commons at
Gaviotas. *La guerrilla* was born of the outrage of peasant soldiers during
La Violencia, who gradually realized that they were fodder to the aristo-
crats of the warring political parties, the Liberals and the Conservatives,
whose platforms barely differed. By the late 1950s, it had become evident
from ten years of mayhem and three hundred thousand dead that those
rulers had merely divided the power and the land among themselves.
With the example of the Cuban revolution flaming on the horizon,
Colombia's tiny Communist Party suddenly found it had an angry, willing constituency, and the FARC—the *Fuerzas Armadas Revolucionarias de
Colombia*—were born.

The children—and now, the grandchildren—of these original *guerrilleros* have been up in arms ever since, and other guerrilla armies have
risen among Colombia's poor urban and indigenous populations. The
FARC, mainly rural, total about ten thousand troops throughout the
country. Their central command is based near—and its eastern division's
headquarters is actually within—the Parque Nacional Serranía de la
Macarena.

There are strategic reasons for this. The practically impenetrable Macarena is only a day's mechanized march to Bogotá. Besides its astounding
array of species, it has also become the refuge of thousands of human
beings. Like the colonists of the adjacent *llanos*, they arrived here fleeing
sanctioned terror, looking for free land, or actually sent by agrarian reform

officials who found it easier to invade a defenseless nature reserve than risk expropriating a few hundred hectares from wealthy landowners. Methodically, they slashed and burned their way in. As the thin tropical soils gave out after one or two harvests, the settlers continued on, farther and deeper, into the Macarena.

The same, in fact, is true for most of Colombia's other thirty-two national parks, and with the government either unable or unwilling to stop squatters, guerrillas take advantage by providing a kind of *de facto* government by jungle law. Besides securing the sympathy of the locals, the FARC have sought support among international environmentalists by claiming stewardship of these fabulous natural treasures. Fisheries biologists do credit them for the first successful ban on seining rivers such as the Río Meta during breeding season (their enforcement technique, reputedly persuasive, entails wrapping poachers in their gill nets and tossing them in the river).

The FARC's environmental credentials weaken, however, when they defend colonists who clear away forest to grow a tall, pale green shrub known as *Erythroxylum coca*. Because there are no paved roads, they rationalized, crops such as cassava or bananas would rot by the time they reached the market. Coca, however, can be processed into flour and packed out by mule with no spoilage. There is truth to this assertion, but also to the government's accusation that the FARC have grown wealthy and tainted from skimming 10 percent from every shipment of coca produced in areas they control.

To the south of the *llanos*, Colombia's jungles are now planted in hundreds of thousands of hectares of illicit crops. An eradication program financed by the United States has left tropical forests here defiled with dead scabs where planes have sprayed defoliants, and pocked with charred holes where coca-growing campesinos continue to advance. The very grace of geography that placed Colombia at the intersection of the Americas and made it so biologically splendid, also made it the perfect transhipment point for narcotic flora found only here and in neighboring Peru and Bolivia.

In the *llanos*, however, soils are so poor that not even coca grows. Paolo Lugari was never tempted by the lush resources of places such as the Serranía de la Macarena. The vision gestating in his subconscious, as the Land Rover crawled across Colombia's huge eastern plain, involved his hunch that someday the world would become so crowded that humans would have to learn to live in the planet's least desirable areas.

But where? His time in the Chocó had persuaded him that rain forests and excess people were a foolish mix. But in South America alone, there were 250 million hectares of fairly empty, well-drained savannas like these. One day, he was convinced, they would be the only place to put bursting human populations. The *llanos* were a perfect setting, he decided, to design an ideal civilization for the planet's fastest-filling region: the tropics.

Later he would tell everyone: "They always put social experiments in the easiest, most fertile places. We wanted the hardest place. We figured if we could do it here, we could do it anywhere."

No one disagreed, but in the beginning no one held out much hope, either. The *llanos* were good for little except inspiring *llanero* musicians to write songs about how mournful life gets on an endless prairie. Biologists believed that about thirty thousand years earlier, this had been part of an unbroken rain forest clear to the Amazon. Then, climate change had created new patterns in the predominant winds. The trade winds that formed over the seas to the northeast blew inland, fanning lightning strikes into fires that burned the jungle faster than woodlands could regenerate. A few trees, including *Curatella americana*—the lonely, fire-hardened *chaparro*, a recurring leitmotif in regional folklore—were able to adapt. Other plants evolved different strategies, such as forming bulbs under the thin, tropical soil. For the most part, the jungle receded south, where the winds diffused, leaving short-cycle, nutrient-poor savanna grasses in its stead. "It's just a big wet desert out there," Lugari was told repeatedly.

"The only deserts," he would one day reply, "are deserts of the imagination. Gaviotas is an oasis of imagination."

~

The Savanna

Two days and four mangled tires after setting forth, the Lugaris had traveled 180 miles. Through much of the trip there had been no road, only the occasional mud-baked grooves left by some intrepid vehicle that had preceded them. They oriented themselves by aerial photographs and by the sun; in the afternoon, when the sun dissolved away in the gray sky, they followed the leafy horizon that bordered the Río Meta, taking care not to approach too closely, lest they submerge the Land Rover in a palm bog and become mosquito food.

At one point, a two-ton truck with a canvas-topped bed roared up behind them out of nowhere, bucking over the savanna and leaving a comet's tail of red dust as it bounced by. By the time the grit settled, the vehicle was out of sight. Two hours later, they encountered it again, tilted against its own crushed fender, one wheel splayed out from a broken axle. A little way farther they met the driver, a Venezuelan who had run out of luck exactly halfway between Bogotá and the border. He was drinking *aguardiente* with a ferry boatman on the last stream they had to cross, at an outpost called Puerto Arimena.

Arimena had been key to the military government's plan for the *llanos*. Surveyors had observed that at the height of the April-through-December rainy season, the land just to the south would inundate all the way to where the watershed tips away from the Orinoco and flows to the Amazon. The government's plan, one that would assuredly open the *llanos*, was to build a canal right here to connect South America's two great northern rivers. Puerto Arimena would then truly become a port, on an inland waterway linking the Caribbean to the south Atlantic.

The trans-Orinoquia highway was begun to service this grand scheme. When the Lugari brothers rattled into Arimena, following the faint traces of the road that might have been, they found six shacks housing a few forlorn campesinos who, for a brief salaried moment in their lives, had worked for the highway department. One day, their foreman had left and never returned; all that remained was a rusting sign announcing the soon-to-be-completed thoroughfare and a tattered Colombian flag, drooping motionless from a bamboo rod.

The Lugaris forded the river on a platform of cecropia logs, nailed to pontoons made of leaking 55-gallon oil drums. Water puddled around their tires and feet; the ferry operator, pointing out the piranhas nosing the edge of the the raft, suggested that they ride inside their vehicle. Once back on land, they entered ten million empty hectares known as *el Vichada*, a territory that went all the way to the Orinoco itself. Vichada was the goal that Paolo Lugari had set out to reach. Nothing looked particularly different, but he was increasingly buoyant as they drove through bevies of hundreds of squealing southern lapwings—the noisy crested plover that *llaneros* domesticate as watchdogs. There were no more white settlers here, just four-sided Guahibo malocas made of moriche palm thatch.

They plunged on, rustling up clouds of birdlife as they ploughed through the grasslands, unchanging but for the ornithological extravaganza: flocks of crested and yellow-headed caracaras, whistling herons, gray hawks, ornate hawk-eagles, savanna vultures, hook-billed kites, and yellow-black cacique birds. An escort of fork-tailed flycatchers, trailing their long, elegantly plumed scissors, flew alongside the Land Rover, inches from their faces. The sun made a cameo afternoon appearance, gilding every feather and wide blade of grass. In the distance, a low, dark shape took form, and Paolo headed for it. The land was so flat that they watched it grow for nearly an hour before they finally arrived.

It turned out to be a pair of long concrete sheds, filled with weeds. These were former warehouses of the road construction camp, now abandoned, that would have been the midway point of the misbegotten trans-*llanos* highway.

"We're here," Paolo told his brother.

"Where?" replied Patricio, removing his driving goggles and scraping caked dust from his face. Perplexed, he looked around. At twenty-three, Patricio Lugari was already making his living in imports. Their sister was attending law school. What was Paolo planning to do in this desolation?

The Savanna

Only a few sections of the warehouses' laminated roofs were still intact. Except for a small thicket of gallery forest, they were surrounded by grass in every direction.

Paolo, meanwhile, was exuberant. These buildings formed the shell casing for the idea that had bored through his mind ever since he had seen them from the air—they could be the first structures in a community expressly designed to thrive in these inhospitable, supposedly uninhabitable lands.

He would later regret this part of the vision, since his first big lesson was that it is often cheaper to build new buildings than to retrofit old ones. But for now, he was home. As they leaned against the Land Rover, tasting the sharp prairie wind, three small yellow-billed terns flew over. "There must be water beyond those trees," Paolo said.

"Why?"

He pointed at the birds. "River gulls. They're *gaviotas.*"

~

JORGE ZAPP, HEAD OF THE MECHANICAL ENGINEERING DEPARTMENT at the Universidad de Los Andes in Bogotá, leaned back at his desk one Friday afternoon with a sketchpad, idly doodling his own approach to the assignment he'd just given his Basic Design class. His students, who had matriculated only that week, had to draw up working plans for an amusement park by Monday. "But Dr. Zapp," one young woman had protested. "You haven't taught us how to design yet."

"Good. I haven't contaminated your minds yet with my version of the right way. You're free to think up anything." He lifted a hand to nip further objections. "That, incidentally, is the most important lesson you'll ever learn from me."

Distressed stares. To ease their anxiety, he took them through an exercise. "How does a blender work?" he asked.

After fielding a few explanations of how armatures spin between electromagnetic poles, he stopped them. "No. Tell me what *really* makes it work." By the end of the hour, the chalkboards were filled with diagrams that went successively backwards from the appliance's whirling blades to the hydroelectric origins of the energy passing through its copper coils, then to a computation of the kilocalories of sunlight needed to make water condense and flow through the hydro-dam's turbines, then to light-emitting fusion reactions on the sun's surface, and, finally, all the way to the genesis of the sun and stars themselves.

Having watched Jorge's compact form bounce from one end of creation to another for the past hour, the students now looked exhausted. "Think big picture," he advised as he dismissed them. "The more you try to grasp, the more possibilities you have."

It was a rare Bogotá day, so clear that the white mantle of the Nevado de Ruiz volcano two hundred miles to the west gleamed through Jorge's window. He was heading out to stroll the grassy hills of the campus when someone knocked on his door. Even as he swiveled to answer, a tall, thick-chested young man wearing a light khaki jacket strode into his office. Extending a large hand as he sank into a chair, in lieu of introduction the visitor demanded, "True or false: Can you build a turbine efficient enough to generate electricity from a stream with just a one-meter drop?"

The stranger propped his elbows on Jorge's desk, rested his bearded chin on his hands and leaned forward. He looked vaguely familiar, and despite his audacious entrance there was something ingratiating about him. Zapp rubbed his moustache and thought a moment. "True," he replied. "Why?"

Then he recognized him. This was the Paolo Lugari he'd seen in the newspapers, the *enfant terrible* son of a brilliant Italian, who, upon returning from the Philippines, had launched a highly visible national campaign to save Guatavita, a picturesque old village near Bogotá, from being drowned by a federal dam project. The power company had purchased all the houses and even the church, and was already pouring cement when Lugari entered the scene. In fiery orations that journalists fawned over, he declared that buying part of public history doesn't convey the right to destroy it. Finally, the government backed off; Guatavita was now a popular tourist area.

More recently, Jorge had heard, Lugari was over in the Chocó. Then some U.S. Peace Corps volunteers who'd dined at his house told him that one loquacious, extraordinarily energetic Paolo Lugari had led their orientation tour around Colombia.

"Come to Gaviotas and I'll show you," Lugari told Zapp. "Tomorrow."

"Come to where?"

"You'll see."

Next, Paolo went to find Dr. Sven Zethelius, a soil chemist at the Universidad Nacional's agricultural chemistry department. Zethelius was the son of a Swedish ambassador who, like Lugari's own father, refused to return to the relative boredom of Europe after a diplomatic stint here. Not long after his first trip to the *llanos*, Lugari learned that Zethelius was delivering a series of stirring lectures on the tropics. On evenings whenever the Universidad Nacional wasn't closed by strikes, he had gone to listen.

The tall, graying, goateed chemist had been sent as a boy to Scotland to study, but he'd promptly returned. "Europe is too organized," he told students. "I want a place where there's no fossilized order. I want a jungle. There are a hundred times more resources here than in developed countries, where everything's been exploited. Colombia can be whatever you want it to be."

Lugari sensed a fellow dreamer. One afternoon he cornered Zethelius in his chemistry lab and explained that he'd staked a claim to the abandoned highway camp he'd found in the *llanos*, along with ten-thousand surrounding hectares. "What can I plant out there?" he asked.

"Probably nothing." The soils around Gaviotas, Zethelius informed him, were only about two centimeters thick, quite acidic, and often high in aluminum toxicity. "Frankly, they're the worst in Colombia. A desert."

"So I'm told. Look," Paolo urged, "the only deserts are those of the imagination. Think of them as different soils. Someday," he continued,

"Colombians who want land will have three choices: burn down the Amazon, do the same to the Chocó, or move to the *llanos*. If we could figure out ways for people to exist in the most resource-starved region in the country, they can live anywhere."

"We?"

"Think of it. Gaviotas could be a living laboratory, a chance to plan our own tropical civilization from the ground up, instead of depending on models and technology developed for northern climates, like the Peace Corps wants to teach everybody."

Zethelius began to nod.

"Something for the Third World, by the Third World," Paolo persisted. "You know what I mean: When we import solutions from the United States or Europe we also import their problems."

Zethelius glanced outside. Protesters were again massing in the concrete plaza. Megaphones, then tear gas would follow. He pulled the window shut. "True enough," he replied. "In Colombia, we've got enough problems as is."

~

THE TROUBLE WITH ORINOCAN TRIBUTARIES, JORGE ZAPP NOTED, looking around Gaviotas for the first time, is that they're so flat they barely seem to flow. But that also meant that the water table had to be relatively near the surface.

"The entire savanna is floating on a sea of good fresh water," Lugari assured him. "We just need to find a way to get at it."

"Okay," Zapp told him. "I think for starters we can build a one kilowatt micro-turbine that will work here. Maybe even two of them. For now, that's enough power for lights, at least during the rainy season. If this stream gets too low in summer, we'll need a diesel generator."

"I'd like to avoid hauling fuel out here, if possible. That's why I came to see you. I think we should try to be self-sufficient."

"That's a goal we should work toward. But it's not possible yet. And,

The Savanna

in any event, we're going to need a lot more than a kilowatt if we want to pump water for drinking and irrigation. Though I've got some ideas about pumps. . . ."

Jorge's voice faded beneath a torrent of thoughts. He was standing, absently swatting mosquitos, at the edge of Caño Urimica, the stream that ran through the property Paolo had claimed in the name of the foundation he'd recently formed, *El Centro Las Gaviotas*. Under the tropical canopy of the gallery forest, the air was cool as mint. Above him, a two-toed sloth slumbered beneath a jacaranda branch. A family of capuchin monkeys swung by. The matter of pumps would be a perfect project to unload on his students. The turbine, too. In fact, there were so many possibilities. His lab director, Luis Robles, was going to be crazy about this. Then he remembered. Damn: Where was Luis when he needed him?

From 1967 to 1970, Paolo Lugari had slipped off to the *llanos* whenever his Chocó duties permitted. He went through a dozen tires, frequently got lost, waited days for ferries, collected medicinal herbs with a Guahibo Indian shaman, camped on river sandbars amid the rustling of mating turtles, stayed in a friendly *llanero's* hut when the chiggers drove him nuts, and contracted malaria twice. ("Light cases. Just a lot of chills," he assured Zapp. "I bring repellent now.")

Traveling alone one night, he was trapped in the Andes by a landslide on the road between Bogotá and Villavicencio, and slept for three nights in his car until the pass re-opened. Usually, though, he invited someone along whose impressions would be instructive. Once it was a botanist. On another occasion, he brought an architect. Sometimes his brother returned with him, the Rover filled with food for the Guahibo families they'd met, and once Paolo convinced his lawyer sister, María, to make the bone-battering journey. Another time, he took Clemente Garavito, a Colombian astronomer whose great-uncle had a crater on the moon named for him. Garavito declared the Gaviotas skies to be the most transparent in all Colombia, ideal for an observatory.

"It rains for eight months here every year," Lugari reminded him.
"Maybe make that a weather station."

Next came Carlos Lehmann Valencia, an expert on Andean condors from Popayán, who urged him to start a natural history museum. Lehmann introduced him to Antonio Olivares, an elderly Franciscan monk who taught ornithology at the Universidad Nacional and who had authored the most indispensable text on birds of the Serranía de la Macarena. "At least half the species in Colombia are in the *llanos*," Olivares declared solemnly after probing Gaviotas with his binoculars for two days. He vowed to return and write *Aves de la Orinoquia*. "All I need is a room where I can sleep and type."

Lugari was in the process of building one. Olivares would in fact return to it one day, and Gaviotas would publish his book, the last of his life. As Lugari's duties in the Chocó wound down, he took assignments with the Colombian-Venezuelan border commission, which gave him excuses to spend time at Gaviotas. Frequently Paolo stayed on the nearby Río Muco with his *llanero* friend, who was growing rice, citrus, papaya, mangos, guavas, and cashew fruit. But in order for a substantial population to live here, Lugari realized, they would need to cultivate the *llano* itself, not just the thin arable strips along its river banks.

At Sven Zethelius's direction, he planted some fruit trees and also tried growing corn, without much success. He lured a pair of university soil chemistry students out to hunt for possible pockets of fertility, as well as to look for sand and clay deposits to use in construction. He hired Guahibo and *llanero* workers to begin reconditioning the old highway camp and build thatched living quarters. Lugari and the researchers slept in hammocks hung with mosquito netting and cooked river fish with oil the Indians sold them, pressed from seje palm nuts in long woven strainers. When an itinerant teacher wandered through, Paolo got the idea of bringing street urchins from Bogotá out to school in the *llanos*, where they could grow up far from the city in a new, healthy community.

The logistics of transplanting poor city kids to Gaviotas proved too daunting, especially since no community of any sort existed yet, but the scattering of families who lived in the area embraced the idea of a school, and soon the teacher had ten *llanero* children for pupils. A nurse from Puerto Gaitán, a tiny port along a branch of the Río Meta, offered to come once a month. Within a year, as more people arrived, she was staying for a week at a time.

"What exactly do you intend to beget here?" Sven Zethelius asked Lugari. They were lying in canvas hammocks under an open-air maloca the Guahibo had built them, consisting of a hip roof of thatched palm-fronds supported at the corners by four thick poles cut from moriche trunks. By yellow Coleman lamplight, they watched a squadron of shadowy bats feast on the buzzing hordes attacking their gauzy mosquito netting.

"Exactly? I'm honestly not sure," Paolo confessed. He'd had a raw, barely formed idea of people coming out to the *llanos* and living together in productive harmony. Who they would be, and exactly what they would do, wasn't yet clear.

"I'll tell you once I know, myself. Or when people like you tell me what's possible."

Night after night, they fell asleep talking in their hammocks. As boys, both were enthralled by a two-volume Jules Verne adventure, *The Superb Orinoco,* about a girl who searches up and down the rivers of Orinoquia for her lost father. Now, actually finding themselves in the novel's setting, they borrowed a launch and cast off down the Río Vichada. Three days later, they arrived at the broad Orinoco itself. In Puerto Carreño, Vichada's isolated territorial capital on the river's Colombian bank, no one had seen the likes of distinguished Dr. Zethelius since early in the century. Back then, the *llanos* had seemed closer to Europe than to the rest of Colombia, with merchant vessels hauling everything from silk to grand pianos up Orinocan tributaries in exchange for animal pelts and hardwoods. The impromptu lectures that Zethelius gave at Puerto Carreño's *colegio* about the future of the *llanos* were so impassioned that even the army's border guards left their post to attend.

Zethelius told Lugari about changes underway that alarmed him and his colleagues, such as a phenomenon called the greenhouse effect, and how the number of the earth's species was inexorably shrinking—both of which were news to Lugari in 1970. If they were going to colonize the *llanos*, Zethelius insisted, they should aim for nothing less than a new, alternative, inhabitable bio-system. Maybe they should invite people from all over the world and make Gaviotas a confluence of cultures, the beginning of a new earthly society.

"I don't know if we should be thinking about saving the entire world out here."

Zethelius hooted. "I've seen what you're reading." Lately, Paolo had been gobbling the canon of utopian literature: Sir Thomas More, Francis Bacon, Thoreau, Emerson, Karl Popper, Edward Bellamy, B. F. Skinner, Bertrand Russell, even revisiting Plato's *Republic*.

"You don't want to just survive out here," Zethelius's voice declared from behind his mosquito netting. "You're trying to create a utopia. In the *llanos*, no less."

Paolo tried to sit up upright in his hammock to look the older man directly in the eye. After flailing about briefly, he gave up. Lying back again, he said, "I want Gaviotas to be real. I'm tired of reading about all these places that sound so perfect but never get lifted off the page into reality. Just for once, I'd like to see humans go from fantasy to fact. From utopia to *topia*."

But how to do that? Lugari started by persuading faculties of universities around the country to send thesis candidates from various disciplines to Gaviotas, to identify the challenges that concocting an ideal society from scratch in the *llanos* would entail and to dream up some solutions. At Colombia's excellent but tumultuous public Universidad Nacional, so many classes had been lost to protests and strikes that students frequently needed seven years to finish a normal four-year curriculum. For some, the chance to complete their work in peace off-campus was hard to resist, even as far off-campus as the *llanos*. Also, engineering graduates needed companies to sponsor their practical research, and many local industries, suspicious that La Nacional was a nest of communists, were staying away.

With a few artfully phrased notices posted on faculty bulletin boards, word spread that Gaviotas was seeking adventurous thinkers with ideas they wanted to test. The reward: Earn a degree by helping to make the empty savannas flourish, in order to siphon off excess population from the cities. About twice a month, candidates could find Paolo Lugari in a small rented house on Avenida Caracas in Bogotá, leaping up from his desk to pump their hands and to listen and nod and assure them that they could be part of the next vital wave of engineering or animal husbandry or anthropology or geology—"pioneer-technicians in a vast tropical frontier!" He already had agreements with their universities, he told them. If they thought they might be happy at Gaviotas, Gaviotas would be their sponsor.

By which, they later learned, he meant that they would get a hammock, mosquito netting, food, and a share in the cooking duties. Usually, they didn't learn this until 500 kilometers of roadless *llanos* separated them from home. Knowing that highway crews once had practically mutinied after being marooned in mud for months at Gaviotas, Lugari had persuaded the national airline, Avianca, to provide weekly single-engine air service to the soon-to-boom heart of nowhere. Researchers would land at a grass airstrip and be left there, often in a prodigious tropical downpour. A quarter-mile away stood a cluster of wooden shacks with roofs of thatched moriche palm leaves, which fortunately proved to be waterproof.

Possibly out of gratitude, the properties of indigenous moriche palm became an early focus of investigation. From the Indians, students learned that ribs of the moriche leaf could be soaked and woven into useful implements such as nets and hammocks. The Guahibo also squeezed an oily juice from the moriche's reddish-brown fruit, which resembled a swollen date, which they fermented into *guarapo*, a refreshing, slightly alcoholic beverage. A pair of chemical engineers from the Universidad Nacional rendered a few kilos of the palm fruit with a corn grinder borrowed from somebody's mother, then extracted pure moriche oil in a

wood-fired still they rigged from a galvanized garbage can. When they ran
 an analysis, they were shocked and delighted to find that both its nutritional value and flavor rivaled olive oil. Its properties not only surpassed those of oil produced from seje, another local palm being studied by a Harvard doctoral student whom Lugari had snared, but the moriche's seed was ten times bigger than that of an exotic oil-bearing African palm being introduced in plantations throughout tropical America.

This was still the early 1970s; the ensuing worldwide clamor for sustainable use of native species was still barely a whisper. At nacent Gaviotas, population approximately twenty, the concept made sense on a more basic level: They needed cooking oil in order to eat, and this stuff already grew here. But now, the exhilaration over finding something with the commercial potential of olive oil had the early Gaviotans toasting each other with *guarapo* around the evening campfires, to the accompaniment of guitars and *llanera* ballads.

Soon, however, they learned that having their habitat and eating it too gets tricky. First, someone noticed that the large moriche seed's oil yield was about six percent, versus thirty percent for *Palmas africanus*. Then they realized that the moriche requires thirty-five years to mature, as opposed to three-and-a-half years for the imported species. These shortcomings produced a totally unintended result: Having exhausted the available supply growing in easy reach to satisfy the researchers' increasing demand, the Guahibos who sold them seeds were chopping down trees to collect the highest clusters.

So oil from native palms became relegated to domestic use only, lest major portions of the gallery forest along the Caño Urimica be leveled. This was less of a disaster than the short-lived attempt to domesticate capybaras, the one hundred-pound rodents known locally as *chigüiros*. Capybaras had been ranched by horseback cowboys in the wetlands of Brazil and Venezuela ever since a colonial bishop decreed that the water-loving creature—whose toes are webbed and whose flesh is often compared to lean tenderloin—was really a fish, and therefore legal for Friday consumption. But the *llanos* had no great swamps, only narrow riparian

The Savanna

ribbons, and breeding them in enclosures proved fatal: The toothy mammals would die trying to gnaw their way out.

"There's no such thing as a failure here," the ever-sanguine Lugari encouraged the researchers. "Every obstacle is really an opportunity in disguise." The idea, he kept reminding everybody, was to try absolutely everything, to see what would work to make *llano* life livable.

Young men and women continued to arrive. Sustained by rice, canned sardines, and metric tons of potatoes trucked or airlifted from Bogotá, they tested the iron-laden savanna soils for pigment production, tried making fiberboard out of *llano* grass, invented a non-polluting tannery, perfected a cheap blend of local soil and cement for paving roads and airport runways, fashioned gaskets from palm leaves, learned to preserve food in a sultry climate with no electricity, turned palm-oil extraction residues into bovine feed supplements, and cooked up a dozen uses for mangos beyond the most obvious one.

Jorge Zapp, meanwhile, had needed no persuading to bring engineering students from the Universidad de Los Andes to Gaviotas. He still sorely wished that his former lab chief, Luis Robles, were around for this, but Luis had disappeared into a place far wilder than even Gaviotas: the jungles of the Chocó. Three years had passed since the lank, handsome Robles had slumped into Zapp's office, his startling blue eyes even more tormented than usual with his mysterious inner anguish, and informed Jorge that he'd had it with university life. *"¡Basta!"*

Luis had threatened this before. Largely self-educated, he'd wandered onto campus a few years earlier and was hired immediately, but never got acclimated to the surrounding academic egos. As head technician at Los Andes' mechanical engineering laboratory—a post Zapp had tailored expressly to Luis's extraordinary talents—he had met with Ph.D.s from all over the world, none of whom suspected he'd never been to college. Nevertheless, this time he was really quitting. He'd filled a Ford panel truck full of gas canisters, a welding torch, a buck saw, two tons of scrap iron, a chess board, and his wife and kids, and pointed for the Pacific. Nobody

knew exactly where they'd landed: the Chocó was even more uncharted
than the *llanos*.

So Jorge Zapp selected a group of his prize protégés and assigned them each a project. "It's fairly straightforward," he told them. "Just figure out how to build the future of civilization from grass, sun, and water."

~

ELEVEN-YEAR-OLD HENRY MOYA HOISTED HIS LITHE BODY OUT OF the water and sat atop the low dam that had created their new swimming hole on the Caño Urimica. It was made of *gaviones blandos*, burlap bags filled with a mixture of fourteen parts soil and one part cement (years later, when cheap synthetics doomed burlap sacks to extinction, Gaviotas would switch to biodegradable plastic). With the addition of water, *gaviones* turned to stone and remained that way long after the bags had disintegrated. Stacked in staggered rows while still in their sandbag stage, when soaked they hardened in interlocking layers that resembled the precisely fitted block construction of the ancient Incas.

"*¡Ya vamos!*" Henry hissed at two friends, Jorge Eliécer Landaeta and Mariano Botello. They left their splashing classmates behind and waded downriver, picking their way around the tubing connected to a pulsating *ariete*. The *ariete*, or hydraulic ram pump, used the river's flow to lift a piston in a cylindrical chamber, until the air compressed inside the chamber forced the piston back down. This particular two-foot-high prototype, adapted by Jorge Zapp's engineers from a 200-year-old British design, was successfully irrigating a cassava patch a kilometer away. The boys lingered briefly, clucking their tongues to imitate the *ariete*'s gentle thunk, then continued, watching out for stingrays and electric eels.

They passed under a small bridge, part of a road that led a half-kilometer north of the original Gaviotas buildings to Villa Ciencia ("Science Village"), a cluster of whitewashed, mud-masonry, two-bedroom houses, each built around a roofed patio with beams left exposed for hammocks.

These had been completed recently, and already there was need for more. When Henry arrived four years earlier, in 1975, there were just ten families at Gaviotas, living in a neat row of thatched cottages. Besides Zapp and his swarm of university students, who buzzed between Gaviotas and Bogotá like *llanos* locusts, those residents had included two teachers, a nurse, a storekeeper, a radio operator, a meteorologist and his wife, and some construction workers. Paolo Lugari spent only part of his time in Vichada; otherwise he was in Bogotá or, Henry had heard, out of the country. Sometimes he would appear accompanied by foreigners with exotic-sounding accents.

Henry Moya was one of six sons of a *llanera* family that lived several hours away on a small cattle finca. His older siblings had attended a mission school equally far from home, but his parents, concerned about increasing guerrilla activity near there, decided to try Gaviotas for their youngest. Henry liked it. The school, books, paper, food, and his room were free: All he'd needed to bring was clothes and a hammock. The workers were paid decently and also received free room and board. The meteorologist let him help launch hydrogen weather balloons. Gaviotas was a tiny, well-organized community of people who were all nice to Henry— except for one.

"*¡Silencio!*" Henry shushed his companions, as the forest along the streambed opened onto a clearing. "Don't let him see us." About a hundred meters away, the biggest construction these remote savannas had ever known was in progress. Besides employing every available laborer within a three-hour radius, about thirty more had been brought from Bogotá. When the new Gaviotas factory was completed, Lugari had told them, 350 people would be living and working here.

The building material was the *llano* itself. At a nearby pit, a ham-shouldered *llanero* named Abraham Beltrán was churning out bricks of soil cement at a pace that awed everyone. His tool was a Cinva-Ram, a name derived from an acronym for an institute at Colombia's Universidad Nacional, where it was invented. The Gaviotas version was a one-meter lever attached to a plate that closed over a rectangular form four inches deep, which one worker filled with a fourteen-to-one soil cement mixture as fast as the operator manning the lever could mash it into the shape of a brick. As the lever was drawn back, the fresh block popped from the mold, and was quickly whisked out of the way of the next shovelful. No additional straw or binder was necessary: *llanos* soil alone was moist enough to cure the cement. For weeks, Beltrán and other workers had been rising at 3:00 A.M. to meet the daily quota of five hundred bricks for the 30,000 square-foot, 40-foot-high factory building that was rising— the largest soil cement structure in the world, which would require two hundred thousand bricks before he was through. The boys loved to watch Beltrán work, barefoot and stripped to the waist, his thick torso bronzed nearly the color of the red dirt, turning out a perfect, smooth block with each satisfying grunt. But they had to sneak their glimpses, because the testy director of the new factory, Luis Robles, permitted no one but laborers and engineers around. He especially didn't want kids.

At that moment, Luis was preoccupied with laying a water line. They could see him wielding a shovel: a tall man in his late forties, with light hair and a high, sun-freckled forehead, wearing only cut-off jeans. As if smelling their presence, suddenly he spun around and squinted. They dived into the foliage, but by then Robles had flung his shovel aside and was sprinting across the clearing. Then he was thundering down the middle of the shallow *caño* after them, as they screamed and splashed their way back upstream. Back at the construction site, even Abraham Beltrán had interrupted his prodigious pace to join the engineers who were convulsed with laughter at the sight of the formidable Robles going berserk again.

Berserk was among the possible diagnoses that had crossed Jorge Zapp's mind the morning early in 1975 when he'd opened the door of his house in Bogotá and found Robles—or something that distantly resembled him—propped against the jamb, barely able to stand. For the past six years, as Jorge learned on the way to the hospital, Luis had been living by an inlet on the Pacific coast, where his sole link to civilization was a fishing boat that passed every two weeks, sometimes bringing provisions. He'd returned to the city because he'd simultaneously contracted each of the three malaria strains that exist in Colombia, and was down to just eighty pounds.

As multiple IVs combatted Robles' fevers, he recounted his technical triumphs over the Chocó jungle. He'd laid an aqueduct, rigged hand pumps, planted two hundred coco palms, and mounted a sawmill. For electricity, he built a wave generator offshore and a ten-kilowatt turbine on a nearby river.

When he was sufficiently rehydrated and recovered, Zapp presented him to Paolo Lugari. "You're coming to Gaviotas," Paolo informed him.

He arrived in his two-and-a-half-ton panel truck, stuffed with home-grown machinery he'd hauled from the Chocó, several tools of his own design, a thousand pounds of salvaged metal, a daughter, his two youngest sons, and an outraged wife who could not believe that he had dragged them from one mosquito-ridden extreme of the Colombian wilderness to another. This time, she lasted not six years but six months. Luis stayed. He was unable to resist what Lugari, Zapp, and the others had begun in this toyland for *técnicos*.

Undergraduates whom he had taught how to weld and to turn a lathe back at Los Andes were now at Gaviotas getting graduate degrees, or simply getting paid, for playing. Their assignment was to invent the kinds of devices that engineers usually only dabble with on Sundays: wind generators, solar heaters, even solar motors. In a drafty workshop converted from the highway crew's former heavy equipment shed, they had recycled a mass of flotsam lugged from the city into prototype windmills, solar water heater panels, micro-hydro turbines, biogas generators, and all manner of pumps, from the compact *ariete* ram pump to a species of water wheel mounted on floating oil drums.

Luis Robles beamed at the piles of junk metal and sections of used PVC, which they were fashioning into machines. He was among kindred spirits. "No *rayadora*?" he asked.

"What's a *rayadora*?"

"Something I needed in the Chocó. So I built one." He'd brought it along: It was a pedal-driven cassava grinder, its drive-train cannibalized from one of his kids' bicycles. His former protégés stood in a circle and admired it, then immediately began thinking up other applications for the pedal principle. It was a natural for Gaviotas, since everyone here was encouraged to use a bike, a practice Luis sniffed at. He'd brought a motorcycle.

This eventually became a raw spot in his community relations, especially with urban transplants, who became so intoxicated by the tranquility of the *llanos* that superfluous motorized activity was deemed pollution of the peace. Luis had to hide the thing in the bushes when Lugari was around, which did nothing to improve his disposition. But even at his most cantankerous, nothing got bad enough to impel Luis Robles to return to Bogotá. Gaviotas was venturing into the miracle business, and the first miracle was having an actual research budget for making design dreams come true.

How had such a wonder come about? It was, Robles learned, the result of one of the seminal events of the century: the initial wail of alarm—later naively dismissed as false—that shattered a lulled planet's delusion of limitless resources. Luis Robles had missed the whole thing. He never even heard of the 1973 global energy crisis until two years later, when he emerged from the Chocó primeval.

Until the Arab oil embargo, Zapp explained to him, Gaviotas was considered an intriguing experiment with little practical relevance. Then, as waiting in gas pump lines gave the world time to contemplate the novel notion of renewable energy, Gaviotas began to attract attention. Journalists appeared. The Colombian National Academy of Science struggled out to Vichada to hold its annual meeting. After the *Wall Street Journal* published a front-page feature about a South American community that had "solved" the energy crisis by devising implements powered by energy that was actually replenishable, a delegation arrived from the United Nations Development Programme.

The UNDP officers looked around approvingly at the truly useful tools being contrived out of cheap, recycled materials. Enchanted, they watched as the Gaviotans lay a drainage culvert—or rather, avoided having to lay one. In a ditch where they had poured a two-inch base of soil cement, they placed a twenty-foot length of inexpensive, meter-wide light-weight polyethylene tubing, normally used for cutting and sectioning into plastic garbage bags. Tying off one end, they filled the tubing with water, so that it resembled a huge transparent sausage or—

"A giant condom," whispered one of the UN observers to Jorge Zapp. "Exactly."

At that point, it was a matter simply of sealing it, burying it with soil cement, leaving the ends exposed, and letting the cement harden overnight. The next morning, they untied the ends, let the water drain away, then pulled out the deflated, reusable plastic sleeve. The earthen-cement tube that remained in its place was strong enough to withstand the weight of a convoy of army trucks driving over it, as one did that afternoon.

"Ingenious," said the UN observer. "How did you ever think of it?"

"It just kind of evolved," replied Zapp. The idea had literally occurred to him one night in a dream, during a week when he was designing cement pipes for the micro-hydro turbine. He'd awakened and tried it, and it worked. This was pure *eureka!*, but that sounded too weird to tell to the United Nations.

Then they posed another question to Zapp: How might Gaviotas' clever solutions to local problems be applied elsewhere in the world?

Years later, after he had been traveling the globe for the United Nations for more than a decade, Jorge Zapp would still reflect on the momentous implications of that question, and not just for Gaviotas.

"At that instant, I realized that the concept of Third World technological development had been born. Until then, we didn't even know the word 'development,' unless it referred to what originated in some wealthy northern country. Now, for the first time, we were being called upon to be the developers."

The United Nations Development Programme's designation in 1976 of Gaviotas as a model community was accompanied by a substantial research grant. Over the years, as their successes multiplied, this support would grow to include travel budgets for Gaviotans to scour the world for ideas they could adapt to their tropical *topia*, and then show that same world how their approach could work anywhere. It was on one such trip in the mid-1970s that Paolo Lugari hit upon a solution to two problems at once.

He was returning from a conference in Rio de Janeiro, when his plane stopped to refuel in the Brazilian jungle port of Manaus. After marinating in Amazonian humidity for two hours on the runway, the passengers were told that the plane needed repairs, and that they would be staying overnight. The situation did little to calm Lugari's anxieties about flying, which had lately increased along with the frequency of his travels. Two months earlier, after a plane went down in a storm, Avianca had cancelled the weekly flight he'd persuaded them to establish between Bogotá and Vichada—providentially, Paolo had just missed the ill-fated flight.

So on this occasion he resigned himself to a delay that, theoretically, meant his aircraft would be safer, especially since the airline was lodging them in Manaus's riverside palace, the Hotel Tropical. But what impressed Paolo Lugari far more that night than the neocolonial architecture were the dinner vegetables.

He collared the maître d'. "Where," he demanded, "are you getting fresh lettuce and tomatoes in the middle of the jungle?" By now he knew that the impoverished soils in the *llanos* weren't much different from those of a rain forest, and despite Sven Zethelius's diligent efforts, Gaviotas was having a dismal time producing anything nourishing from them.

"Aren't they lovely?" the maître d' agreed. "Some priests deep in the *floresta* have a *cultivação*."

"Where, exactly?"

He canceled his flight, rented a boat, and went to find them. A few hours upriver, he was led to local Catholic missionaries growing greens in box planters made of palm wood, set on blocks above the slick clay jungle floor. The Brazilian priests had analyzed the soil to determine which minerals were lacking. In the boxes, they mixed dirt with decomposing jungle detritus, and compensated for the absent nutrients by adding extra cobalt, manganese, and traces of magnesium, zinc, and copper. The result was a bountiful crop of onions, chard, lettuce, and tomatoes.

Excited, Lugari went back and told Zapp and Zethelius. They had some concerns: Using fertilizers would be controversial among the purists in Gaviotas. "They told me they're only adding minerals," Paolo said.

"Same thing."

"What's wrong with minerals?"

"Probably nothing, the way they're using them in confined beds," Sven surmised. "Runoff into the Amazon would be insignificant. The problem is when too much fertilizer washes downstream, and algae starts to clog waterways and suck up all the oxygen."

"I think someone should go down there and study their system," Lugari said. "Who can we spare?"

It occurred to Lugari and Zapp exactly who. Before Gaviotas, each had connections to the U.S. Peace Corps. Paolo was an orientation guide for newly-arrived volunteers. Jorge, who spoke English, became a mother hen to the homesick whenever an earnest young gringo felt especially shell-shocked in a country where the local surrealist and future Nobel-laureate novelist, Gabriel García Márquez, claimed to be simply a journalist chronicling everyday events. Peace Corps workers were always looking for a pretext to visit Gaviotas, and some had offered to share American know-how in the quest to grow foodstuffs viably in the *llanos*.

They were welcomed to try: Lugari had wondered about raising chickens, and the Peace Corps came to test these and rabbits as well. Both thrived, but only as long as they were being fed, which brought Gaviotas back to its original problem. Neither grain for the chickens nor legumes for the rabbits would grow in the soil of the *llanos*, and importing animal feed from Bogotá made little economic sense. But here was a method that actually portended to work. And so, reversing the customary North-to-

South flow of expertise, at its own expense Gaviotas sent a pair of United States Peace Corps volunteers to Brazil, to learn from South Americans how to grow vegetables in the tropics.

Nine months later, Paolo Lugari, Sven Zethelius, and Jorge Zapp stood under a plastic-roofed enclosure, in an aisle between two fifty-foot-long platforms raised on blocks of soil cement. These were covered with shallow, dirt-filled flats, each a meter square, planted in tomatoes, eggplant, cucumbers, and lettuce. The initial harvests had been encouraging, although gardening had not gone as easily here as for the Manaus missionaries. Zethelius confirmed that the aluminum-laced mantle that passed for topsoil at Gaviotas was far poorer than even the leached earth of the Amazon rain forest. They had needed much more soil compensation here than the Brazilians required, he explained.

"Meaning what?" Lugari asked.

"Meaning more fertilizer. Besides lacking all the minerals those priests have to add, we're missing potassium, phosphorus, calcium, and boron. But that's not the biggest problem. Fertilizer is fairly cheap. At two parts per million, a few grams of cobalt will last us years."

"So what's the problem?"

The big problem was root disease. Introduced species, such as carrots, cucumbers, and lettuce, had no natural defenses against the local insects, fungi, and bacteria. Apparently, a Peace Corps volunteer had been discovered fighting back with doses of systemic fungicide, and an argument broke out over dinner. "Does this mean," someone demanded, "that we have to poison the soil in order to grow something in it, and then risk poisoning ourselves by eating the results?"

Jorge Zapp, recalling the ruckus, chuckled as he examined a purple eggplant. Another issue, he added, was that *llaneros* had no idea what eggplant was, and cucumbers weren't part of their traditional diet, either. The gringo had planted a lot of these, and as a result the pigs were getting plenty of fresh produce these days.

"Suppose," Jorge asked Zethelius, "that instead of poisoning the soil, we just sterilized it?" Before Sven could reply, Zapp's mind raced ahead,

The Savanna

and he held up a hand until his complete thought unspooled. As they waited, a pair of green honeycreepers landed on the tomato flat, chirped briefly, and flew on. "Got it," he announced, smiling at the others. Instead of trying to sterilize soil, he concluded that it would be a lot easier to make their own, adding whatever minerals were necessary, as the Brazilian priests were doing.

"Make it out of what?" Lugari asked.

"Anything. All you need is something to hold the plants in place so they don't fall over. Sand from the riverbank beaches. Rice husks."

Nearly four years later, in 1979, an evaluator from the United Nations Development Programme made a site-visit to Gaviotas. He was there to see the appropriate technology that Gaviotas had produced with its original $350,000 grant, to determine whether a second funding phase would be justified. Expecting to see machines, he was unprepared to also find greenhouse enclosures covering a third of a square kilometer, filled with Spanish onions, tomatoes, chard, lettuce, cilantro, peas, peppers, parsely, garlic, cabbage, balm, and radishes.

"Hydroponics," Zapp told him. He explained that this approach, using wastes from rice farms along the Río Meta as a growing medium, had evolved from the Brazilian system they had adapted, and was now spreading around the country, even in the flower industry. In their hydroponic nursery, they had plants germinating in trays of sawdust and wood chips. "It lets us grow food where nothing would grow before. Including the mint leaves in your tea this morning."

The UN official became thoughtful. "What about poor people?" he asked.

"You mean like us?"

"I mean wherever there's a lack of food. Could you do this in, say, the misery belts around cities?"

"If we can grow it here, it can grow anywhere."

"Didn't we budget you some money for outreach?"

"Thirty thousand dollars. To hold an international seminar to spread Gaviotas technology."

"Charity starts at home. Use that money to make something grow in the slums. I'll find some more to send Gaviotas around the world."

~

ALONSO GUTIÉRREZ NEVER WORRIED ABOUT FOOD: IT WAS EVERY-where. When he first arrived in the *llanos* as one of Dr. Zapp's protégés, he chomped happily on the mangos and guavas planted along the forest edge during the military dictatorship, and stained his tee shirts black with the deceptively clear juice of the astringent native cashew fruit. He was aware of Gaviotas' ban on hunting, which made sense to him, since the riparian habitat bordering the Caño Urimica was so small. But nobody had raised any objection to fishing; as a boy, he had made yearly fishing trips to the Orinoco with his father, a coffee grower. During his first week at Gaviotas, Alonso homed in on the Río Muco, returning with pails of golden *cachama* and wolf fish and earning an ovation from the cooks.

In May, the end of the four-month "summer" or dry season, he started watching for termites. He'd eaten them before (as well as every other kind of ant, grub, and butterfly he'd encountered) but termites weren't the prey he was after. Upon arriving, he had noticed immediately that the other-wise flat *llanos* were riddled with short red earthen cones. These baby volcanoes, he knew, were the homes of colony ants.

Once, wildly curious to see how colony ants avoided flooding during the rains, he'd torn apart one of their impressive four-foot-high nests, and discovered a series of siphons, complete with U-shaped traps, to divert water and wick it away. He tucked the lesson into his memory to use in some future design, and waited for May. Finally, it happened, on the eleventh. He was in the courtyard of the Gaviotas school, spinning tops he'd carved out of *chaparro* root with the *llanero* kids, when one of them alerted him to the air-borne termite swarm he told them to watch for:

"¡*Comejenes!*"

Why the tiny black termites with their huge wings always emerged the night before their distant cousins the colony ant queens made their annual nuptial flight, no one knew. "Ants tomorrow!" the kids were chanting, but Alonso reminded them that it all depended on a good rain, followed by strong sun.

Which is exactly what they got the next day. The *llanos* soaked all night under a downpour that dumped off the moriche eaves in a continuous liquid sheet. The clouds broke apart at dawn, sliding around the sky like gray tectonic plates and casting a morning rainbow to the west. Another fainter arc appeared, parallel to the first, and everyone murmured, *"Macho y hembra"*—a female had joined the male. Green parakeets flew through the pair of colored hoops, bumblebees converged on the fragrant red hibiscus, and excited children swarmed around Alonso Gutiérrez.

"Keep your eyes on the *tijeritas* and the *águilas*," he instructed them. Luckily, it was a Saturday. By ten o'clock, the sky was blue as the Caribbean, but so laden with humidity that the sun burned as if through a magnifying glass—"a rain sun," they called it. If the moisture condensed again before the ants—

"¡Tijeritas! ¡Aguilas también!"

Flocks of fork-tailed flycatchers and caracaras could be seen spiraling near the airstrip. By the time Alonso and company arrived, the birds had commenced dive-bombing thousands of soldier ants, identifiable by their red eyes popping from oversized Martian heads, as they poured from the cones to sweep the immediate area so that their royalty could emerge. Like the queens themselves, the soldiers could deliver swift, cutting bites that caused blood to spray. Wearing plastic bags over their hands and rubber irrigation boots, the children moved in cautiously. Suddenly, they started shouting as small, hairy-faced drones appeared, because they knew that immediately after would come the queens—one for each of the hundreds of colonies inside each anthill. With ravenous birds wheeling overhead and ecstatic woolly anteaters loping nearby, the humans pounced. As the inch-long queens paused to spread their tissuey wings at the edge of the hole, the children grabbed them by their fat abdomens and shoved them into plastic sacks.

That afternoon, over a fire pit, Alonso showed them how to snap off the heads with their fingernails, then fry the plump thorax and stomachs. "Some people add butter and salt. In Santander province, they cook them in their own fat."

"How do you like them?" the children asked. He grinned and showed them.

"*¡Ay no*, Alonso!—you're not supposed to eat them raw!"

Alonso Gutiérrez was born on a coffee plantation in northwestern Colombia. His father had a workshop full of gadgets, and Alonso figured he had a head start on things like turbines—they even had their own version of a *trapiche*, a manual sugar cane crusher that Gaviotas would later refine into a commercial model. When he entered the Universidad de Los Andes in 1970, Luis Robles had already fled to the jungle, and the mechanical engineering lab had become neglected. Alonso led a group of students who more or less comandeered it.

He didn't do his thesis on an apparatus for Gaviotas—pumps and windmills were just diversions for him. His own research dealt with gas dynamics: specifically, the thermal conductivity of air directly in contact with airplane wings, a critical factor in the design of supersonic jets. But when Gaviotas received its first UN grant, Alonso began flying to Vichada on weekends to help Zapp and his classmates make the place functional. Stocky Alonso Gutiérrez was a little reminiscent of a bulldog pup—friendly, but powerful and even a little spooky. Yet with a tool in his hand, he had an exquisitely delicate touch: When the final pieces for the first Gaviotas hydro-turbine needed to be fitted at the site, he had machined them on a hand lathe, since as yet there was no electricity.

He could design practically anything, his university colleagues believed. What he couldn't, or wouldn't do, was write. For years, it appeared he would never graduate because he hated to document his research. This foible, coupled with a similar distaste for drawing, worked to his advantage at Gaviotas, where action was always prized over theory. "Doing a blueprint is an inefficient way to make something," Alonso would answer his exasperated professors. "Just because you see it on paper doesn't mean it'll work. Since you have to build it anyway to find out, why not just do that in the first place?"

Since he couldn't build his own supersonic aircraft, he honed his ideas by working on everything else. Besides devices for Gaviotas, for five years he secretly labored over a camera to photograph human auras. He actually got it to work, but didn't tell anyone for fear it might get him kicked out of the university. In 1975 he finally graduated and went to live in the *llanos.*

"*Now* where is he going?" Luis Robles asked Jorge Zapp. Over lunch, Zapp had just challenged his students to come up with a design for a thus-far elusive concept: a solar refrigerator. Everyone headed for the work-shop, except for Alonso Gutiérrez, who had just pedaled past the dining commons with a fishing pole strapped to his back and a circular hunk of sheet metal tied to his handlebars.

Zapp watched him disappear into the savanna. "He's thinking. Alonso can't do anything unless he's doing something else." Or being somewhere else: He'd even devised a bicycle-mounted portable desk, so Gaviotas engineers wouldn't be chained to some stifling workshop. On this occasion, he was headed for the Río Muco to pan for gold, a pursuit in which he persisted for years, though he never found any. In the process, however, he met every *llanero* living in a radius of several hours, helped them build irrigation systems and—after these were perfected—set up Gaviotas windmills on cattle tanks for many surrounding fincas. He showed the Guahibo how to lay rudimentary sewage lines to remove human wastes from their sad little settlements, in exchange for learning how to build waterproof moriche roofs on the new buildings going up at Gaviotas.

"Beautiful," Lugari said to him one afternoon. Alonso was sitting in the grass at a building site, whittling a top as he supervised roof construction.

"Too expensive," he replied.

"Why? Palm leaves are free."

"Right now they are. I found out it takes eighty leaves per square meter to make a roof watertight. If Gaviotas keeps growing, and especially if the idea is to populate the *llanos,* we need to switch to clay shingles or metal unless we intend to chop down the *caños.*"

"It would be better not to depend on materials we have to bring in."

"It's very romantic to build out of local natural materials, but it's dumb to be purists all the time. And impractical. The future will need nature *and* technology. We can't make solar panels out of whole-wheat bread."

How *would* they harness solar energy? Alonso became friends with a boyish engineer named Jaime Dávila, one of the current crop of students to whom Zapp had assigned that very problem. In his first year at the university, Jaime had designed a solar panel similar to the rectangular boxes that the fledgling, energy-poor nation of Israel began hanging on houses during the 1950s to heat water. At Gaviotas, Jaime and Jorge Zapp first experimented with a large parabolic trough designed to concentrate the sun's rays, built from scrap metal in front of the open-air, roofed dining commons.

From its nearby pen alongside a stand of bamboo, an orphaned ocelot kit rescued by the Gaviotans watched young barefoot engineers, lacking any other way to devise a curved reflective mirror six meters long, cover the trough with aluminum foil. It worked fine; the blue-gray tanagers that scrounged rice and bread crumbs off the lunch tables soon learned not to light on its scalding surface. But to pipe solar heat from a central plant made less sense than siting rooftop panels on individual houses, so Gaviotas turned to designing smaller collectors efficient enough to heat water under rainy savanna skies.

"What do we do with that?" Jaime asked Zapp, gesturing at the forlorn parabolic trough. They were sitting in the dining commons one morning, waiting out an eight-day downpour so that a plane could take Jaime back to Bogotá. Not anticipating being stranded, Dávila hadn't brought textbooks to study for a coming exam in solid mechanics, so Zapp was coaching him.

"Paolo wants a solar kitchen. Maybe that's our oven."

"World's longest baguette."

The Savanna

Alonso Gutiérrez took Jaime Dávila and Jaime's biologist girlfriend, Juana, daughter of noted Spanish emigré painter Juan Antonio Roda, along on jeep excursions out into the surrounding sea of grass. Juana's brother, Marco, also a painter and photographer, made increasingly frequent trips with his wife, Mireya, to join them. Alonso invited them all to see his new finca: He had claimed his own piece of property on the far edge of Gaviotas, and one day intended to be part of the new colonization of the savanna. Marco Roda set up a tripod and made endless exposures of the *llanos,* whose shimmering horizon mocked the limitations of a mere camera. "Couldn't we find a way to live here?" Mireya asked.

"We have to live here, too," Juana told Jaime. She and Lugari were discussing the prospects for raising edible native fish in ponds at Gaviotas.

"We have to graduate first," Jaime reminded her. "Who knows if this will even be here by then?"

"Get Zapp to move his department out here. He may as well."

It was true—Jorge Zapp was in the *llanos* so much that he'd run out of excuses to justify the time he spent at Gaviotas to his university. He had achieved mythic status among students for an office that, according to campus lore, once remained locked for more than a year. In 1974, with everyone getting sick of his prolonged absences, he stepped down as faculty dean; by 1976, with a grant from the United Nations Development Programme to coordinate Gaviotas' research and travel, he astonished his colleagues by leaving the Universidad de Los Andes altogether.

Alonso Gutiérrez, meanwhile, was having so much fun designing water lines and septic systems at Gaviotas that he eventually managed to earn a master's degree in hydraulics. He helped develop the pliable building blocks made from burlap sacks filled with dirt and cement known as *gaviones,* and built a closed-system soil washer that used recycled water to make *llanos* grit usable for soil-cement. About that time, he decided that the *llanos* soils couldn't possibly have always been so terrible. His theory was that if the savanna was once covered with forest, it would have deposited organic material that might have dissolved in rain water and percolated below the surface, maybe as far as a hundred meters.

"Well, it's not doing us much good down there," remarked Sven Zethelius.

"Then let's go get it."

"And how do you suggest we do that?"

Alonso planned to build a large drilling rig to seek buried topsoil. "If we find it, we can pump water down the hole to dissolve it, and then spray it over the surface."

Zethelius didn't even try to stop him. As a scientist, he respected the particular fever that gripped Alonso Gutíerrez's brain: the insatiable passion to experiment. So Alonso and his friends built the thing, sank several holes, and found absolutely nothing. Alonso remained undaunted. How else were they going to know if they didn't try?

They had so many ideas that they could barely sleep. The only despair was not having enough hours to attempt them all. Frequently, they stopped everything to try one out. All that digging in the dirt, for instance, had Alonso contemplating the expansive nature of clay, which can swell enough to lift a building, with sufficient humidity. Then he discovered that a Universidad Nacional student named Edgar Gómez who was hanging around Gaviotas was writing a thesis on a truly original concept: a non-electric irrigation system that employed clay to allow plants to water themselves.

Gómez's system consisted of flexible quarter-inch tubing through which water flowed directly from a faucet to a plant's roots, as in a typical drip-irrigation system. The difference was that a one-foot length of the tube was packed in an inch-thick coating of clay, surrounded by a protective shell of porous ceramic. The ceramic-encased clay cylinder with tubing running through its center was then buried alongside the plant.

If the surrounding soil was moist, the clay in the cylinder expanded enough to pinch the tubing shut, cutting off the flow of water from the source. When the soil became dry, the clay inside the cylinder would dehydrate and contract, allowing water to pass through to the plant's roots. Once the ground dampened again, the clay did likewise, again swelling to control the flow.

The Savanna

Alonso was delighted by the simplicity of a device that allowed the garden itself to decide when it need water—not some costly computer, like the Israelis were trying to deploy in the Negev. He was dying to build one—for that matter, he reasoned, they should be designing solar pumps, using liquids that dilated in sunlight to make a flexible siphon that would expand and contract to suck water out of streams and aquifers.

But after some promising early tests, developing the clay irrigator was postponed, because of an idea that struck Alonso Gutiérrez like a jolt from the engineering gods themselves, an idea that would transform life for peasants in and far beyond Colombia.

"Civilization," Paolo Lugari likes to observe, "has been a permanent dialogue between human beings and water." From soil studies undertaken the year after he founded Gaviotas, Lugari had learned that the region of the *llanos* was like a gigantic mattress suspended above a huge underground reservoir of clean, sand-filtered runoff water from the Andes. Nevertheless, eighty percent of the maladies suffered by *llaneros* and local *indígenas* were caused by water contamination near the surface. The first important task, as Jorge Zapp had confirmed, was to get at the pure water below.

Their first attempt used an ancient hand-driven mechanism called an induction pump, possibly the oldest hydraulic tool invented by humans. Because it depends on air pressure to lift water when a piston is raised within a cylinder, an induction pump's well can be no deeper than 34 feet, the height to which atmospheric pressure can support a column of water. The true range of such a hand pump is actually less, because the weight of a piston rod capable of moving 34 feet of water would be prohibitive for most people: Gaviotas' model reached only 13 feet, too shallow to assure purity, and was used mainly to irrigate guava trees.

In such unremittingly flat country, the next logical step would be to harness the wind to do the work of humans. But windmills present a challenge in the equatorial doldrums, where breezes often seem to give up rather than try to budge the torpid air. The original Gaviotas windmill was a design gleaned from a book written by a Finnish missionary, consisting of two 55-gallon drums sliced in half and welded end-to-end to form two pairs of S-curved scoops, then stacked on a pole one atop the other. Their weight proved impractical for the tropics: The drums functioned best as a weather vane, managing to spin whenever rising storm squalls started blowing hard enough to move them.

Fifty-seven more windmill prototypes would be built on the way to a design responsive to gentle tropical zephyrs, yet able to withstand sudden tempests. Zapp's chief assistant was a rangy former student named Geoffrey Halliday, the Colombian-born son of a British expatriate, whom Zapp plucked from the boredom of managing a factory in Bogotá. Together, they tried canvas-covered wings like those used in Holland and Crete. From sections of PVC pipe, they cut windmill blades in shapes that resembled twisted wood shavings. Next came air-foils made of aluminum sheeting, which performed beautifully until unexpected gusts would rip them away. They experimented with four-bladed and five-bladed models, with and without tails. They hooked their devices up to a dynamometer and a torque meter and tested them in the back of Geoffrey's jeep, rising at 5:00 A.M. to bounce over the savanna at a hundred kilometers per hour in the stillness of dawn, scattering shrieking flocks of southern lapwings. They made an important leap forward the day that Jorge handed Geoffrey yet another piston-driven pump he'd tooled and told him to stick it in a bucket of water to see what would happen.

"You mean pump water *from* the bucket, or actually put the pump in it?"

"This is a submersible version. So submerge it."

Geoffrey did. It gurgled as water displaced air in the cylinder. When he lifted the piston, it displaced—pumped—the water that was inside, as Jorge had hoped. The big surprise was that, when he returned the piston to its original position, it pulled more water along, pumping that, too.

"Look at that!" Zapp breathed. "*¡Doble efecto!*"

"Pumps in both directions," Geoffrey agreed, continuing to work the gizmo until the sound of sucking air confirmed that all the the water formerly in the bucket was now puddling around their feet.

Without intending to do so, Jorge Zapp had invented the Gaviotas double-action pump. Two more years would pass before he and Luis Robles finally perfected an ultralight windmill to connect to it. In the meantime, no matter how simple and cheaply they could be built, windmills would remain beyond the budget of too many peasants, who would continue to lug contaminated water from streams or draw it from unsanitary, shallow wells, their depth limited by—

Wait. Alonso Gutiérrez sat bolt upright and looked around. He had fallen asleep lying in the grass on his land in the *llanos*. By the tilt of the Southern Cross at the horizon, it was maybe halfway between midnight and dawn. He closed his eyes. The answer was still there. So obvious.

Alonso knew all the problems of pistons—they were more than a thousand years old. One problem, for example, was the seal created by the water against the sides of the sleeve. To move a piston in order to make the enclosed water rise, you spent energy lifting it against the pressure of that seal, as well as against the weight of both the water and of the rod and piston. But what if . . . ?

Alonso fumbled in his pockets for a pen, then scribbled notes on his palm and down the inside of his forearm. Over the next week, he carried a notebook constantly, until he realized what he was doing and threw it away and disappeared into the shop and just built a model of the thing. Instead of wasting energy by lifting a heavy piston, why not leave the piston in place within a lightweight plastic sleeve, and *lift the sleeve instead?*

Almost timidly, he went to find Jaime Dávila. Jaime was in the workshop, half-hidden behind a stack of solar water-heating panels. His bench was strewn with sections of copper pipe, some welded together, some sliced lengthwise. "Heat exchangers," he explained, brushing his thick black hair out of his eyes. "I'm still not there."

For some time, Jaime had been attacking the clean water problem from the opposite direction: He was trying to design a purifier that would use the sun to boil tainted water, then somehow deliver it at a temperature cool enough so that it could be drunk on demand. Such a device could prevent a lot of disease. He and Alonso and Geoffrey Halliday were always talking about inventing something that would make them heroes— something that would change *everything*. Alonso looked down at his crude pump mock-up. Could this be it?

"What's that?" Jaime asked.

Alonso explained. Jaime whistled.

As in much of the tropics, during the dry season the water table in the *llanos* usually dropped below the limit of conventional hand pumps, leaving disease-ridden surface streams as the only water source. But because Alonso's sleeve pump didn't require applying force against atmospheric pressure, he was certain that it could pump water from a much deeper well.

"Not only that, it's so light even a little kid can work it. A woman can do it with her little finger."

"How much deeper?" Jaime asked.

Alonso hadn't had a chance to sink a shaft for his model yet, but he'd made some calculations. Basically, it depended on the length of the plastic sleeve. Since PVC tubing didn't weigh much compared to the stationary piston inside, Alonso figured that it could easily go four times the conventional depth.

"Forty meters!"

"That's with a normal pump handle. Theoretically, with an extension, it could go much deeper."

Once, they had built an Archimedes pump. Based on the principle of the screw, it used a rotating internal spiral to lift water, but this pump was also limited by the weight of its moving parts. But now Alonso felt like Archimedes himself: With a lever long enough and a place to stand, with his sleeve pump he could suck water from the center of the earth!

"Have you showed it to Zapp yet?"

"He's in Bogotá."

"All the more reason to celebrate. Let's find Magnus."

The Savanna

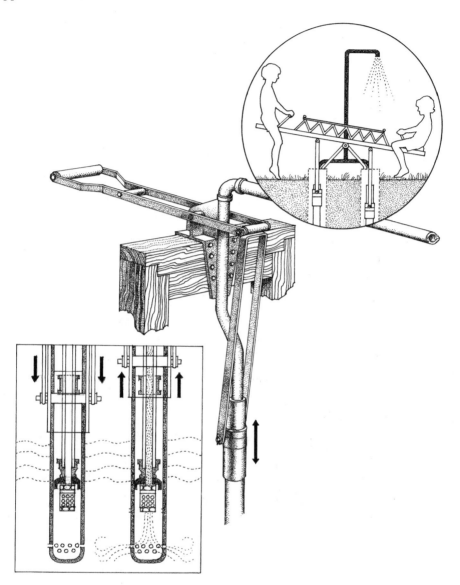

Gaviotas Manual Sleeve Pump

Magnus Zethelius, Sven's son, had recently inherited the position of doctor at Gaviotas. After medical school at the Universidad Nacional, he had come to Gaviotas to give the obligatory year of rural service the Colombian government required of all new graduates in medicine. He had brought his U.S.-born wife, Arianna, a teacher whom he'd met in Bogotá. After Magnus completed his year of service, he and Arianna decided to stay on. It was too interesting in the *llanos* to leave.

Jaime and Alonso found Magnus, uncombed as usual, sitting on the steps of the two-room brick clinic, his tall form bent over the unlit cigarette that he was holding.

"You smoking now?" Alonso asked Magnus.

"No. But maybe I should take it up."

"How's the patient?"

"He's going to make it. It's amazing."

A week earlier, a young adult male Guahibo Indian had been carried into Gaviotas. He'd been bitten the day before on the right leg by a local pit viper called a *montañosa*—a South American lance head. Magnus saw immediately that the man was in an advance state of septicemic shock. Gangrene already discolored his toes, and the lining of his mouth had begun to hemorrhage. Blood pressure and body temperature were both way down. Zethelius pumped bicarbonate fluids, anti-venom serum, and tetracycline into him, but the patient sank deeper into delirium.

This was the rainy season; trying to get him to a hospital would take three days. "I'm sorry," Magnus told the family.

The Guahibos huddled briefly, then returned. Peering up at Zethelius, they asked shyly if they could consult a *brujo*, a shaman. "Of course," he told them. There wasn't much more he could do himself. "Where will you find one?"

"He's here."

Unbeknownst to Magnus, a gnarled old Guahibo he'd been treating for a hernia was a medicine man. He had arrived from his village near the

The Savanna

Orinoco, three days away by horseback, in great pain. Now he shuffled forward, his dark almond eyes mirroring the slanted lobes of his thin moustache. For a minute he loomed a few inches above the dying patient. Then he straightened. "Bring tobacco," he told the Guahibos.

What he wanted was a wild species whose nicotine content was nearly hallucinogenic in strength. They told him that it didn't grow in their part of the *llanos*. The *brujo* closed his eyes. "Then bring me three cigarettes."

Magnus sent a nurse to find them, and also to hunt up Michael Balick, the doctoral candidate in ethnobotany from Harvard who had been at Gaviotas for nearly three years, researching his thesis on indigenous use of native palms. Balick had made friends with the Guahibo, gathering seeds with them and learning their language. He would want to see this.

A breathless Michael Balick soon appeared with a notebook and the cigarettes. The *brujo* lit one. Leaning near the patient's head, he began a repetitive monotonous chant, like the nocturnal keening of a dove. At the end of each phrase, he drew deeply on the cigarette and exhaled smoke in the patient's face. He repeated this over the stricken man's arms and legs. Then he doused the cigarette in a glass of water and let it soak.

Still chanting, he sprinkled the patient from head to foot with tobacco water. This continued for a half hour with the remaining cigarettes. Balick recorded Zethelius's observations as Magnus monitored the vital signs of the patient, who had noticeably calmed. Objectively, Magnus knew that the man still had to be in a clinically toxic state. Nevertheless, minutes after the ritual ended, he asked Balick to note that his patient was now totally relaxed, his heartbeat and temperature normal.

Except for the gangrenous leg, within four days he was well. When told that the leg would have to be amputated, he remained serene. He accepted the prosthesis that Jorge Zapp's engineers made for him and, after learning to use it, returned to hunting and gathering. The paper that Zethelius and Balick later wrote about the shaman's miraculous emergency treatment was published in the international *Journal of Ethnopharmacology.*

As he heard about Alonso Gutiérrez' prototype sleeve pump, Magnus
Zethelius realized the number of lives it could save. "How hard is it to drill
to forty meters?" he asked.

"Remember that silly rig I made us build to find buried topsoil? We
went down nearly a hundred meters."

The sleeve pump meant that women and children would no longer
have to spend hours each day carrying water jugs balanced on their heads.
It was an enormous technological step, reinforcing the Gaviotans' faith
that it was truly within their grasp to change fundamental circumstances
and preserve life. But could technology begin to address the needs of the
spirit, that incorporeal quality that the Guahibo shaman breathed back
into the dying patient? Could anything revive the future for an entire
people?

Only a decade earlier, the Guahibo had still been following hundred-
year orbits around the *llanos*, as they had done since the beginning of time
as they knew it. Settling periodically in a given area, they would hunt
tapir, deer, and finally monkeys when larger prey grew scarce. After about
five years, protein deficiency propelled them on again, and the wildlife
population gradually recovered behind them. But ever since fences began
to lock the Guahibo Indians out of their ancient nomadic rhythm, both
indigenous wildlife and indigenous *Homo sapiens* were visibly declining.

Those same fences, the Gaviotans understood, were actually locking
everyone else in. The sane little civilization they were trying to build was
an attempt to pump sense back into a human race steeping in its own
toxins. Signs of irreversible shock were already evident, and Gaviotas was
such an infinitesimal antidote.

～

Magnus Zethelius's predecessor at Gaviotas was a doctor
from Cali. In 1975, Oscar Gutiérrez had been headed to the Amazon for
his year of rural service when a chemist uncle told him about a colleague,

Sven Zethelius, who was off with a bunch of romantics trying to settle *los llanos*, like pioneers in the North American Old West. Intrigued, Oscar tracked down Paolo Lugari in Bogotá, who told him that the difference was that Gaviotas was helping to save Indians, not shoot them. They had a vacant building that could serve as a clinic. "Are you ready to go?"

A week later, when Gutiérrez was mopping his face in the savanna heat, trying to convert a snake-ridden brick shed into a health post, a group of Guahibo Indians appeared to see the new doctor. Cases of smallpox, they said, were appearing in their village, Caribey. Oscar dropped his mop and bucket and followed them. Smallpox supposedly had been eradicated—he would have to report this to the United Nations. Caribey was just twenty-one kilometers away. If the village were truly infected, everyone's pioneer days might be numbered.

To his relief, it turned out to be measles. But he had never seen so many adults affected at once. They were lying in rows on the earthen floors of the mud-daubed huts. Women were sponging the sick with buckets of river water, trying to keep them cool. Oscar handed out all of his fever and cough medicine. A few days later, the Guahibos returned to tell him that Indians were dying. He went back and saw how serious the situation was. All he could do was distribute more palliatives. "There is no cure for measles," he explained helplessly. "If a person isn't immunized, it can be fatal." Obviously, nobody here was immunized. A horseback priest who rode up from the Río Muco informed him that there were more cases all along the river.

Having arrived just two weeks earlier at Gaviotas after three aching days of overland travel, Oscar Gutiérrez turned around and returned to Bogotá to seek enough vaccine to halt an epidemic. In the federal health department, they told him that none was available, that measles was a common ailment and not to worry. He returned to Gaviotas empty-handed. Within a week, he was back in Bogotá.

"There's no vaccine," he was told again in the Ministry of Health.

"They're dying!" he insisted.

"So what? They're Indians."

He called Cali and Medellín. In Cartagena, he finally located four
thousand doses of measles vaccine and a civil patrol pilot interested in
seeing Vichada. The immunization campaign they undertook saved
many lives, but it was too late for many others. The epidemic, which the
health ministry had chosen to ignore, eventually spread all the way to
Venezuela. Despite high mortality, it merited mention only in the back
pages of Bogotá newpapers.

Originally at Gaviotas to fulfill his rural service obligation, Oscar
Gutiérrez remained an extra year, leaving to study cardiology in Europe
only after being assured that Magnus Zethelius, his former assistant who
had recently earned his M.D., would replace him. Together they drew up
plans for a health system, based on their experiences in the measles campaign, to deal with the great distances between the villages of the *llanos*.
They envisioned doctors flying in airplanes, and boats and jeeps to carry
them across rivers. They wanted radios in every settlement, so Indians and
llaneros could call the central clinic at Gaviotas for emergency instruc-
tions or an ambulance. They wanted the Gaviotas school to be a center for
teaching indigenous people the rudiments of Western medicine and also
a repository of the Indians' knowledge of medicinal botany.

They submitted a funding proposal to the Ministry of Health.
Michael Balick's field assistant, a Guahibo named Eutemio Vargas, helped
them with one of its critical components: a translation into Sikuani, the
Guahibo's language, of the superb manual written in Mexico by American
health worker David Werner, *Donde No Hay Doctor* (Where There Is No
Doctor). Vargas, who had learned Spanish in a mission school and had
served in the army, accompanied them to Indian villages to translate first
aid classes and explain the health organization Gaviotas was founding.

Their work was featured in a film about Gaviotas shown at the United
Nations' 1976 World Conference on Human Settlements and Habitat in
Vancouver. Both Paolo Lugari and Oscar Gutiérrez attended and spoke.
Two years later, at the World Conference on Technical Cooperation
Among Developing Countries held in Buenos Aires, Gaviotas was named
the leading example of appropriate technology in the Third World. Nev-

ertheless, the Ministry of Health rejected their proposal for medical services in the *llanos*.

"It's unconscionable," Magnus said.

"It's votes," Paolo replied. "In *los llanos*, there aren't any. Indians don't. Nobody would count them if they did. That's the way things work."

"I'm sick of how things work," Magnus said. "Maybe we should start our own hospital."

"We will," Paolo said. "We will."

~

IN COLOMBIA IN THE LATE 1970S, NOTHING WAS WORKING AS WELL AS it might have. From 1958, the end of the military dictatorship, until 1974, the two opposing Colombian political parties by agreement had alternated four-year presidencies. This unified "National Front" was meant to gradually over sixteen years institutionalize cooperation throughout the land. This cooperation came to pass, in fact, but not as originally intended.

Over nearly a generation, instead of providing credits, land, and opportunities to raise the mass of their country's population from poverty, the leaders and powerful families of each side mostly divided these among themselves. Indians and poor peasants watched the best property be usurped by large cattle ranches and commercial plantations. Under this transition back to democracy, not only funds for Indian health programs but promises of roads and electricity for far-flung places like the *llanos*, made during military rule, became distant dreams.

As hopes for government aid receded in the hinterlands, the guerrillas grew bolder. Like an allergic reaction to overindulgence, the country found itself breaking out in heightened insurgence in various places at once. One guerrilla group, the M-19, raided the arsenal of a Bogotá army base, where commandos stole hundreds of weapons and proceeded to use them. Soon thereafter, they trapped half the foreign diplomatic corps, including the U.S. ambassador, at a banquet in the Dominican Embassy, keeping them hostage for months.

Las Fuerzas Armadas Revolucionarias de Colombia, or the FARC, which had grown from a peasant defense force to twenty-seven well-armed fronts operating nationwide, kidnapped a U.S. Peace Corps botanist named Richard Starr in the Serranía de la Macarena and held him in a black plastic tent for three years. When he went mad, they finally released him, but within months he committed suicide; that same year, the Peace Corps withdrew from Colombia.

After competitive elections resumed in 1974, initial overtures by the civil government to negotiate an end to political violence were blunted by the army. Prodded by U.S. advisors not to let Colombia succumb to the Castro-inspired revolutionary fervor infecting Latin America, the military was now trying to eradicate two new groups, the Cuban-inspired ELN (National Liberation Army) and the Maoist ELP (People's Army of Liberation). Four years later, a new president declared all-out war against *la guerrilla*, sanctioning what amounted to martial law throughout the land. Arbitrary arrests, torture, and assassinations became routine. For crimes such as painting anti-government graffiti or carrying a concealed jackknife, alleged subversives could be jailed for six months. Villages suspected of leftist sympathies were burned. But rather than suppressing opposition, the conflict only intensified.

Increasingly, Magnus and Arianna Zethelius and the Guahibo paramedics, while making their rounds through the *llanos* by jeep or bicycle or while paddling a string of dugout canoes laden with medical supplies down the Río Muco, encountered insurgents. Some were the children of old *guerrilleros* from the decade of *La Violencia*; some were recent migrants with tales of families massacred during new land seizures. The encounters were usually at roadblocks between villages, where guerrillas would sometimes charge *llaneros* a protection toll while they awaited army convoys to ambush. The Gaviotas medical team was always allowed to pass, a fact that filled them with both relief and dread. The *llanos* were increasingly perceived by the military as *zona guerrillera*. All of its residents were therefore politically suspect, and a doctor could be accused of being a collaborator.

Occasionally, residents awoke to find Gaviotas papered with FARC leaflets. Terrified, they discussed what to do. After their nearest neighbor was abducted one night by silent men with guns, some Gaviotans wondered if they should arm themselves.

"Never," said Lugari. "The best defense is to be defenseless. Otherwise, each side will accuse us of being with the other."

They had always known that their little paradise was a fragile bloom in the harsh, uncivilized *llanos*. Now, the encroaching human threat to their peace seemed a far greater menace than worthless soils and man-eating insects. Their policy became never to ask who anyone was. Like the Red Cross, all factions respected Gaviotas. It became known throughout the region that no one came to Gaviotas armed. It was fair to assume that some *llaneros* who arrived to trade at the commissary for corn or coffee or fish hooks, or who wanted to buy a pump or windmill, might be with *la guerrilla*, but they had to enter Gaviotas like any other neighbor, never carrying a weapon.

There was no way, of course, that this rule could also apply to the army. One day, Blackhawk troop-transport helicopters descended with nearly seven hundred soldiers, who bivouacked on their airstrip. The commanding officer reminded Lugari that before he ever saw it, Gaviotas was a military camp.

"They were a highway crew."

"They were an engineering division of the government of General Rojas Pinilla, constructing an outpost to protect Colombia's strategic eastern sector from Venezuelan and Brazilian expansion."

All the Gaviotans could do was pray that *la guerrilla* didn't choose that moment to attack. A few days later, the army engaged the guerrilla at Tres Matas, twenty kilometers away. As would happen frequently over the next decade, especially after Gaviotas built its magnificent all-solar hospital, the Gaviotas clinic was used by the military for emergency medical support. Helicopters carrying the army's wounded arrived at all hours. In the meantime, a coincidental surge in the arrival of injured civilians suggested that the guerrillas were also bringing their casualties. At times it was not simple to manage this equilibrium. Once, Magnus Zethelius discovered

that he had bedded two opposing combatants in the same room. One had
seventeen lacerations; the other had taken a bullet in his neck. Magnus
had worked so many hours straight that week that he forgot which was
which. Earlier they had been trying to kill each other; now the one who
could still walk was bringing the other water.

Once, when he was a university student, Gonzalo Bernal had considered
but quickly dismissed the idea of joining *la guerrilla*: The idea of creating
a peaceful society through armed conflict seemed doomed by its own con-
tradiction. Yet, as he and his college companions searched for alternatives
to the callous world awaiting them, only two paths seemed open: become
an artist or become a *guerrillero*. There had to be another choice. Gonzalo
was studying communications, and frequently gathered with a group of
friends pursuing degrees in engineering, medicine, and economics, to
speculate about designing an ideal citadel. For a while they contemplated
starting a kibbutz, but no one had money for land or tractors. After
graduation, Gonzalo watched as, one by one, his former classmates joined
the M-19, or went off to the United States, or hocked their high ideals for
a chance at high salaries.

Gonzalo became a secondary school teacher. One evening in late 1978
he returned home from the *colegio* to find that his wife, Cecilia, was still
at the university. Gonzalo switched on the television and flopped on the
sofa. The educational channel was showing a documentary on some development project in the *llanos*. Suddenly, he sat upright.

What he had fantasized, he realized, already existed. The program
mentioned that Gaviotas had an office in Bogotá. The next morning,
Gonzalo Bernal was knocking on the door. Paolo Lugari, wearing a dark
suit and tie, opened it. He couldn't see any university students just now,
he told the thin, dark-haired young man who stood there. He was meeting in a few minutes with officials from the United Nations.

Gonzalo apologized for arriving unannounced. "I'm not a student. *Yo
soy profesor*. I saw the TV program. Can I come back later?"

Paolo paused, regarding him with new interest. He'd forgotten to watch the documentary, he said. "Can you wait? I want to know what they said about us."

He waited. Hours later, Gonzalo Bernal was talking to Lugari, who drummed large, nail-bitten fingers on the desktop as Gonzalo explained why he had come. "Look," Paolo finally said. "A plane is taking medicine to Vichada this weekend. It'll return in two days. Come take a look for yourself. See if it's what you've really been dreaming about."

Startled, Gonzalo replied, "I need to talk to my wife—"

"Bring her along. There's room."

Gonzalo's wife, Cecilia Parodi, was finishing her university degree in occupational therapy. They'd bought a tiny cottage in the mountains near Bogotá, and she had planned to work with handicapped children in a neurotherapy clinic, but now they were leaving everything to go to the *llanos*.

Their weekend visit had been strange. They barely saw Lugari. A Guahibo man who worked with the livestock took them around, showing them the orderly living quarters, each with a solar panel suspended on its palm-thatch roof for heating water. They went to the school, which wasn't in session. They met some *llanero* and Indian children boarding there, who heard their city accents and asked if they were gringos. They saw the site where the new factory was planned and toured the existing workshop, filled with piles of brushed steel windmill parts, colorful pumps, and other unidentifiable contraptions.

They stopped by the little brick clinic. The doctor, they learned, was out vaccinating *los indígenas*. "Not many women here," Cecilia observed.

"Not many anybody," Gonzalo replied.

Most people were gone fishing, their guide said. In the open-air dining commons, a government forester named Pompilio Arciniegas, who was on loan to Gaviotas, sat on a bench at a wooden table, drinking coffee. For three years, Arciniegas had been trying to coax native species and even some exotics such as eucalyptus to grow here. Cheerfully, he admitted that everything they planted dried up after a month. "Either the summer is too hot, or the rain is too intense and washes the soil off into the *caño*. Either way, the roots die."

"Why do you stay?"

"Sometimes I think the government forgot about me. But we're still trying. And I like it. Very peaceful here."

On the flight home, Paolo didn't talk, but kept reading a book that, Gonzalo noticed, he gripped with whitened knuckles. Finally, as the dairy farms of the Bogotá altiplano came into view, Lugari turned around and asked them, "Can you start next week?"

"Start what?" Cecilia asked.

Gonzalo was being offered a job as teacher and administrator at the school. Gaviotas would find something later for Cecilia. Not much pay, and they had a three-year-old daughter. "It would be impossible to just pick up by next week and—"

"Fine. You'll start in January, then."

Afterward, they couldn't remember exactly why they'd said yes. They were even less clear when they returned two months later, having quit their jobs, sold their car, and boarded up their new house. This time when the plane deposited them on the airstrip, no Guahibo guide was there to meet them. No one at all. Instantly, they were perspiring. Their daughter, Tatiana, who until that moment in her life had only tasted cool mountain air, began to wail.

Gonzalo picked up their bags. Cecilia picked up the baby. They looked at each other, then started walking.

They found the man who Lugari had told them was the administrative coordinator. Luis Adelio Gachancipá, a *llanero* of medium build in his late thirties, combed the fingers of one hand nervously through his wavy hair while he relieved Cecilia of her suitcase with the other. All the houses were occupied, he apologized. "So where are we supposed to live?" Cecilia inquired, gathering her own blonde hair with a barrette to allow what little breeze there was to reach her neck. Gachancipá didn't have a ready answer to this question. Temporarily, he put them up in the kindergarten.

Their main luggage was supposed to arrive on a truck bringing provisions from Bogotá; it never did. They got a bit luckier after the first week, however, when the remaining Peace Corps volunteer finally gave up, because the *llaneros* kept insisting that lettuce from his hydroponic garden was good for cows, not people, and that eggplant wasn't good for anything. Gonzalo and his family moved into the house he vacated in Villa Ciencia.

"Hardly anybody approaches us," Cecilia told Magnus Zethelius, the doctor who seemed to be their one friend that first week.

"*Llaneros* are very guarded with new people," he said. "Wait."

They were seated over lunch trays in the dining commons. Lunch was stewed meat and potatoes, corn chowder, salad, and lemonade. *Llanero* workers and their families ate at adjacent tables; on the other side of a low partition, all the engineers were gathered. Heads turned as Luis Robles loudly broadcast his disapproval of the cabbage and beet salad in the direction of the kitchen.

Magnus, embarrassed, seemed about to say something when they noticed Luis Adelio coming up the path. He was accompanied by a short, trim man with thick hair and a wiry moustache, who walked with purposeful, springy steps that had the administrator straining to catch up. "Have you met Jorge Zapp yet?" Magnus asked.

At that moment, Zapp looked over at them and waved. After pausing to exchange greetings with the engineers, he hopped over the partition and joined them.

Magnus made introductions. Jorge explained that he had just returned from a conference in Mexico. "I hear your clothes haven't arrived. Are they taking care of you?"

Cecilia thanked him for asking, and replied that Luis Adelio had kindly provided for them from a community storeroom.

"When we first started here, it was always like that," said Zapp. "Our clothes, shoes, boots, bedsheets, cars, and jeeps all belonged to Gaviotas. It was like socialism almost. Except don't think we're a bunch of socialists."

"So what are you, then?" Cecilia asked.

Jorge looked around. "We're still designing what we are. And really, not much has changed. Our houses, our school, and this dining room all belong to Gaviotas. We all live off grant money we've received, plus the food we raise. We don't have job descriptions—everyone just sort of falls in where needed, or creates something original to do. But it's not anarchy. Social rules here are unwritten, but everyone respects and observes them."

"Such as?" Cecilia inquired.

"Alcohol, for one. It's easy to get drunk in this climate and get into trouble, so if people drink at all, they only do it inside their houses. Same with guns: no one brings them to Gaviotas. Nobody hunts, and—have you noticed?—no dogs. They scare away the wildlife."

Gonzalo gestured at the dining room partition. "Who made the rule segregating the scientists from everyone else?"

Jorge frowned. "It just kind of happened. Ever since we got funding for the UN projects, we get so caught up that we end up bringing work to meals and sometimes stay at the table for hours, still at it—sometimes Alonso sleeps out here. Meals are an important time for creative exchanges, and Luis gets a little testy when that's interrupted."

"The children say Luis is an ogre."

"Did they show you the toy train he built them?"

"It's great," said Gonzalo. "But it's not good for the engineers to be separated from everybody else. You can't build an ideal community without sharing. Alternative technology isn't enough. This also has to do with people."

Zapp looked at Gonzalo curiously. "You know," he said slowly, "just last night, I realized again that we're much more than a field laboratory. Gaviotas is really becoming some wonderful, new kind of community. It took my own children to show that to me." Grinning, he said, "I have to tell you this . . ."

He had been in Cuernavaca at a conference about becoming economically competitive in the Third World. He was sent by the United Nations

Development Programme, which was hinting at a final round of funding to help Gaviotas make their technology not only viable, but attractive enough to compete with conventional systems in the marketplace. Their model alternative society, the UN hoped, was aiming for fiscal as well as energy self-sufficiency. Gaviotas couldn't and shouldn't count on grants forever.

"So I went to the conference," Jorge said, "and the keynote speaker told this parable about an old king."

Realizing that one day he must die, the king had decided that his legacy should be more than castles and an army. He sent for all the wise men of his kingdom, and from all the surrounding kingdoms. When they had gathered, he charged them to write down all the knowledge of the world. They worked for ten years and produced a great encyclopedia, which they presented to him. "This, sire," they said, "is a synthesis of the entire world." Yet the king's eyes filled with concern. "You have labored well," he acknowledged. "But it's thirty volumes. Who's going to read it? You have to condense it to one book."

They got back to work. Ten years later, when they lay the single enormous tome at his feet, he still looked glum. "It's a great accomplishment," he said, "but it weighs a ton. You must digest it further."

Another decade. The king was seriously advancing in years. This time, the wise men returned with all worldly wisdom reduced to a chapter. The hoary old monarch shook his head.

Next, they got it down to a paragraph. Still no good. Finally, as the 110-year-old king lay on his great silken deathbed, breath fluttering in his brittle old ribcage, they brought him all the wisdom of the known universe, boiled down to a single sentence.

"Can you guess what it was?" asked Jorge. Nobody tried.

"There's no free lunch."

They groaned and nodded. "So last night I return to Gaviotas and tell my kids I'm going to tell them a fairy tale. And I did. And at the end, all they say to me is, 'So if there's no free lunch, *Papá*, what will *we* pay with?'"

Zapp looked almost sheepish. "At that moment, it struck me that without even trying, we've been creating another kind of world here. It's based on solidarity, one in which no one knows when he'll be paid for what he does, let alone get rich. It may just be survival, but it's survival in the best sense of the word: People surviving as considerate, sharing beings. No one demands anything of anybody except to get along with each other and work hard, in cooperation. We do this simply because we love to. In Gaviotas, we're driven by something different than competition or pecking orders. And we're content here. Whatever this is, it can't be underestimated."

In the weeks following their arrival, Gonzalo Bernal and Cecilia Parodi looked for signs of this dynamic, humane coexistence. They discovered that Zapp wasn't merely rhapsodizing about no one expecting to be paid promptly. Salaries were chronically late, sometimes even three months. Since everybody received room and board, this wasn't fatal, but it was difficult nonetheless, especially for workers supporting families elsewhere. As a result, the turnover rate in paradise, they learned, was higher than it ought to have been.

A week before the academic semester began, Gonzalo discovered that there was nothing in the school budget. Gaviotas didn't have a telephone, but the national cattlemen's association, FEDEGAN, maintained a radio-phone network, which lately had become even more vital because ranchers were becoming so vulnerable to guerrilla invasions. FEDEGAN had given Gaviotas a unit, which they hooked to a photovoltaic module, and Gonzalo used it to call Bogotá. "How are we supposed to teach and feed 120 kids next week without money?"

"It's coming, it's coming," Paolo tried to soothe him, aware that any cattleman tuning in could hear this conversation. "I've been working on something big. Everybody'll get paid soon."

"Fine. We'll start classes then."

In the meantime, Gonzalo Bernal organized events to keep everybody's mind off money. He held a soccer tournament, then put together an all-star squad and invited teams from settlements up and down the rivers. He and Cecilia built a sand court for playing barefoot volleyball, and started a theater.

The children started arriving from all over the *llanos*, carrying their belongings in cardboard boxes. From his pupils, Gonzalo learned that Gaviotas' current financial crisis was nothing unique. Elsewhere around the savanna, professors employed by the government sometimes didn't get paid for eight months. Some teachers took their classes armadillo hunting in order to eat.

Gonzalo led all the fourth and fifth graders into the engineers' workshop. No children had entered there ever since a few sneaked in and accidentally toppled a cane crusher onto a stack of neon tubes that the engineers were recycling into solar collectors. "What the devil?" hissed Luis Robles.

Gonzalo explained that they were holding class. "I want students to spend an hour every week here, in the carpentry shop, in the greenhouse, and with the cattle. And in the kitchen." He draped his arms around young Henry Moya's and Mariano Botello's shoulders. "If the idea is to show people how to live out here, then someday these kids are going to be running this place, or places like it. We'd better start teaching them how."

In 1973, two years after the first researchers had arrived at Gaviotas, the Colombian government started its own experimental agricultural station along the shores of the region's only freshwater lake, Carimagua, about fifty kilometers to the west. The research at Carimagua was mainly devoted to testing strains of cattle forage imported from all over the world. Unlike deliberately defenseless Gaviotas, where anyone could wander in, vehicles entering there had to pass armed checkpoints with chain barriers at guard booths, where visitors had to surrender their government identification cards before they received passes. A permanent army base was established alongside Carimagua's agricultural station, which from time to time was attacked by the guerrillas.

Many people who came to live at Gaviotas arrived by way of Carimagua. There were jobs there, but the men and women who journeyed across the *llanos* looking for work were frequently given only six-month contracts. Between that and the guerrilla threat, the tranquility of Gaviotas was often more appealing, even if payment was a bit slow. No one ever had to leave Gaviotas; as long as the food and lodging remained free, money wasn't all that mattered.

Yet everybody envied Carimagua's recreation budget, which the government calculated was a necessary perquisite to keep technicians in the lonely *llanos*. The Carimagua soccer team, with its leather spikes and shiny uniforms, was the best-equipped for hundreds of square kilometers. It had been four years since anyone had beaten them, and Gonzalo Bernal decided that, in 1979, Gaviotas was going to do exactly that.

"Never happen, *Profe*," Carlos Sánchez told him. Sánchez, a pale, husky *llanero* from Villavicencio, had taken over the hydroponic greenhouse after the Peace Corps' final retreat. Gonzalo had become friends with him in the school, because Carlos was courting one of the teachers, Mariela Gerenna. Carlos removed his straw hat and scratched through wiry black hair. "We'd have to get up before dawn to practice enough."

Gonzalo began ringing the bell at 4:30 A.M. daily. Cecilia organized the women to sew names on the jerseys. Gaviotas upset Carimagua 2-1 and never lost a match over the next three years.

Spirits were high among the two hundred Gaviotas residents, but money was nearly nonexistent. With the San Pedro's Day festival, a June tradition, approaching, Gonzalo asked Carlos Sánchez and Abraham Beltrán for suggestions of how to celebrate. "We're broke," he reminded them.

"We don't need money, *Profe*," said Abraham. "We just need food, music, and women."

They borrowed a truck and took up a collection of beer and soda at all the neighboring ranches, inviting everybody. Outside El Porvenir ("The Future"), an optimistically named collection of shanties halfway to Carimagua, they found a bus half-entombed in the *llano* mud. Inside was a Villavicencio band named The Vultures, which had already missed the fiesta where they had originally been headed. Gonzalo explained that he had no spare *pesos*, but offered to pay them all the food and drink they could ingest if they'd play at Gaviotas. He had mimeographed bills of varying denominations, featuring pictures of windmills, cassava-grinders, sugar cane crushers, and sleeve pumps. At the party, the band was treated to food and drink that people bought with this scrip, which was redeemable for real cash at Gaviotas if and when there ever was any. Neighbors chipped in so that The Vultures would keep playing. The party lasted three days.

A few days later, Paolo Lugari called on the radiophone to tell Gonzalo Bernal that there was a position open for Cecilia. "She's taking your place at the school. You're now the coordinator of Gaviotas."

"But Luis Adelio—"

"Luis Adelio's been ready to step down for a long time. He was just waiting for the right candidate to replace him. When Magnus suggested you, he and everyone else agreed: Jorge, Luis Robles, me—"

"Luis Robles?"

"Especially Luis."

"He says that I don't understand the first thing about engineering. Which I don't."

"He says you know about engineering a community. Since you got there, worker turnover is practically down to zero."

Gonzalo thought. "Look, Paolo. If I'm administrator, I'm taking a hammer to the partition in the dining hall. Just because some Gaviotans might not have had the luck to get a university education doesn't mean they aren't intelligent or creative. The engineers could use some fresh ears to listen to all their table talk. They might even learn what we need invented around here."

"Fine. Whatever you think we need."

"We need more women."

"Did we lose some cooks?"

"I don't mean cooks. If we get the money for this new factory to mass-produce pumps and windmills, we need to train women to work there. Otherwise we'll be so top-heavy with single men in the middle of nowhere that—"

"You're absolutely right. That's why you're in charge. Starting now."

"But I'm not—"

"Don't worry about making mistakes. All it takes is to be right fifty-one percent of the time. Do that, and we'll be doing fine."

∼

THE EVALUATOR SENT BY THE UNITED NATIONS DEVELOPMENT Programme in late 1979 to decide if Gaviotas would receive another infusion of funding was a Peruvian named Luis Thais. Thais had recently been appointed the UNDP's representative in Colombia. When Paolo Lugari and Jorge Zapp offered to arrange his flight to Gaviotas, he refused. His office had just acquired a new four-wheel drive Ford Bronco, and he couldn't wait to try it out. What better way to get to know the country than a drive to Gaviotas?

"How much time do you have?" Jorge asked.

"All weekend."

Paolo and Jorge glanced at each other. They knew the road, and they both knew how badly Gaviotas needed money.

They left Bogotá at 3:00 A.M., and were over the mountains and past Villavicencio by dawn. Luckily, the dry season had begun. With only one tire change, they bounced into Gaviotas by three that afternoon. After the suffocating dust of the drive, Thais gazed with pleasure at their immaculate white-washed oasis, filled with birdsong and the scent of fruit blossoms.

The original buildings left by the highway department had been refurbished into mechanics and carpentry shops adjoining an engineering lab. Across from them, separated by a maintenance yard, was a commissary and supply warehouse. On the other side of the compound, the Gaviotas school was housed in six individual classroom structures with red-tiled roofs, arranged around a concrete patio. Nearby, more than a hundred boarding students lived in two single-story, U-shaped dormitories. Along one edge of the bamboo-shaded commons area in front of the roofed open-air dining hall was a barracks comprised of single rooms for laborers and researchers. Opposite was another residential wing for couples, and behind that was the two-room brick clinic.

Several private cottages for workers with families had been built within sight of the main compound, and, west of the school, a series of polygonal, one-story modular family apartments known as Villa Armonía was nearly completed. The rest lived a half-kilometer away in Villa Ciencia, across the Caño Urimica. A grove of mango trees planted two decades earlier by the highway crew, close enough to the *caño* to take advantage of rich riparian soils, had grown tall and stout. Hibiscus and allamanda shrubs had been interspersed with guava and cashew trees alongside a new low white building that contained the coordinator's office and guest quarters.

After the travelers refreshed themselves under solar-heated showers, they went off to see the engineers. In the mechanics shop, Zapp and his crew led Thais through the stages of their windmill research. The typical sheet-metal rotors used in the United States, they explained, were too heavy for the *llanos*. Dutch-style canvas blades had made sense in the laboratory back in Bogotá, but the frequency of prairie fires in the savanna quickly changed their minds. Now, blending ideas from Holland, Africa, Australia, and NASA, they were close to achieving a *llanos* model that would pump thousands of gallons per day: a compact unit weighing barely 130 pounds, its blade tips contoured like airplane wings to trap soft equatorial breezes, even under four miles per hour. This was coupled with Jorge Zapp's submersible inverted double-action pump—which, his team of engineers told Thais as Jorge modestly studied the ground, had been awarded the 1978 National Science Prize in Colombia.

They showed Thais the micro-hydro turbines, the original one-kilowatt model and their newly installed ten-kilowatt version, and the dam

on the *caño* made of *gaviones*. Nearby, two sizes of ram pumps were tapping the energy of running water that bubbled past them. Further downstream, on floats made of 55-gallon oil drums, two paddle wheels pumped
water through coils of hoses as they rotated on the current.

He saw the hydroponic gardens and the Gaviotas culverts made with
the giant condoms. Next came the *tanque Gaviotas*, a low-cost technique
for building artificial ponds by pegging chicken wire against the sloping
sides of an earthen pit and swabbing it with thin layers of soil cement
(blended in another Gaviotas innovation, a one-man manual cement-
mixer). There was a series of levers designed by Luis Robles that created
and maintained tension on wire fences, even when gates were open. The
engineers demonstrated the cork-screwing manual well-digger, the parabolic solar grain dryers, the rotating-drum peanut shellers, the ox-drawn
land graders, and the manual baler that compressed hay in a manner
much like the Cinva-Ram formed soil-cement bricks. In the engineering
lab, they showed him hot-water solar panels made from burned-out neon
tubes, the pedal-powered cassava grinder that reduced ten hours of work
to one, the one-handed sugar cane press, and—still in the early stages of
experimentation, but fascinating nonetheless—a solar refrigerator.

They saved Alonso Gutiérrez's sleeve pump for last. "This one," Zapp
told him, "is going to make a lot of women happy. And healthy." Thais
immediately grasped its significance. But what really disarmed him was
an adaptation that Luis Robles had rigged up outside the kindergarten. It
was a see-saw attached to a sleeve pump: As the children played, they re-
plenished their school's water tank.

He was still talking about it over dinner. "How on earth," he asked
Luis Robles, shooing away a flying cockroach that had chosen that moment to dive-bomb their table, "did you ever think that up?"

"It wasn't me," Luis replied. "I was showing students from the school
how a pump handle is a kind of lever, and one of them said, 'You mean
like half a see-saw.' I built one that afternoon. I've got a design for connecting a set of playground swings to a pump too, but there hasn't been
enough time to build it. Or money."

The Savanna

At that, the table grew quiet, except for the cockroach, which kamikazed into Alonso Gutiérrez's lentil soup. Everyone froze except for Alonso, who pounced with his spoon and happily crunched into it.

"Well," said Thais finally. "I see you could use some cash here, before somebody starves."

Part II ～ THE TOOLS

It was Paolo Lugari's suggestion to move Saturday to Wednesday. By the early 1980s, so many visitors were traveling to Gaviotas on the weekends that, instead of resting, Luis Robles found himself spending fourteen hours showing them around. Then too, when celebrated guests such as the president of Spain or Gabriel García Márquez appeared, or the daughter of some cabinet minister with twenty classmates from her Bogotá *colegio*, there was great disappointment if they found that everyone had gone fishing.

Reinventing the days of the week also was safer: In surrounding settlements, weekends were often soaked in alcohol, then ignited with gunfire. By moving theirs to Wednesday and Thursday, the unarmed Gaviotans had a better chance for survival when they ventured out into the wild *llanos*.

With the new United Nations funding that was approved after Luis Thais's 1979 visit, the factory was completed. The grant was intended to help Gaviotas commercialize and distribute inventions and adaptations, to show that appropriate technologies weren't just novelties, but viable alternatives. One of Jorge Zapp's first goals when the money arrived was to perfect the windmill. Several earlier models worked fine but required more maintenance than could be expected from struggling peasants. The problem was driving Jorge crazy: Wind power was the cheapest source of energy in the Third World. They *had* to find a design that could be assembled easily and that would operate at least five years without repairs.

On the fifty-eighth try, he had what he was looking for: a five-bladed beauty, its individual aluminum vanes patterned after the cross-section of landing flaps they found in a NASA airfoil catalogue, each torqued to turn leeward, eliminating the need for a tail. Luis Robles tweaked the angle of rotation so the ultra-light assembly wouldn't blow apart in a gale. By late 1980, seventy men and women were employed at machines designed by the Gaviotas engineers, bending aluminum sheets into windmill blades and stamping out parts for ram pumps in dies hand-tooled by Alonso Gutiérrez to mass-produce petroleum-free Gaviotas energy technology.

Until they figured out a way to levitate materials over the Andes, they would still be dependent on fossil-fuel-based motorized travel—but overcoming that was one of the challenges on their list. Teresa Valencia, an education major who arrived at Gaviotas to write her graduation thesis on rural community development, was astonished en route by caravans of trucks slogging across the *llanos*, hauling in loads of plastic pipe, hoses, aluminum, stainless steel, and glass. "Is the idea to build a city here?" she asked Alonso Gutiérrez.

"Cities don't work. The idea is to build something that does."

"But does it take all this stuff?"

"We need materials to design the tools for a survivable future. The reason cities are so awful isn't technology's fault. Technology just gets corrupted there like everything else. With as many people as this planet is going to have, we're going to need technology's help." He looked at her, and the grimace that had filled his face softened. "We'll need all the help we can get."

He took her to the mechanics workshop. His area was in a corner surrounded by free-standing metal shelves filled with sheet metal, plastic tubing, copper coils, rubber tires, and assorted industrial trash. Teresa picked up one of several wooden spindles lying on a hand lathe that was clamped to a short tool bench. The spindles looked like tops. "What are these?"

"Tops." He took one, coiled a string around it, and spun it across the floor. It continued until it disappeared out the doorway. "Helps me think to make toys. And to play with them."

The only chair was piled with books. No desk. "Where do you draw up your plans?" she asked Alonso, who sat on the floor winding another top.

Alonso tapped his receding hairline. "I hate blueprints. Very inefficient to stop and draw ideas. It's much faster to write in three dimensions."

He took her to the land he owned adjacent to Gaviotas. He took her night fishing on the Río Muco, floating in a dugout canoe the Guahibo had made for him. When Teresa finished her thesis, she stayed on as a Gaviotas schoolteacher.

It was a golden time for the Gaviotans. Gonzalo Bernal and Cecilia Parodi were expecting a baby. Even Luis Robles had mellowed, setting up a household in Villa Ciencia with Mérida Rodríguez, the secretary in the factory. Instead of an overseer, he became a kind of father to the young engineers, using his great innate technical gift to give three dimensions to their ideas, just as he had done for Jorge Zapp for so many years at the Universidad de Los Andes. Luis modified Alonso's ingenious sleeve pump, substituting durable materials for the scraps Alonso had used in his model, and added the ultimate touch: a lever mechanism that allowed it to function on a covered well.

Neighbors—anyone in a four-hour radius—brought their kids to school and stayed to inspect the novel tools coming out of the factory. Soon, the landscape became dotted with what resembled a scattering of bright aluminum sunflowers, as *llaneros* realized that they could sell a couple of cows to buy a new Gaviotas windmill and come out ahead. Before, cattle would die of thirst in the dry season or get stuck drinking in the muddy *caños* and be too weak to pull themselves out. Not only did bovine mortality decline, but with improved access to better water, so did human ailments. The *llanos* began to feel like a livable place.

In February, 1982, an airplane landed unexpectedly, bearing a presidential candidate. "Probably nobody here will actually vote," Paolo Lugari admitted to Belisario Betancur.

Betancur replied that if he lived in Gaviotas, politics would never cross his mind, either. He eyed the solar panels atop the guest quarters and inquired if they were for sale. They were, Paolo said.

"If I'm elected, we'll put a set on the presidential palace."

A few years earlier, in 1977, U.S. President Jimmy Carter had done just that. Carter went on to create tax incentives and significant budgets for research in solar and wind energy. Then his successor, Ronald Reagan, dismantled Carter's solar heating apparatus on the White House roof in 1981, and the tax breaks and funding for alternative-energy research along with it. With Belisario Betancur's election in October, 1982, the Gaviotans found themselves not only engaged in solving the problems of life in the *llanos*, but also part of a visionary international movement. With the loss of support in the most technologically sophisticated nation on earth for clean, sustainable energy, the vanguard of that movement was now partially vacant. Why shouldn't people like themselves from the so-called developing world fill it?

"It's the blackest color that humans can make," the British engineer informed them.

Jaime Dávila and Alonso Gutiérrez nodded. They knew that.

The black to which their host referred consisted of layers of chromium dioxide and nickel oxide deposited on a copper-plated silica film, whose surface was so devoid of light their eyes got lost trying to focus on it.

"The thickness of the film," the engineer continued, "has to be an exact multiple of the wave length of the light used in the oxidation process. Unless you have a computer capable of strictly calibrating the procedure, I'm afraid you simply can't duplicate it."

Jaime and Alonso thanked him. After exchanging business cards, they excused themselves and exited into the gray London afternoon. "Got it?" Jaime asked, grinning.

"*Sí*. Easy."

"What about the computer?" The British process depended on an imposing main-frame.

"Who needs it? They're letting it tell them what to do. Ours will be better without one."

They now knew, they were pretty certain, everything they needed for the solar hot-water panel of their dreams. Since 1979, at the UN's request, Gaviotas engineers had been globe-trotting to solar energy conferences to collect ideas for adaptation to tropical conditions and Third World budgets, and to share their own findings. Jaime had just been to France and Greece. Now they needed to move fast. From London, they flew back to

Bogotá and caught a cab directly to a shabby industrial neighborhood. The taxi dropped them in front of five connected warehouses. The first four had been converted into plumbing, carpentry, mechanics, and electrical shops. The last was for assembly.

It was a little after dawn. They hauled themselves up a makeshift staircase in the fifth building, which led to the experimental lab they'd built on the roof when they moved the solar panel manufacturing operation to Bogotá a year earlier, in 1982. "Ah, home," Jaime sighed.

"Home to our kids," Alonso agreed.

Their kids were thirty street urchins, who, under their tutelage, were turning out forty solar collecters each day. This had all begun with a phone call Paolo Lugari received that same year from a friend of President Betancur's. During the late 1970s, economist Mario Calderón had served with the Inter-American Development Bank in Washington. Calderón was from Caldas, a province of northwestern Colombia whose provincial seal featured a hatchet felling a tree. He was proud of his heritage, but the global energy crisis of 1973 had given Mario Calderón a new economic gauge to measure the effects of development in the modern world.

He returned home to direct Colombia's Central Mortgage Bank, charged with financing public housing projects in cities overextended by rising populations. Mario Calderón had no intention of building instant slums. He wanted livable, dignified dwellings that anticipated the future. A 544-unit apartment complex in Medellín that the bank had financed before his arrival caught his attention, because it heated its water with solar technology designed by a research center in Vichada called Gaviotas.

"Can you come see me?" Calderón asked Paolo over the phone. "I have more projects to propose to you. Bigger than Medellín."

Lugari silently thanked the ancient sun gods. The Medellín venture had turned into a near disaster, for which Gaviotas apparently had now been forgiven. At the time, Gaviotas engineers had been designing a new solar collector prototype nearly every week. In conventional solar panels, water circulates through a grid of copper tubes laid on a black surface inside a box sealed with a pane of glass. The glass allows solar rays to enter but traps their heat—the so-called greenhouse effect. For the public housing in Medellín, instead of costly imported copper, they used recycled neon and fluorescent lamps. In this, an original Gaviotas concept, water flowed through hollow lengths of inexpensive aluminum, painted black and inserted in the salvaged glass tubes to create a greenhouse effect. It featured a thermostatic valve to control internal temperature, alleviating a tendency of early solar collectors to overheat and explode.

The one concern was corrosion. Because mercury can attack aluminum, Gaviotas requested tests to verify that none was present in Medellín's water. An analysis for mercury by a local university was negative. Yet four months after the installation was completed, an agitated Paolo Lugari called Alonso one night to say that a heater had ruptured, flooding an apartment. "Get on the first plane up there and find out what happened!"

Alonso flew to Medellín, sawed apart a collector, and confirmed aluminum corrosion. But the reason was one they hadn't anticipated. The aluminum was being attacked by a compound formed when the chlorine used to purify Medellín's drinking water reacted with organic contaminants. Investigating, Alonso learned that the presence of chlorine, which wasn't needed in the water they drank at Gaviotas, can decompose aluminum at the high temperatures present inside solar collectors. Gaviotas had no choice but to install new collectors, this time made from corrosion-free copper. The error cost thousands of dollars, an outlay only partly mitigated when Alonso devised a way to weave copper tubing into a grid to reduce at least the expense of solder.

Mario Calderón was aware of what had happened. "But you accepted responsibility and solved the problem," he assured Paolo, "and very creatively, too." Now Calderón showed him plans for Niza VIII, a 683-unit housing project in Bogotá. "What would it take to do the whole thing with solar energy?"

"The whole thing?"

He explained to Calderón that if by "the whole thing" he meant deriving electricity from solar energy, the cost would be high. "Photovoltaics are too expensive to buy or make here. It's not Gaviotas' mission. The research to make them cheaper, and their manufacture less toxic, is for First World budgets. But one-fifth of all electricity consumed in Colombia is used to heat water. That's a waste. We can show the country how to save twenty percent of its electricity costs, by doing that for free with the sun."

Not exactly for free, of course. But Paolo believed that the initial investment was affordable.

"Say the cost per living unit of a solar installation runs 35,000 pesos.* Over five years, that comes to less than a 600 pesos a month. If people's monthly utility bills average 1,000 pesos, they could pay for a solar water heater and still have savings left over."

Calderón stood and clasped Paolo's hand. Taller even than Lugari, in his tailored dark gray suit and maroon tie he was the picture of a distinguished senior banker, except that he couldn't stop grinning. "This is so exciting!" he declared.

Calderón assured Lugari that he foresaw many more collaborations between the Central Mortgage Bank and Gaviotas, projects that would entail thousands of solar panels. It would make no sense to build them out in the *llanos:* The weight of transporting glass and the certainty of breakage on the Orinocan trail were prohibitive. Recalling his old dream of helping homeless children, Paolo Lugari visited two Salesian priests who ran a school and shelter in Bogotá for street kids, and promised to turn as many as he could employ into solar energy technicians. Alonso Gutiérrez mourned the prospect of plunging back into the city, but liked the idea and agreed to help. Soon, thirty street kids were helping ten engineers assemble and modify solar panels, stamping out parts on a hydraulic press and using a contraption Jaime built to fold sheet metal. "Sometimes," Alonso murmured, "I just want to stick my finger in that machine to see what happens."

A Gaviotas engineer named Alberto Rodríguez came up with a water-

---

*about U.S. $500 in 1982.

saving distributor mechanism to ensure that shower heads on all floors of the planned multiple-level dwellings expelled the same amount of hot water. After experimenting with various shapes, the Gaviotans chose spherical water storage tanks to compress the greatest volume into the least space (the resulting metal globes seen on many Colombian rooftops became widely known as "Lugari's balls.") A thermal siphon, through which denser cold water constantly displaces hotter, would recirculate the water through the system with no moving parts, creating a virtually maintenance-free solar panel the designers guaranteed for twenty years.

But the biggest challenge for the engineers was that Bogotá is one of the cloudiest cities in the world, and at nearly 9,000 feet, frequently chilly. Out in the torrid *llanos*, no one cared if their bathwater was a little cooler after nine straight days of rain. For Bogotá, they would need a design that could not only soak up direct sunshine, but also gather the warmth of diffused, overcast light.

Then they learned about the British silica film with the ultra-black oxidized layer and ultra-high price tag. An hour at the London factory told them what they needed to know. Back in Colombia, Alonso stripped a copper sheet clean in a bath of nitric acid, rinsed it, then violently oxidized it by dipping it into a solution of copper sulfate dissolved in sulfuric and hydrochloric acids. The result was a texture dense and velvety as a butterfly's wing, and black as fear itself. Since the oxidation was deposited directly on the copper without an intervening layer of film, it was, as Alonso had predicted, even more efficient than the British version. They tested it for a typical week of dank Bogotá weather; it was as though the warmest, most inviting place in town was their shower.

"This is a long way from aluminum foil," remarked Jaime Dávila.

～

In March, 1983, the lovely colonial city of Popayán, birthplace to eleven Colombian presidents, was smashed by an earthquake that shook the land from Bogotá to Quito, Ecuador. More than four hundred people died in Popayán alone. President Belisario Betancur appointed Paolo Lugari to head the historic city's reconstruction, and Mario Calderón to finance it.

Paolo Lugari returned to his hometown. There was gray in his beard now and his hair was thinning, but his energy and self-assurance were even greater than when he was Mariano Lugari's brilliant *enfant terrible*. People who'd watched him grow up wondered why this ebullient, imposing figure, who obviously enjoyed the attention of women, had never married. "I did," he told them. "To Gaviotas."

In the town plaza, he delivered a rousing oration in front of the demolished cathedral, exhorting the populace to restore their heritage. In lieu of payment, Paolo asked that a plane be put at his disposal so he could move between Vichada and Bogotá, even as he was working in Popayán.

So much was going on at Gaviotas that he needed to be everywhere at once. At one point, Paolo was snatched from his Popayán apartment by the M-19 and held captive, but after listening to him for two days, the guerrillas released him out of sheer exhaustion. He jumped back to work. Already Mario Calderón wanted Gaviotas technology for another public housing project he planned for Bogotá. This time it was for a five-story, 5,500-unit apartment complex called Ciudad Tunal, intended to house 30,000 people. To Paolo's knowledge, there wasn't anything comparable: This would be the largest solar-water-heated construction in the world.

In Medellín, Gaviotas' reputation apparently had survived its initial setback, because they'd had to add another factory there just to keep up with orders for solar water heaters. And at home in the *llanos*, they were finally beginning what would be their masterpiece of that era: *El Hospital Rural Autosuficiente para el Trópico "Gaviotas."*

President Betancur named Paolo Lugari his presidential adviser for technical development. Zapp and the engineers rolled their eyes: Paolo wasn't even a scientist. What he had was a prodigious imagination and a memory like magnetic tape that, when called upon to dazzle foundation directors or government contractors, spewed forth in astonishing detail things that they explained to him in their laboratories. Fortunately, he did listen. He, Geoffrey Halliday, and Alonso Gutiérrez traveled to a photovoltaic cell factory in California. They had agreed that the new hospital would be completely solar, which meant buying photovoltaic semiconductor technology to produce its electricity. Maybe, Paolo reasoned, the cost of generating energy with solar cells was dropping within reach of Third World countries.

Looking around San Francisco, Alonso rather doubted it, seeing as solar electricity wasn't exactly catching on yet in the First World. In the factory, Alonso and Geoffrey noted the costly diamond bits in the lathes and the enormous temperatures required in the crystallization process. "It'll take years to give back the energy they use to manufacture these cells," Alonso whispered.

They guessed that ARCO, which owned the plant, was aware of this, because it was for sale. The principal reason, however, was that the Reagan administration was abolishing all federal tax-credits for renewable energy investments in the United States, effectively gutting the U.S. solar energy market. But even if photovoltaics still had a future elsewhere, Alonso and Geoffrey told Lugari that cheaper, more efficient photovoltaic film currently under development would replace cells like these. "They want to pawn this stuff off on some unsuspecting poor country. Can we go home now?"

Yet the idea of sunlight actually making something move was a magical notion that stuck in the engineers' minds. Apparently Paolo Lugari was similarly seduced, because one night he called them together for a secret meeting. "I have something to show you."

From a box he produced what appeared to be a toy in the shape of a small dumbbell, consisting of a foot-long stick with a small glass ball on either end, in each of which liquid could be heard sloshing. The stick was suspended by a pin at its midpoint between two parallel wooden uprights;

if pushed, the dumbbell would spin between them, one end rising as the other fell.

Instead of pushing, Paolo held the dumbell in a vertical position, lit a short candle, and placed it under the lower ball. After a while he let go, and it began to rise. It wasn't hard to guess what was happening: As the heated liquid inside one ball vaporized, it grew lighter compared to the other, which eventually fell and came to rest under the candle. At that point, the process repeated itself.

"So?" somebody asked after a while.

"Use your imaginations. We put several of these together, arranged like spokes on a wheel, use mirrors to focus the sun's rays as the heat source, and we'll have a solar engine."

The engineers could see what was flickering in Paolo's mind: A solar turbine could generate electricity without the high cost of making photo-voltaic cells, nor the expense of controlling toxic contamination from chemical compounds employed in their manufacture. Nevertheless, they had been to solar energy conferences from the Middle East to Florida's Epcot Center, and were pretty aware of how inefficiently sunlight converts to motion. But how could they resist trying?

The wheel they finally produced, after several explosions and considerable expenditure, was nearly five meters across, positioned above a 200-square-meter parabolic mirror. At one revolution every five minutes, their solar motor generated two horsepower. They hooked it up to a cassava grinder and ran it for Paolo. "That's all?" he asked.

Alonso slapped him on the back. "That's how we learn. Scientists have to build absurd things in order to find out what actually works."

～

DURING THE LATE 1970S, THE WORLD BANK HAD FUNDED A COLOMbian government project to colonize virgin territory, using Gaviotas as its model. The first new village, Tropicalia, was to be twelve hours further east into the Orinocan savanna. Gaviotas was contracted to clone its ideas and architecture; a crew spent an entire dry season there, duplicating their living quarters. But support for Tropicalia quickly fizzled "for budgetary reasons," they were told. The lack of a national will to forge a new society had discouraged the Gaviotans at the time—their attempts to fight the madness around them sometimes seemed as futile as trying to change the history that had spawned it.

But now, in the mid-1980s, it appeared that the Gaviotans' moment had come. There was a perception among them of tremendous momentum, a growing, glowing sense that they had not just discovered but fashioned the key to a beautiful future in harmony with an exquisite ecosystem. President Betancur had made good his promise to have them install solar panels at his executive mansion, and had them doing the same on public works projects all over Colombia—even Bogotá's electric utility now had Gaviotas solar water heaters atop its headquarters. Next, Betancur told Paolo, he planned to resurrect the Tropicalia idea of a technological colonization.

Seventy street kids were now trained Gaviotas factory employees. Jorge Zapp had teams of technicians teaching the newly urbanized poor of Ciudad Bolívar, the swelling squatters' colony on Bogotá's southern flank, how to plant hydroponic gardens on their rooftops. The harvest was so generous that a women's cooperative there was supplying lettuce and cucumbers to the city's top grocery chain. And Sven Zethelius had actually found something that would grow in the *llanos*.

Paolo had brought the idea back from Venezuela, where he'd heard an agronomist mention the hardiness of *Pinus caribaea,* the tropical pine that grew in a variety of soils throughout Central America. Zethelius obtained seedlings from Guatemala, Nicaragua, Belize, and Honduras. So far, everything was still alive and even getting taller, with the *hondurensis* variety performing the best. Sven's little plot of foot-high, long-needle pines became a Gaviotas curiosity.

"What will we do with pine trees?" an engineer asked him.

"Who knows? At the very least, we'll learn something from them. What did we do with your five-meter solar engine?"

And, Gaviotas was at last ready to build something that would be a synthesis of all their ideas. A hospital, they all agreed, was appropriate: It was both a practical necessity and a symbol of healing. It was also a matter of security: A new threat was making the *llanos* increasingly risky for their traveling medical teams. In the past, *cultivos ilícitos* were only known in Colombia's volcanic highlands, where, during the 1960s, marijuana had become a cash crop. But news from Guaviare territory, directly to the south, told of something once virtually unknown in Colombia: coca cultivation.

Except for small ritual tribal plots in Colombia's Amazon and in the mountains near Popayán, coca had mainly been grown in Peru and Bolivia. Nevertheless, during the early 1980s an illicit agro-industry began spreading through Colombia's eastern lowlands, to the growing accompaniment of gunfire. Magnus Zethelius, slicing through an emergency patient's jacket one day to remove the bullet in his chest, encountered thousands of pesos hidden in the lining. He sensed that the Gaviotas ban on firearms would not be easy to enforce among the jeepful of men that arrived to take his patient away, each with a semi-automatic Israeli Uzi protruding from under his rain poncho.

The architect for the new hospital was a self-described city rat who had no interest in living in Gaviotas, but he understood the urgency of preparing viable human habitats in remote regions. Before meeting Paolo Lugari, Luis Alfonso Triana had been assigning students at the Universidad de Los Andes the task of designing Amazonian cities for the year 2020—about the time, he figured, that massive populations would be spilling into the jungle. Rather than burn trees out of their way, he envisioned delicate buildings poised on metal legs, suspended at a respectful distance above the foliage.

He had no illusions regarding the difficulty of convincing urban developers to respect nature rather than squash it. Then he was hired to design scale-models of the projects that Mario Calderón's bank was financing around the country. After seeing his work, Paolo Lugari asked him if he'd like to take a little trip.

The first time Triana saw Gaviotas, he was only partly impressed. "The palm roofs are quite *folklóricos*, but it's the wrong aesthetic for solar energy. The solar panels look like giant metallic spiders that just landed from Venus. Metal roofs would not only look better, but if you factor in labor, they're a lot cheaper."

"So I've heard," Paolo said.

Luis Alfonso Triana was turned loose on Gaviotas. Stroking his huge moustache, Luis pronounced the L-shaped cottages of Villa Ciencia, built around roofed hammock patios, as "too normal. We need something related to nature. Something familiar enough to live in but original enough to say 'Gaviotas'." The result was several airy family dwellings, whose hexagonal roofs of thin, corrugated steel, studded with solar panels, consisted of two radically pitched, triangular wings joined at their longest edges, rising to a crest that dipped to resemble a beak.

The galvanized steel roofs of the *gaviota*-shaped homes, cheaper and more durable than corrugated aluminum, were a precursor for the structural columns of the hospital, which he decided should be sleeves of the same metal, filled with concrete. Luis Alfonso loved steel. Gaviotas also needed an all-purpose community center, whose roof "needs to give a dramatic impression," he told a group of Gaviotans, gathered at the chosen site between the school and the dining commons. "It has to be useful, but be symbolic as well. It has to be . . ."

They waited.

". . . stainless steel."

It would be expensive, but Triana had an idea for how it could pay for itself. A mathematician at the university calculated the parabolic shape, which, Triana predicted correctly, would focus and reflect heat away from the building, even at dead noon at the equator. This shape was not unlike the solar collector trough the Gaviotas engineers had once made out of aluminum foil.

"Exactly," said Triana. "If we properly calculate the axis of the parabola, we can harvest solar energy by heating oil in a tube at the focal point." Jaime Dávila examined the blueprints Triana had brought, a rarity at Gaviotas. He turned them upside down. "Hmmm," he said, and wan- dered off toward his lab.

For the hospital itself, Triana proposed a blend of classical Spanish design and the modern materials Gaviotas used in its technology. He wanted a main patio with a fountain, from which a corridor would lead to the surgery and convalescent rooms. The corridor would be of glass and brushed steel, like taking a walk inside a solar collector—half its vaulted roof, in fact, would *be* solar collectors. The entire building, Triana insisted, should be somehow transparent: "Part of the beautiful open space of the *llanos,* not closed off from them." This would be partly accomplished with glass, and partly with the cunning use of ventilation ducts. He had no particular design for the latter, but he was sure the Gaviotas engineers would come up with ideas.

They had to. Magnus Zethelius had reached his limit with the current clinic. It had been built, he told Triana, by people from the highlands who had no idea what happened inside a building in the tropics. Patients had to lie on the floor to stay cool, and Guahibo Indians did what they had always done before white men appeared: remove their clothing. Drugs spoiled so rapidly in the stifling pharmacy that Magnus had tried tacking up cardboard to keep the heat out. "Architects," he told Triana, "should have to sleep in the buildings they design." Luis Alfonso understood that he was being warned.

To boil water, the existing clinic used propane, whose supply depended on trucks that often arrived days late. In the kitchen, they cooked with firewood—a scarcity in the *llanos*, especially since Gaviotas refused to cut the gallery forest along its *caño.* They had to invent solar mechanisms to accomplish all these functions, even if it meant using photovoltaic cells that they couldn't produce themselves. "No place on earth stands apart from the rest of the world anymore," Zapp reminded his engineers. "Not even Gaviotas."

Triana, immersed simultaneously in yet another Gaviotas solar water-heated public housing project in Bogotá, realized that he would need help with the hospital. He brought the best design student he'd ever trained, a

The Tools

recent graduate named Esperanza Caro, to Gaviotas in early 1982 and handed her several notebooks overflowing with the deluge of ideas he had gleaned from hours of listening to Magnus, Lugari, and the engineers. Esperanza poured over Luis Robles's remarks on thermodynamics for a self-cooling roof he'd proposed. The Gaviotans wanted a kitchen equipped with solar pressure cookers. Jorge Zapp had suggested the underground ventilation used in Arabian mosques, whose minarets had high windows through which rising heat escaped, sucking cool air from subterranean tunnels into the main chambers. Esperanza was still reading a month later when Paolo Lugari stopped by to ask when she was going to actually do something.

She stared at him, thoroughly glazed. "At least tell me what you're thinking," he urged.

"Give me a couple more days," Esperanza mumbled.

With Alonso Gutiérrez, she walked the land to look at possible building sites, and what impressed her most was the *llano* wind, always coming and going like a living creature. It convinced her that the hospital must be transparent to the breeze as well as the light. Now she actually began to see a shape jell out of thin, sunlit air. Concentrating, she wedged a short passageway between Triana's patio and solar corridor, oriented to lure the prevailing northwest wind. The vision snapped into focus.

Back at her desk, she started constructing a scale model composed of her thoughts, of everybody's thoughts. Forty-eight sleepless hours later, she showed Lugari a mock-up of his hospital. For several minutes, he stared at the spatial embodiment of years of research and ideas, expressed in intricate, miniature detail. Then he looked up at this petite, exhausted young woman, whose haggard face was nearly hidden behind a wild tangle of curls. "*Magnífico*," he breathed.

"When do we start already?" demanded Paolo. "We need a schedule. We need a flow chart—"

He was drowned out by their howls. Alonso Gutiérrez swung from his hammock and yawned. "We start at the beginning, Paolo. We end when we finish. There's your schedule."

Alonso proved to be correct: Once construction began, the hospital would take four years to complete, something they couldn't have possibly known in advance because no one had ever built anything like it before. But Lugari's urgency was not entirely misplaced, as every day during the 1980s in Colombia came reminders of how fragile the future was. By the time the Gaviotas hospital was completed in 1986, its doctor, Magnus Zethelius, was long gone.

"You can't leave," Lugari had implored.

"We have to. What happened to Luis Adelio decided it."

Paolo didn't argue any further. Luis Adelio Gachancipá, their former administrator, had opened a small store with his wife in a tiny *pueblito* just west of Gaviotas. Gaviotans often stopped by for a beer. Then armed men came for him. No one knew why. After his captors led him off, never to return, people were too frightened to talk.

A new word had crept into the national vocabulary: "paramilitary." *Los paramilitares* were frightening alter egos of both *la guerrilla* and the army. Like the former, they were vigilantes—but for hire, not for a cause. Their usual prey was anyone suspected of leftist sympathies, either correctly or haplessly, but unlike soldiers, the paramilitaries weren't bound by a code of conduct. They were paid either by emerald barons and cattle ranchers tired of being terrorized and extorted by *la guerrilla*, or by the new monster on the block, the cocaine *capos*. In their free time, they often behaved like uncontrollably loose cannons.

Guerrillas, *paramilitares,* and common delinquents increasingly turned to kidnapping for terror and profit. Just before Luis Adelio disappeared, American missionaries in the southern *llanos* were abducted. *Norteamericanos* were choice trophies; in defenseless Gaviotas, Magnus Zethelius's American wife and five-year-old son were now too vulnerable.

Gaviotas resumed using young doctors who were giving their obligatory year of rural service. To assure that *médicos rurales* would continue to serve in remote areas where even the government feared to tread, the country had been color-coded. A freshly graduated doctor might fulfill his or her *rural* requirements by serving as little as three months in a red zone such as the central valley of Colombia's principal river, the Magdalena, which, beginning in the early 1980s, seemed perpetually locked in mayhem between *la guerrilla* and *los paramilitares*. Another hot spot was Urabá, the banana-growing region near the Panamanian border, where union workers were practically used for target practice; another encompassed the skirts of La Serranía de la Macarena. The *llanos* ranged from yellow to orange, indicating that stints of six to nine months were sufficient to comply, but Gaviotas only accepted candidates willing to promise at least a year.

Hospital construction proceeded, a maze of angles rising above the savanna, formed by white walls, glass awnings, skylights, brushed steel columns, floor-to-ceiling slatted-glass window blinds that opened to the breeze, and exposed metal supports finished in blue and yellow enamel. When people elsewhere asked how such apparently cold materials could fill a patient with a sense of warmth and well-being, Lugari and Zapp replied that they had to see for themselves. Somehow, Luis Alfonso Triana, Esperanza Caro, and the engineers were creating an aesthetic and humane healing environment out of what looked like machine parts. The hospital embodied their belief that technology could be as Thomas Edison intended it: an enrichment of human existence, not a steamroller that turned on its inventors and crushed them. As it sprang from Esperanza's model onto the landscape, the hospital thrilled everybody.

Triana's central patio fountain was a film of water flowing over a one-meter cube, providing five times the evaporation surface of a conventional catch-basin to deliver cool moisture to the air. With the combination of her wind corridor and Luis Robles's self-cooling roof, Esperanza Caro became convinced that they didn't need the subterranean ventilation used in Arabian minarets—an idea that dated to the Egyptian pyramids. But the engineers were set on demonstrating that the concept would work. Tunneling through the hospital's perimeter terrace of *gaviones*, they added a series of underground ducts whose hillside intakes opened to the prevailing breeze, to further freshen the interior.

Luis Robles's roof was hailed as a master stroke of simplicity. The old clinic's roofing of corrugated asbestos cement was so sizzling hot that Magnus Zethelius had nearly heaved a rock through it. To avoid sunlight's tendency to turn a roof into a broiler pan, it occurred to Luis to use not one layer of corrugated roofing, but two. By bonding another atop the first, he created a row of honeycombed air chambers, open on either end and sloped at an angle, which absorbed and bled away the solar heat.

The net effect of all these natural cooling techniques was cost-free, maintenance-free air-conditioning. For the patients' rooms, Luis went a step further, borrowing an idea from the drying compartments used in the coffee industry. Recalling from his malaria convalescence the depressing ceiling at which he was forced to stare, he turned these into the equivalent of giant double-hung windows. Atop each room he built a segmented galvanized roof, which slid open by means of a hand-cranked pulley. The result, weather permitting, was a retractable ceiling that gave patients fresh air and the blue sky by day and turned their nights into planetarium shows.

The psychological healing benefits of such gadgetry were obvious, except to their Guahibo neighbors, who considered any hospital insufferable. To wall someone away from family members was, to the Guahibo, the ultimate unhealthy confinement. The Indians themselves designed and built the solution. Just beyond the infirmary, the glass-roofed solar corridor led to a short vine-covered walkway, connecting the Gaviotas hospital to a separate wing: a large square Guahibo maloca. Instead of beds, indigenous patients and their families could lie in hammocks hung from wooden vigas under the broad thatched roof. To earn their keep, relatives of the sick were invited to tend tomatoes, lettuce, cabbage, and onions in an adjacent hydroponic greenhouse.

$\sim$

The Tools

DAWN. THE *SAUCELITOS,* MUSICAL, GOLDEN-EYED THRUSHES THAT dwell in the shrubbery at Gaviotas, faithfully signalled 5:00 A.M. Within a half hour, Gaviotans were parking their bikes by the dining commons and wandering up the paths with their coffee cups. By 5:40, stragglers arrived to find the rest of the community, nearly 250 people, assembled in the garden in front of the *comedor.* Facing them were two rows of young men and women, at rigid attention. They wore short-sleeved khaki uniforms, black rubber irrigation boots, and khaki jungle caps with a red star at the forehead. Each carried a rubberized green backpack, a full cartridge belt, a canteen, and a semi-automatic rifle with an attached banana clip.

The Gaviotans looked at one another and shrugged. This had happened before. The guerrilla *comandante,* a blond man in his mid-thirties, addressed the group. "Which of you is in charge?"

Gonzalo Bernal and Paolo Lugari were both in Bogotá, but had they been present it wouldn't have mattered. "We all are," replied several voices.

The *comandante* paced in front of them. He and his troops, he said, were the *Fuerzas Armadas Revolucionarias de Colombia,* as if everyone didn't know. They were here to discuss the current need for armed struggle.

"We don't fight."

"This is neutral ground."

Their voices were calm. "There is no neutral ground in Colombia," said the FARC *comandante.* "You're either with us or against us."

"We're with people. Not politics."

"We're fighting for the people's rights," the commander replied.

"If you believe in the rights of *el pueblo,* then just let us go to work."

"And please take your guns. They're not allowed here."

Nobody moved except for small children, who approached the *guerrilleros* to inspect their weapons. No one stopped them. Finally, a woman asked, "Are you taking us hostage?"

The *comandante* relaxed and smiled. "Our orders are not to touch anybody here."

"Because what you're doing is too valuable."

Paolo Lugari had more troubles than *la guerrilla* on his mind. Gonzalo Bernal and his family were leaving Gaviotas.

Despite his trepidations, as administrative *coordinador*—a position that everyone in a community that spurned governance agreed was necessary—Gonzal Bernal had made relatively few mistakes. During a lice outbreak in the school, he learned that *llaneros* consider shaving a child's head tantamount to mutilation, for which he accepted responsibility and apologized to each offended family. The hair grew back, as did Gonzalo's esteem in the *llanos*. People continued sending their children to the Gaviotas school, where his wife, Cecilia, was now the director.

Their daughter, Tatiana, swam in the *caños* and ate grasshoppers with her Guahibo playmates. When their son Juan David was born, the *llaneros* filled their cottage in Villa Ciencia with gifts of chickens. Juan David learned to swim before he could walk. It was apparent, in fact, that he was more comfortable in the water than on land. At the age of one year, he still didn't crawl. Earlier, his parents had noticed that, except when he slept, his left hand remained closed. Two Bogotá pediatricians who examined him told Gonzalo and Cecilia that he was simply showing early right-handed preference. But Magnus, who had performed the boy's delivery, had noted that in an otherwise routine birth, Juan David's umbilical chord bore only one artery instead of the normal two. He recommended a specialist.

A neurologist found a lesion on the right side of Juan David's brain. It had caused functional impairment in his left limbs, eye, and ear. After three years of exercises, physical therapy, medication, trips to clinics, and more specialists, Gonzalo and Cecilia finally concluded that they needed to live close to rehabilitation and medical facilities.

Gaviotas grieved. Gonzalo had helped turn a research station into a community, where everyone worked, ate, and played together. He and

Cecilia had started a secondary school, attended by Gaviotans who took nightly correspondence courses via shortwave radio, which Gonzalo supervised. "*Profe*, what will we do without you?" mourned Henry Moya at the last class. When he wasn't reading his lessons, Henry was in charge of planting guava, citrus, papaya, and avocado trees in soil dug from the *caño*.

"Keep studying. All of you. Maybe you can come to school in Bogotá. I'll be helping at the Gaviotas office."

His *llanero* students looked down at their bare feet. Bogotá?

~

ESPERANZA CARO COULD BARELY BELIEVE THAT SHE HAD SPENT five years working for so little pay, yet working with a passion she'd never dreamed could be shared by so many colleagues. Years later, as she designed wind parks for the city of Fukuoka and on Shikoku Island after receiving her doctorate in Japan, she would realize that Gaviotas was the place where she'd first embraced the elements that breathed through all her works. It was also where she had learned how human values can lift technical vocations to higher planes, an understanding affirmed by a Japanese architectural journal that named Gaviotas' hospital among the forty most important buildings in the world.

While Jaime Dávila sweated over the concept of solar pressure cookers for the hospital kitchen, Geoffrey Halliday and Luis Robles collaborated on the methane-fueled stove-top burners. The source of the methane would be cow pies.

Like every other colonist in the *llanos*, Paolo Lugari originally hoped to make cattle prosper in the endless savanna grass. Ever since the Philippines his real dream had been to use water buffalo, but as they weren't found in Colombia, in the early 1970s he'd convinced a rancher to donate twenty pure-bred Brahma bulls to his fledgling foundation. Three years later, he was still touting his good fortune in acquiring such superior beasts, but, far richer in ideas than money, he had yet to buy any cows to go with them. One of the Peace Corps volunteers, an Iowa farmer named Don Mason, finally managed to relieve the all-male herd's bovine loneliness by acquiring a few heifers.

After Mason departed, Omar Marín, a *llanero* with some veterinary training, became the head cowboy. For years, he grazed the cattle on the open savanna, herding them into conventional corrals during roundup. Then, in 1985, Luis Robles designed a big circular pipe-corral with moveable partitions to divide it into pie-shaped holding pens. It featured self-latching gates that a horseback cowboy could open with his boot from either direction, and a watering tank fed by a windmill-powered pump. On one side was a cattle chute with a floor consisting of two parallel spring-loaded steel planks. As cows trod over these while funneling single-file down the chute, they activated a pump that fed a series of overhead showers, rinsing the animals off prior to branding, vaccinations, or slaughter, or simply refreshing them during the dry season.

A hundred meters from the hospital, Luis and Geoffrey built a second watering tank surrounded by a sloping cement floor. As cattle were brought to drink, their cow pies slid down the floor to a gutter, where running water sluiced them to an enclosed concrete vat. Using an attached handcrank, the vat's aromatic contents could be churned into a sort of dung soup. Natural fermentation rapidly converted this slurry to compost and methane; the methane "biogas" flowed through underground pipes to the glass-and-steel hospital, emerging at the stove burners.

That solution was simple compared to the solar refrigerator. How could Gaviotas cool with the sun? The easy answer, which they rejected, was to produce electricity with photovoltaic cells, then plug in a conventional refrigerator. But the possibility of a refrigerator that used the much cheaper technology of thermal solar energy had immense implications for the tropics, and was yet another irresistible challenge.

Jorge Zapp handed Geoffrey Halliday a Danish brochure for a refrigerator whose coolant was ammonia instead of conventional Freon. Shortly thereafter, the discovery in late 1985 of the Antarctic ozone hole, caused mainly by the chlorofluorocarbons contained in Freon, would make this choice especially prescient. At this point, though, what interested Zapp was how the Danes were using calcium chloride, a salt that absorbs ammonia.

Geoffrey studied Danish for a month to get the gist of their system. Granulated white calcium chloride was allowed to soak up ammonia. When the calcium chloride was heated, the absorbed ammonia boiled and was released. Rising pressure forced ammonia gas through a coiled tube that led to a chamber where it cooled, condensing again into liquid. At that point, the ammonia flowed back to the calcium chloride, which again absorbed it.

Why this cycle served to chill food was explained by a principle of evaporation: As a fluid absorbs heat and changes from liquid to a gas, it lowers the temperature of everything surrounding it. To make liquid ammonia undergo this change to a gaseous state simply required applying heat. Why not use the sun, rather than an electric power plant, to provide that?

"A solar version makes sense," Geoffrey assured Jorge Zapp. Unlike most refrigerators, which use a compressor to force room-temperature Freon gas into a liquid state, this solar rendition would require no moving parts, since heat and chemical absorption kept the ammonia circulating. Geoffrey built a test model out of copper. He hooked it to a solar panel that incorporated a Phillips vacuum tube to focus heat on a single point. The cup of water he placed inside turned to ice. That left just two problems to solve: how to keep everything cold at night, when the sun doesn't shine, and how to mitigate ammonia's tendency to corrode metal.

The first proved easier, because the Gaviotans could use the earth's own rotation to regulate the absorption-evaporation cycle. During the day, water heated by a solar panel was directed through a pipe that ran straight down the middle of a canister packed with ammonia-saturated calcium chloride. As heat radiated from the pipe, warming the salt, the ammonia evaporated and cooled the water. By night, without the sun to warm it, that water in turn cooled the calcium chloride, allowing the absorption process to begin again.

Geoffrey had fun solving that problem: The hydraulics and physical behavior of the materials were elegant and dependable. The critical factor, though, was insulation—unless he maintained temperatures in a narrow operating range, everything would stop working. He purchased a normal refrigerator in a Bogotá department store, ripped out the interior trays and the egg shelf, doubled the insulation, and then spent a week redesigning the door so that it would still open. After two years of breakdowns and repeated additions of insulating foam, he came up with a big white box, swaddled with about seven inches of polyurethane. It was ugly, but it worked, except that the commercial solar vacuum tube collector used to boil the ammonia kept shattering. So he and Zapp built their own.

For a container to hold the ammonia-rich calcium chloride, the Danes used specially-treated, non-corrosive aluminum panels soldered around a double thickness of glass. Since soldering aluminum was so costly, Geoffrey packed his calcium chloride into a large pipe of conventional aluminum and hoped for the best. He had to figure out how to vent it against gas buildup, an experiment that lasted two months, during which the whole community of Gaviotas reeked of ammonia. But finally, he had two working models. They installed one in the hospital kitchen and one in Jorge Zapp's house. People came from all over the *llanos* to see the wonderful refrigerator that kept milk and vegetables cold without electricity. Everyone wanted one, until three months later when an aluminum pipe blistered and popped.

Geoffrey was in Bogotá with Alonso Gutiérrez at the time, organizing the workspaces in the new Gaviotas factory-office complex at the base of Monserrat peak. They consulted materials specialists at the Universidad Nacional, who suggested thicker aluminum walls to compensate for surface embrittlement. They tried that; the eventual result was a rather loud noise. To determine at what point metal fatigue set in, they decided to take a pipe that was tested to withstand a thousand pounds' pressure and simply heat it until it burst. They packed it with ammonia-laden calcium chloride, set it on a flame, and retreated to the far end of the 2,000-square-foot shop.

They neglected to inform anyone else of what they were doing. This was 1986, a time when the collective nerves of the Colombian citizenry were rawer than anyone could recall since *La Violencia*. The phenomenon of drug mafias, initially a novelty that TV newscasts had likened to Al Capone movies, had mutated into a live and daily horror. *Narcotraficantes* were using drive-by assassins on motor-scooters to settle scores as casually as businessmen elsewhere used messenger services. Bombs were demolishing police stations, prosecutors' automobiles, and residential neighborhoods where judges lived, as well as seemingly random targets.

Therefore, following the impressive detonation of Geoffrey and Alonso's overheated aluminum pipe, it took a while to round up the Gaviotas factory and office staff from the street where they'd fled. They never did solve the problem. "I'll keep trying, Paolo," Geoffrey promised Lugari.

Paolo sighed, in the process inhaling a large gulp of ammoniac air. "Wonderful, Geoffrey," he gasped.

~

"Pepe Gómez wants to meet you," Guillermo Perry told Paolo Lugari.

"Who's Pepe Gómez?" asked Paolo. They were chatting after a meeting in Bogotá of the Instituto Geográfico Agustín Codazzi, which had undertaken extensive soil studies in the *llanos*. Both Lugari and Perry, then the director of Colombia's federal tax bureau, were board members.

"Pepe Gómez is a very bright friend of mine. A social scientist. He's also a great-grandson of Pepe Sierra."

That got Paolo's attention. "Why does he want to meet me?"

"He's heard that Gaviotas is very interesting."

A legend about Pepe Gómez's great-grandfather Pepe Sierra tells of the day he went to a notary to have a deed copied. The clerk who had him put the request in writing read it and smirked. A little too loudly in the adjacent office, he announced to a colleague that this ignorant bumpkin had spelled *hacienda* without an *h.**

"You know what, *carajo?*" remarked Pepe Sierra when the clerk returned. "I own two hundred forty-five haciendas without an *h.* How many have you got *with* one?"

Semi-literate or not, during the first part of his life Pepe Sierra acquired many square kilometers of what was then vacant land beyond the northern outskirts of Bogotá. He spent the rest of his years watching the city come to him, an inexorable process that left him the richest man in Colombia.

His descendents diversified the family holdings into dairy farms, Caribbean shrimping fleets, Maryland cornfields, New York real estate, French factories. Their children attended lustrous schools; great-grandson Pepe Gómez graduated from Exeter and went on to Cornell.

Instead of business, Pepe studied sociology. He was inflamed by human struggles. While in college during the early 1960s, he joined a network that smuggled Jewish refugees from Hungary, Romania, and Czechoslovakia. As the decade proceeded and his convictions grew more extreme, his family, replete with executives and financiers, soon suspected that they had a black sheep in their midst, albeit a sensitive and brilliant one.

After Cornell, Pepe put oceans between himself and the rest of the flock. He raced cars in Germany, then waded into the political-pharmaceutical ferment of Paris in the late sixties. He drifted to the Punjab with the Sikhs, then to Tibet with the Buddhists, to Algeria with an agrarian reform crusade, to Katmandu, to Yemen, and, finally back to Bogotá, into psychoanalysis. For a while he was married to a militant in the Colombian Maoist worker's movement. Several trips to Red China ensued. China assumed nearly divine ideological status for him, but, ultimately, home was still Latin America, where he found his family's resources useful to a quick study like himself. Just before discovering Gaviotas, he was a con-

---

*In Spanish, the letter *h* is silent.

The Tools

sultant to Fidel Castro's brother Ramón on a dairy project in Cuba's Picadura Valley.

"What do you want from Gaviotas?" Lugari demanded. With Jorge Zapp, they were flying to a meeting with officials at El Cerrejón, the world's largest open pit coal mine, whose financing they were hoping to obtain for a windmill project in northern Colombia. Unexpectedly, Paolo had invited Gómez along, although they had only met a week earlier. Pepe knew what was on Lugari's mind. Was Gaviotas just another refueling stop on this aging rich kid's quest for spiritual identity? The last thing Gaviotas probably wanted was a fabulously wealthy socialist, fearing that either the guerrillas would kidnap him or the army would suspect them all of being communists.

Pepe knew what *he* wanted: Gaviotas potentially rolled all his ambitions into a single reality. Here was an attempt to create a sensible social paradise, to alchemize a good life not only from the barren *llanos*, but from his woebegone Colombia! If they could build a bright future here, people would truly know they could do it anywhere. He saw opportunities Gaviotas was missing to channel its accomplishments into the greater world. Pepe was sure he could find customers who could buy the community's technological wares, and ways to help those who couldn't. Fluent in three languages, Pepe Gómez had plans, contacts, a pilot's license, a mountain bike, and his eye on a cottage at Gaviotas' Villa Ciencia.

He almost blew it during the meeting with the El Cerrejón executives by interjecting frequent remarks that contrasted the purity of Gaviotas' mission with the crass profiteering of the fossil fuel industry, until a glare from Paolo silenced him. Afterward, he promised to stifle his impulses for the greater good of Gaviotas. "Try me," he appealed to Lugari and Zapp.

What the hell, they decided. There was something about wiry Pepe Gómez both maddening and lovable. In only a week at Gaviotas, he had charmed everybody and absorbed an amazing amount of information. He had opinions about everything, which drove Paolo crazy, but he made many shrewd suggestions and possessed the energy of Alonso Gutiérrez.

And with Gonzalo and Cecilia gone, Gaviotas badly needed someone who actually liked to organize.

"Remember," Paolo warned him. "We aren't communists. And we aren't a commune, either."

"What are we then? A company? A community?"

"Both. Neither. We're Gaviotas."

"How hot can solar energy heat?"

Pepe Gómez and Jaime Dávila, necks craned upward, were in the glass-paned corridor of the Gaviotas hospital watching Juan Novoa, one of the former Bogotá street kids, soldering stainless steel tanks to the trusses of the roof.

"Theoretically, as hot as the surface of the sun—about six thousand degrees centigrade. The trick is capturing it," Jaime answered.

"How about here?"

"You mean in Gaviotas? Depends on what we're trying to do."

Before building the solar kitchen, Jaime had set up a laboratory in the new Gaviotas office-factory complex in Bogotá to study fluid mechanics. He especially needed to observe how high-temperature liquids behave when pumped. Jaime had decided to circulate solar-heated, low-viscosity cottonseed oil around the pressure cookers in the kitchen, because to maintain the necessary high temperatures, oil presented fewer problems than water. To test his idea, he'd used a set of Sanyo vacuum-tube solar collectors imported from Japan—supposedly, the highest-temperature solar collectors available.

Now he was showing Pepe the results. Above the kitchen, vacuum solar collectors adapted from the Japanese models were heating the oil to nearly one-and-a-half times the boiling point of water. "When I consulted with the Japanese, they told me they had never worked with such temperatures. So we made our own improved version, by reinforcing the internal hydraulic connections and adding insulation at the extremities of their tubes, and got it to work."

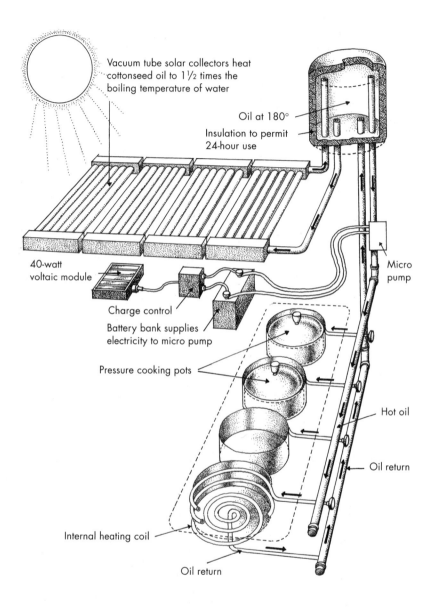

Vacuum tube solar collectors heat cottonseed oil to 1½ times the boiling temperature of water

Oil at 180°

Insulation to permit 24-hour use

40-watt voltaic module

Micro pump

Charge control

Battery bank supplies electricity to micro pump

Pressure cooking pots

Hot oil

Oil return

Internal heating coil

Oil return

Solar Kitchen in the Gaviotas Hospital

As sunlight super-heated the oil, a heat siphon sucked it into a holding tank. When Jaime flipped a toggle switch, a forty-watt micro-pump, run on batteries charged by photovoltaic cells, forced the hot cotton-seed oil through coils that looped around six stainless-steel pressure cookers, then back up to the roof to re-heat. Insulation in the roof-top oil tank kept the closed system hot enough to operate twenty-four hours a day, and there was adequate charge left in the battery bank to illuminate the hospital all night with compact fluorescent bulbs, designed to operate on twelve-volt direct current.

Pepe rubbed his bearded chin, thinking hard. "You use no fuel, but you can pressure cook. Incredible. I'm sure we could sell these things."

"Maybe. All this equipment is pretty expensive." But, he added shyly, he saw more possibilities for two of his other inventions, whose materials were considerably more reasonable. "Let me show you."

The first, in the hospital laboratory, was a simple solar distiller, also powered by their solar vacuum-tube collectors. As concentrated solar heat turned water into steam, a heat siphon pulled it into a spiral-shaped glass condensor, through which four liters of distilled water dripped per day.

The second, known as the *hervidor solar*—the "solar kettle"—had taken Jaime six years to develop after Jorge Zapp showed him the original concept. There wasn't much to see: a stainless steel spigot, connected through the transparent roof to a compact solar panel and a pair of shiny steel tanks. But the solar kettle, all the Gaviotas engineers agreed, had enormous implications.

"The principle," Jaime explained, "begins with an old country custom: boil water one day to drink the next, after it cools. People usually store it in a clay pot in the shade, then later dip the water out. The problem is that frequently it ends up getting dirty again. Or, all the water gets used, and people are too thirsty to wait until more boils, so they end up drinking unpurified water."

Jaime's goal was an inexpensive solar-operated system that would give unlimited boiled drinking water, already cooled to room temperature, straight from a tap any time of day. Furthermore, the device had to work under cloudy skies. Using their oxidized copper formula, Gaviotas solar collectors already heated water to 120° Fahrenheit under diffused light. Since pasteurization begins at 135° F., tweaking their normal operating temperature just 10 percent would eliminate a lot of unwanted microbes. From there, he and Jorge Zapp had calculated, to kill all pathogens meant raising the water to full boiling temperature for at least two minutes.

They accomplished this with a very efficient heat exchanger, which Zapp had begun developing years before and Jaime Dávila finally completed. As untreated water was pumped into the solar panel, it traveled through one chamber of a double copper pipe. At the same time, water that was already boiled was flowing in the opposite direction through the pipe's other chamber, toward a reservoir tank connected to the tap. When the hot and cold water passed each other with just a thin copper membrane between them, the boiled water cooled down and the "raw" water warmed up—the heat exchange.

Once inside the solar panel, the untreated—but now pre-heated—water's temperature rose quickly, often to 160° F. From there, it only needed a little push to hit boiling. That little push was provided by direct sunlight. After studying meteorological records, Jaime realized that even on cloudy days, the sun nearly always breaks through, even if only for a few minutes at a time. The system he built worked like a coffee pot: Whenever a burst of sunshine brought the temperature to boiling, pressure forced the steam that formed through a one-way valve into an upper tank. From there, it condensed back into water, which flowed down through the heat exchanger to the faucet tap.

Using a one-meter-square solar collector as its heat source, Jaime's kettle needed only one minute of direct sunlight to make water start to boil and pass through the one-way heat valve. Because the upper tank couldn't fill unless direct sunlight actually pushed purified water vapor through the valve, any water reaching the tap was always trustworthy. The storage capacity was great enough that, even allowing for days when the sun never broke through, the kettle delivered about eight gallons daily of pure drinking water—more than enough for an average family—only two degrees warmer than when it left the ground.

Like Alonso's sleeve pump, Pepe Gómez realized that this device could change the quality of both water and life for millions of people. He watched as Juan Novoa jumped down from the hospital roof with his welding torch and stood unflinching as Jaime, who looked too young to have designed something so portentous, picked flecks of solder out of Novoa's eyes.

"Please wear your goggles," Jaime begged again, but Juan just grinned, convinced that all the trouble in his life was behind him now. When he was six, Juan had been stolen from his mountain village, taken to Bogotá and used as a domestic slave by a man who regularly beat him until he bled. After running away, for years he slept in buses. He was thieving for his meals when a nun took him to the mission run by the Salesian priests. They gave him clean clothes, a bed, and a choice: learn carbon welding and how to run a lathe, or return to the street. He was fourteen; five years later, Paolo Lugari offered the Salesians' most promising boys a chance to become solar energy technicians.

And five years after that, Jaime Dávila invited him out to the *llanos* to help install the solar works on the hospital. When Juan first saw the boundless space and the flowing *caño*, he told Pepe, he nearly cried. "Then when they said I could stay here, I did. Gaviotas is my family."

Next, Juan and Jaime would be building a solar clothes dryer for the hospital linens. They were basically inverting the concave parabolic roof of the community center, which was designed to reflect heat away, by building a convex parabola out of clear plastic to concentrate the sun's rays inside and trap them like a greenhouse. The floor of the dryer was two hundred-fifty square meters of soil cement, painted black. When they finished, Juan said, the internal temperature should reach 130° F.

Pepe Gómez couldn't get over it. These people could become wealthy off their resourceful technologies, but from the beginning, the Gaviotans had refused to patent their innovations, preferring to share them freely. Gaviotas, Pepe was sure, could show the world how to be environmentally

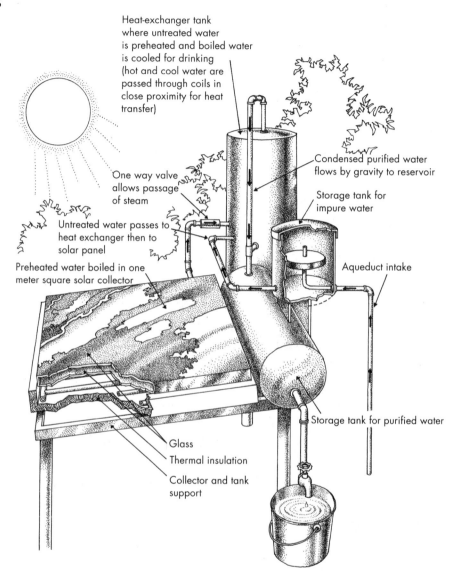

Heat-exchanger tank where untreated water is preheated and boiled water is cooled for drinking (hot and cool water are passed through coils in close proximity for heat transfer)

Condensed purified water flows by gravity to reservoir

Storage tank for impure water

One way valve allows passage of steam

Untreated water passes to heat exchanger then to solar panel

Aqueduct intake

Preheated water boiled in one meter square solar collector

Glass

Thermal insulation

Collector and tank support

Storage tank for purified water

The Gaviotas Solar Kettle for Sterilizing Water

aware, creative, egalitarian, and still make a decent living. Already, Gaviotas-trained *llaneros*, Guahibo Indians, and former street hoodlums were teaching urban architects and engineers how to install solar energy systems in Colombia's cities. It made Pepe dare to envision Colombians changing the wretched image the world had formed about their country, by teaching the entire planet how to live sanely.

The world needed to know about Gaviotas, and Pepe Gómez was going to make sure that it did.

~

BETWEEN 1983 AND 1987, PEPE GÓMEZ MADE SIX FILMS ABOUT Gaviotas. He and Lugari showed them in Curaçao, Canada, Venezuela, Nicaragua, Haiti, and the Dominican Republic. Jorge Zapp did the same in France, Holland, England, Peru, and Paraguay. Technicians from Chile and Costa Rica came to Gaviotas to learn pump designs. Hondurans came for windmill technology. Bolivians began reprocessing their spent neon tubes into solar collectors. A Mexican women's cooperative came to learn how they could stop hauling buckets of water more than a kilometer for their cornmeal business. A team of Gaviotans went back to Veracruz to help them assemble their own sleeve-pump factory.

China, Pepe Gómez learned, was also interested in sleeve pumps. He convinced Paolo Lugari to accompany him there: He wanted to show him Peking, the communes, the fish farms, everything. Paolo was impressed that such a populous country could achieve food self-sufficiency, but for the most part he did not enjoy being in China. He and Pepe argued constantly over the definition of a workers' paradise. "You're just cranky because the beds are too short for you," Pepe said. But Paolo could never get comfortable there, lying down or standing. The only part of China he really liked was all the bicycles.

"We need a bike repair shop at Gaviotas," he told Pepe. "In fact, we should design an appropriate bicycle for the *llanos*. In fact, we need our own bicycle factory."

The Tools

They had a better time in Israel. Lugari loved the kibbutzim—it was the closest thing to Gaviotas he had seen. He liked the *moshavim shitofim*, which blended communal living and private enterprise, even better. He and Pepe were still debating what Gaviotas was, or should be. How could they really be a community, Pepe demanded, if all the land belonged to one person?

"It doesn't belong to me. It belongs to *El Centro Las Gaviotas*, a non-profit foundation."

"A lot of your people don't understand that. They think that they can only live there if they're working for Gaviotas, so it's the same as a company town."

Paolo colored, then finally nodded. "One day," he said, "we'll have a mixed economy. Collective services, communal businesses, but private ownership. People seem to have an obsession about owning a piece of land. Not all people—the Guahibo certainly don't. But we have to be flexible."

An Israeli minister who'd recently visited Colombia had invited them to look at energy projects. Sporting an Arab *keffiya*, Pepe steered them around the desert in a tiny rented Fiat. The current Gaviotas doctor, Marcela Salazar, who'd come along to see the Holy Land, sat next to him. Paolo, his bulk squeezed into the back seat with a big bag of Israeli citrus, peeled orange sections for his companions. At Sede Boker, site of Israel's National Solar Energy Laboratory, they stood at the windy gravesite of Israel's first prime minister, David Ben-Gurion, overlooking a canyon where Jews were believed to have re-entered the Promised Land after forty years in the desert. Two millennia later, Zionist dreamers such as Ben-Gurion had returned again to establish a Jewish homeland. Ben-Gurion was a visionary, but also practical. He noticed that the Promised Land was the only place in the Middle East where The Almighty neglected to put petroleum. In order to survive, he realized, his young nation had better find other sources of energy.

During the early 1950s, he met a Jewish physicist from Oxford named Harry Tabor, who'd emigrated from England with ideas about harnessing the plentiful Israeli sunshine. Tabor assembled a team of researchers, and

the result was the modern hot-water solar panel. By the time Paolo Lugari
and Pepe Gómez made their solar pilgrimage to the Holy Land three decades later, Israel had the world's highest percentage of buildings with
water heated by the sun.

They saw banks of photovoltaic cells in the Negev. They visited solar
ponds filled with heavy brine from the nearby Dead Sea, capable of generating hundreds of kilowatts: The Israelis were pumping the hot saline
solution that naturally concentrates on the bottom of shallow, sunlit salt
ponds through a heat exchanger, which vaporized a fluid to drive a turbine. In Jerusalem, they visited LUZ, a corporation that had built seven
350-megawatt solar power stations in southern California, based on the
same parabolic trough principle as Gaviotas' first aluminum-foil-covered
collector. Near Tel Aviv, scientists at the Weizmann Institute planned to
aim sixty-four curved mirrors at a fourteen-story tower, to generate electricity by concentrating sunlight ten thousand-fold on a single point.

Yet more impressive to the three Gaviotans than all these grand generating stations was an Israeli law requiring simply that water in all buildings up to eight stories high be heated with solar energy. This made more
sense, it seemed, than giant solar utilities: Since sunlight falls everywhere,
the sole reason to centralize solar energy production was to keep utility
companies in business. In Bogotá and Medellín, they had proven that
solar heated water could be affordable to almost everybody. Getting a law
like Israel's passed in Colombia, they agreed, would be one of Gaviotas'
greatest contributions to the Third World.

But Colombia, consumed by other troubles, wasn't ready. During 1985, as
Belisario Betancur neared the end of the single four-year term allowed to
Colombian presidents, his dream for a nation transformed in Gaviotas'
image had been overwhelmed by events. Earlier in his presidency, he,
Paolo Lugari, and Mario Calderón had traveled to a spot on the Río Tomo
twelve hours east of Gaviotas, not far from the World Bank's abandoned
Tropicalia project. There, as a young man, Betancur had once watched a

Guahibo shaman correctly foretell events by reading the wind that blew through a cloud of tobacco smoke. "Marandúa," the shaman had called the jungle wind's messenger spirit, and Betancur now proposed to begin something far more ambitious than Tropicalia here and name it Marandúa. It would be Gaviotas writ large, a citadel gateway to the jungle— on the scale of Brasilia, except built to harmonize with nature, not obliterate it.

In early 1985, a group of settlers was actually sent to the Río Tomo to begin the colonization. Gaviotas was scheduled to provide technology and to plant millions of Honduran pines trees in the surrounding savanna. But before this ambitious project could begin, hell exploded.

Over the previous few years, a huge cocaine mafia had coalesced around a corrupt Medellín congressman named Pablo Escobar. Men who had once smuggled Colombian emeralds now found far more profit in white powder. They dispatched police and politicians with cash, bombs, or bullets. They suborned military commanders with not only currency but collusion, by unleashing their private armies against suspected civilian sympathizers of the military's hated enemy, *la guerrilla*.

With nearly one hundred fifty paramilitary organizations at large in the land, Betancur's peace process was soon doomed. So many elected officials from the Unión Patriótica, the party formed by amnestied ex-*guerrilleros*, were being slaughtered that they'd begun to videotape their meetings to document faces of colleagues who would be dead by the next gathering. In retaliation, *la guerrilla* arose in arms all over the country, their war chests increasingly augmented by profits skimmed from coca harvests and processing laboratories. In an audacious assault in November, 1985, the M-19 seized the federal Palacio de Justicia, just opposite Betancur's solarized executive mansion. After a brief siege, the army rolled tanks onto the national plaza and literally reduced the august building to rubble. A hundred *guerrilleros* and half the Colombian Supreme Court justices died.

As if it were time for nature to punish the misdeeds of humans, that same month the Nevado de Ruiz volcano erupted in Colombia's central

Andean cordillera. On November 16th, an avalanche of steaming mud rolled down its eastern slope toward the pleasant coffee-zone town of Armero, in one of the country's most peaceful areas. It was 11:00 P.M.; most who weren't asleep were listening to a championship soccer match. Seconds after power lines snapped and their radios went dead, twenty-five thousand Colombian citizens were buried.

In the face of multiple catastrophes, President Betancur's great expectations for Marandúa, the next step beyond Gaviotas, were postponed. But at a conference back in 1982, early in his administration, he had broached another plan, and Pepe Gómez had been there to hear it. This involved a contribution that Gaviotas could make to the country, and Pepe decided that it must come to pass. Instead of creating entire new civilizations, Betancur had proposed to infuse practical Gaviotas technologies into the frightening reality of Colombia's most convulsed areas. Rather than promises, this time the government would bring to regions that for years had been, *de facto*, conceded to *la guerrilla*, something they could actually use.

~

JOSÉ IGNACIO LÓPEZ, HIS SUNBURNT LEGS COATED WITH MUD TO WARD off gnats, hoisted the hundred-pound section of cement well-casing on his back and started to climb a sandy path that led past banana trees and coco palms to the village of Canaletal. Behind him flowed the Río Magdalena, the longest and widest river in Colombia, which earlier in his life José Ignacio had never thought he'd see.

José Ignacio was born in a Bogotá squatters' colony, in a hut made of scraps. Through a stroke of fortune, a family friend who had gone to live in the *llanos* learned that a colony of scientists there needed someone to run the kitchen. José Ignacio's mother, María Elisa, became the head cook at Gaviotas, and José Ignacio, instead of haunting the city streets, worked construction, trucked supplies across the savanna, and helped deliver Gaviotas implements to market. Later, he learned to install solar panels.

Thanks to Gaviotas, he'd exchanged a precarious existence for an interesting life and a real future. For this current assignment, offered to him by Pepe Gómez, he'd been trained as a field technician in Gaviotas water technology. But the opportunity was proving a little more interesting than he'd expected.

He turned to watch the boat depart. In it, two more technicians, Hernán Landaeta and Omar Marín's brother, Agusto, were headed downstream to Boca del Rosario, a pueblo with a lovely white church along the riverbank, where José had already installed four sleeve pumps. A few minutes earlier, the boatman had eased the long, narrow launch alongside the shore and dropped him off, along with well-casings, picks, shovels, mosquito netting, hammocks, and piles of plastic and galvanized pipe. Canaletal was on a ridge that separated the river from a broad, reedy marsh filled with ducks and ospreys. It was sometimes hard to fathom how, in a region blessed with so much water, water could be Canaletal's biggest problem.

Yet in villages all along Magdalena Medio, the Río Magdalena's tropical central valley, water-borne disease was the principal cause of death. Women had the choice of lugging their gourds from either the stagnant marsh or the river, brown with human waste, petroleum scum, and agricultural chemicals. Gaviotas planned seven wells at Canaletal, deep enough to insure clean water only a few steps from everyone's doorway. This was a happy notion toward which José Ignacio tried to divert his thoughts from what he'd seen on the river that morning.

The first body had bobbed up alongside the dock as they loaded the boat. People pretended to ignore it, but they couldn't fail to notice that, like others they encountered as they motored downriver, it was missing its head. No one knew for sure who was responsible, but mutilation suggested *los paramilitares*. There were unconfirmed rumors of yet another paramilitary massacre upstream in a town called Puerto del Río. Not that *la guerrilla* was particularly chaste in Magdalena Medio. The Gaviotas technicians already had lost one driver they'd hired locally, killed by the FARC for some unknown infraction.

When the Gaviotans first arrived at their base of operations here, a river port of about 20,000 inhabitants named San Pablo, they were visited by a small detachment from the EPL—the Maoist-aligned People's Liberation Army. Although dressed in mufti, with their automatic pistols, assault rifles, grenades, binoculars, and two-way radios, they were better armed than the police. After a polite but thorough interrogation, the EPL decided that Gaviotas was on a humane mission and could be granted safe passage. "From us, at least."

Their humane mission's official title was the *Plan Nacional de Rehabilitación*. Gaviotans also referred to it by the name Belisario Betancur conceived when he was still president: *Agua Para Todos*—Water for Everyone. It was a war on thirst. The goal was to install appropriate technology—sleeve pumps, ram pumps, windmills, even see-saw pumps—to ensure clean, potable water in hamlets throughout Colombia.

Betancur's term in office had ended in October, 1986. Under his successor, President Virgilio Barco, instead of another amnesty for guerrillas, a National Rehabilitation Plan was designed to undermine the insurgency movement peacefully, by bringing infrastructure and services to areas the government had long neglected. The plan's maps were identical to those used by the Colombian army to denote guerrilla territory. The new battle would be for loyalty: Who could serve rural people better—the government or *la guerrilla*?

Agua Para Todos, which had proposed to bring Gaviotas technology to the nation, was incorporated into this new Plan. The *Plan Nacional de Rehabilitación*, however, lacked the budget to live up to its ambitious title. Spending money to develop the impoverished hinterlands was still widely viewed as bleeding resources away from productive areas—better to pay the military to keep rural rabble in their place than finance long, costly programs whose fruits might take generations to ripen.

Paolo Lugari went to the United Nations and pleaded for funds so Colombia could truly incorporate what Gaviotas had begun during *Agua Para Todos* into the new Plan. "Otherwise," he said, "nothing will happen. A village that needs water will have to wait until a commission from the capital makes a site visit. Then they'll go back and decide. If they agree, next they'll send a surveyor, also from the city. Then a hydrologist. Then a company contracted to lay the pipeline. By the time it's built, the system costs fifteen times more than originally projected, and it's usually obsolete, because by then the community has changed."

The Gaviotas plan, by contrast, sent teams of rural people trained as technical social workers in trucks already loaded with everything needed—pipes, cement, pumps, windmills—directly to the community. "If the people agree, everyone pitches in on the spot. Something that takes a government two years gets done in a week. While they install in one pueblo, they invite neighboring communities to watch. They give classes on how to combat water-related illnesses. By the time they finish in one place, they have the next one already organized."

Luis Thais of the United Nations Development Programme, who had helped fund the expansion of Gaviotas in the 1970s and early 1980s, was now director of the UN's Regional Project for Overcoming Poverty. Thais's experience with the UNDP had proven to him that the problem of poverty was not just ethical but structural. Wealth failed to percolate down to the growing masses faster than it was sucked back upward. At some point, if the spread of desperation went unchecked, it would undermine the rest of society's best efforts and there would simply be no more development. The Gaviotas plan to provide everybody with clean water addressed one of the most basic human needs of all, and the UN agreed to back it.

There was something else, however, that the United Nations wanted from Gaviotas: Jorge Zapp. Zapp's travels for Gaviotas in Latin America had prepared him to be the ideal science and technical evaluator for a comprehensive UN poverty study to be undertaken throughout the Americas. With the hospital complete except for the solar refrigerator, and with his urban hydroponics projects flourishing, Zapp requested a leave of absence from his duties at Gaviotas. "What about *Agua Para Todos?*" Paolo Lugari asked him.

"Its challenges aren't technological," Zapp said, "just organizational

and social. You don't need an engineer. You need a brilliant *loco* to orches-
trate it. And you have him. Pepe Gómez."

Pepe Gómez surely felt richer than his great-grandfather had ever dreamed of being. He took no salary at Gaviotas, but had his own house in Villa Ciencia. He had a commanding view of the world's biggest hacienda: the seemingly infinite landscape of the *llano colombiano*. He lived in a blissfully tranquil community, filled with fragrant blossoms and glittering birds. Their village was now far more beautiful than when he found it. One of Pepe Gómez's first acts as coordinator was to tell Lugari that all the whitewashed buildings "look like a convent. I'm buying a zillion gallons of colored paint."

"Forget it," Lugari growled.

"Go back to Bogotá. We'll do it while you're away."

Paolo had stalked off, muttering. But later, after families had painted their houses however they chose, even Lugari admitted that the place looked great.

Pepe had horses to ride, a mountain bicycle to cross the savanna, and, as he told dubious friends back in Bogotá, "a Mercedes with wings"—a single-engine Piper Dakota that Gaviotas had rented for *Agua Para Todos*. He virtually had his own private landing strip. And, he was running the most fascinating, worthwhile project that he knew of.

Dozens of technicians had been trained. As Jorge Zapp proudly recounted all over Latin America on his UN travels, under *Agua Para Todos* the Gaviotans had begun in the *llanos* like medieval knights errant, going pueblo to pueblo, as many as eight teams in the field at a time. After four months, they had installed Gaviotas equipment in seventy villages in the *llanos* territories of Vichada, Meta, and Casanare. The factory at Gaviotas had geared up, and was now bursting with boxes packed with bright red ram pumps, yellow sleeve pumps, blue see-saws, and polished aluminum windmill parts. Gaviotas technicians were ready to cross the Andes and tackle the nation for the *Plan Nacional de Rehabilitación*.

Off they went, in jeeps, buses, motorboats, and canoes, sometimes remaining in the field two months before coming home for a week's break. They worked as far south as Amazonas province and all the way north to San Andrés and Providencia, Colombia's island possessions off Nicaragua's Caribbean coast. In every village, they would meet with the townspeople, ask the oldest farmers where the best water lay, ask whether enough wind blew there for windmills, ask if they would like a *balancín*— a see-saw—for the schoolyard. Each time, they watched to see who seemed most interested, and they would hire that person—often the local well digger, or bicycle repair man, or mechanic. They paid him in tools and parts as well as cash, so that when they left, somebody remained behind to maintain the equipment.

They became known as *el grupo de Gaviotas*, identifiable everywhere by their white caps and tee shirts with a logo showing Gaviotas' namesake tern flying over a green and yellow landscape. They used no pneumatic tools, only picks, shovels, Gaviotas-designed manual drills, and narrow bamboo ladders sized to fit down wells. Sometimes the army asked what they were doing with jackknives and radios, especially in villages that were considered guerrilla strongholds. Why were they supplying water to the enemy?

"The president hired us to supply water to Colombian citizens."

Usually, by word of mouth, the guerrillas already knew who the Gaviotans were. "Just make sure you stay away from our women," a FARC *comandante* told Pepe Gómez.

On some days, Pepe would begin near the Ecuadoran border in southwestern Colombia, fly the Piper to check installations on the northern Caribbean coast, and make it back to Vichada to sleep in his bed at Gaviotas. But by the second year, the *Plan Nacional de Rehabilitación* primarily focused the Gaviotans' efforts in the central valley of Colombia's main artery, the Río Magdalena. Magdalena Medio contained some of the most coveted soil in the country, as well as key oil reserves, and was therefore where much of the trouble lay—and where the government needed the help and example of Gaviotas the most.

From a source high in the mountains, near where the Andes enter Colombia from Ecuador and fan into three cordilleras, the Río Magdalena brings tons of rich sediment to deposit as it flattens into Magdalena Medio, its broad, fertile central valley. Lush grasses make Magdalena Medio a cattleman's paradise, and therefore an opportune setting for *la guerrilla* to replenish its treasury. A FARC platoon appearing at a wealthy rancher's home would offer two alternatives: Either submit to a monthly "vaccination," often the equivalent of three thousand U.S. dollars, or be kidnapped. In the early 1980s, when some ransoms began to top eighty million pesos,* ranchers began organizing self-defense units.

By mid-decade, the spectre of *narcotráfico* arrived in Magdalena Medio in what became known as the "counter-agrarian reform." Drug barons laundered excess dollars by purchasing farms and ranches at any price, not to grow illicit crops but for their country estates. A hint of what might happen to a farmer's children if he refused to sell usually changed his mind. When *la guerrilla* tried to charge *narcos* the monthly vaccination, armed goons responded. A natural alliance formed between the drug lords' private armies and several ranchers' self-defense units, and the *paramilitares* were born.

Paramilitaries began making pre-emptive strikes against suspected centers of guerrilla activity. Hundreds of peasants were killed, thousands more displaced, and *narco-rancheros* absorbed the lands abandoned by these refugees as well. Along with choice farmland, Magdalena Medio's wealth was also due to great oil deposits. The navigable river, nearly a mile wide in places, had ports for shipping and refining petroleum. Union leaders who organized the oil workers became favorite prey for right-wing paramilitary assassins, as did pro-labor village councilmen and mayors. In response, the guerrillas pledged protection to both leftist union workers and small farmers whether they wanted it or not, and the spiral of terror

---

*U.S. $1,000,000 in 1983.

The Tools

escalated. Not long before the Gaviotans arrived in 1986, the first congressman of the party formed by amnestied *guerrilleros*, the *Unión Patriótica*, was assassinated in Magdalena Medio. With two years, the number of dead UP politicans had reached six hundred; within a decade, the toll was more than two thousand.

Pepe Gómez, scion of one of Colombia's most celebrated family fortunes, worked for nearly three years in full view of the FARC and other guerrilla groups, who never realized who he was. Wearing shorts and his Gaviotas cap and shirt, he traversed the entire Río Magdalena, blending with everyone else. When Rafael Pardo, director of the *Plan Nacional de Rehabilitación* and later Colombia's Minister of Defense, wished aloud that he could see the Gaviotans at work, Pepe dressed him in the same disguise and smuggled him in. Pepe filmed the pump installation at Canaletal, and *la guerrilla* accommodated by rounding up straw-hatted fishermen with cast nets in dugout canoes for the establishing shots.

Somehow, the Gaviotans moved unharmed through their anguished country. With *la guerrilla*, the army, and paramilitary groups all wearing khaki or camouflage and favoring the same Israeli automatic weapons that seemed so plentiful, they rarely knew who was who. As *la guerra sucia*, Colombia's dirty war, deepened during the late 1980s, the community of Gaviotas felt more like an oasis of peace and reason than ever.

The number of pueblos to receive Gaviotas technology topped six hundred. Some teams working in Magdalena Medio traveled with a retired police sergeant who—no one ever understood exactly how—seemed to possess an intimate history with all sides and smoothed the way for the technicians. Such entrée was particularly welcome when they worked in territory controlled by the National Liberation Army—the ELN—which, due to its tactic of blowing up oil pipelines, had become a major polluter of Colombian rivers.

The ELN contended that the government was selling off Colombia's birthright through contracts that awarded foreign companies half the

country's unrefined light crude in exchange for exploration technology.
The damage from oil spills resulting from ELN pipeline sabotage was insignificant, they argued, compared to the messes left by American and British oil firms, who had no stake in the country except the profits they could pump away. Neither their vandalism nor their abductions of oil executives had much impact on Colombia's petroleum policies. But the multi-million-dollar ransoms provided the ELN steady income, so that locals were doubly terrified whenever oil was discovered near their homes—both of heightened guerrilla presence and of petroleum contamination ruining their water and soil.

As Colombian *petroleros* grew increasingly active in the *llanos* north of Vichada, the ELN followed. Might they ever reach as far south as Gaviotas? During the late 1970s, exploration rigs contracted to Ecopetrol, the state oil corporation, had appeared ten kilometers away. *Llanero* drivers and laborers were hired at five times the local salary, and alcohol consumption in the region became epidemic. For two years, trucks with huge tires had roared through Gaviotas, knocking over new trees and scattering cyclists. Then, in 1980, just as suddenly they were gone, leaving the regional economy an imploded wreck. No one knew what Ecopetrol had found. Because oil was a strategic national resource, the corporation would make no explicit acknowledgements until some future time when they might come to claim their asset.

Far from feeling shielded by the purity of their mission, the Gaviotans knew well that environmental endeavors could be perilous. Recently, ELN guerrillas had captured the entire staff of a national park, Parque Natural El Cocuy. Nature reserves, they declared, were elitist contrivances to deny people their rightful access to land. With the others watching, the guerrillas made the park superintendent, a biologist and a celebrated *llanero* harpist, kneel and confess to this crime. Then they summarily executed him with a bullet to the back of his neck.

Gaviotas' *Plan Nacional* technicians, sometimes installing their seesaws in schools occupied by bivouacked *paramilitares,* carried papers stating that they were helping the people, and hoped for the best. There were no assurances. Nearly half the preventative medicine faculty of the biggest university in Medellín had been wiped out by paramilitaries for "subversive" organizing in squatters' colonies surrounding the city. Their principal activities involved teaching people to drink and cook with clean water.

The Gaviotans were interrogated by all sides, demanding to know if they had seen "enemy" troop movements. "A few days ago," Pepe Gómez would reply, "cleaning their rifles." Yet his biggest battle was not with subversives, but with bureaucrats. Via a lottery, the government had chosen which pueblos would receive Gaviotas pumps. But technicians sometimes found themselves working in villages whose water was too brackish, something unknown to officials in Bogotá who had never set foot in Magdalena Medio. Nevertheless, the *Plan Nacional de Rehabilitación* contract didn't permit Gaviotas to make changes.

Pepe called project officials and wrote letters, to no avail. He also begged the government for an ongoing service contract, which Gaviotas offered practically at cost. Maintenance, all agreed, should be the responsibility of each community. But any new technology, Pepe Gómez argued, no matter how simple, took years to firmly establish itself.

But there was no more UN money available to finance this follow-up, and the government had other worries. Murders had risen beyond fifty per day. Ever since the minister of justice was gunned down in 1984, politicians seldom ventured forth without a swarm of bodyguards, a measure which failed to help the attorney general, shot with his escorts four years later. Newspapers advertised armored cars with bullet-proof tires, driven by models dressed in flak jackets. The cultural pages announced lectures by "violentologists," who described death as a growth industry: armored vehicles, bodyguards, short-term life insurance packages for traveling to Medellín, weapon sales, security systems, and "funeral cooperatives." Free-lance motorcycle-mounted assassins could be hired practically like catering services. After years of peace gestures and rehabilitation programs, the country seemed only to be entering a deeper vortex. Anonymous killers drove four-wheel-drive campers into villages, firing with impunity into bars and ice cream parlors and houses: One Saturday in a single Magdalena Medio town the death toll was forty-three, including children and grandmothers.

In 1990, a new president was elected, who favored applying economic tactics to Colombia's problems. President César Gaviria phased out many of his predecessors' social programs and opened the country's markets to the world, in accord with the strategy known as Enterprise for the Americas, outlined in U.S. President George Bush's New World Order. Popular but costly projects such as the *Plan Nacional de Rehabilitación*, intended to stabilize the nation by developing rural areas, were reduced sharply; instead, military presence and spending were increased in *las zonas guerrillas* to maintain peace.

An era of government social programs had given way to leaner fiscal policies that favored incentives and credits for the private sector over public expenditures. The plan to bring water to everybody was just the first of Gaviotas' contracts with the Colombian government to succumb.

∼

IN EARLY 1989, PEPE GÓMEZ, PRESIDENT OF THE CHINESE-COLOMBIA Friendship Society, escorted a group of diplomats from the People's Republic of China, including the ambassador, to Gaviotas. In the hospital, they encountered a family of Guahibo Indians, whose Oriental appearance bore a marked resemblance to their own features. A Guahibo elder gravely examined the ambassador, who might have been his cousin, and asked whether he were Indian or white.

Pepe translated the question. "Which do you think?" the startled ambassador asked the *indígena*. The Indians discussed this among themselves, and finally decided that the ambassador was white, because of his clothes.

The Chinese found this quite amusing, and were enchanted by Gaviotas. To Paolo Lugari's deep alarm, the ambassador announced that Gaviotas was "a socialist paradise."

The Tools

"People will think we're communists," he groaned. A subsequent visit by Alvaro Gómez, the dean of Colombian right-wing politics, who declared that Gaviotas embodied "profound conservative principles" only partly calmed his concerns. "Why does everyone want to classify us? We're not ideologues. All ideologies do is start trouble."

"You're too paranoid," Pepe Gómez said. Paolo didn't rise to the bait, as he had on many other occasions. For six years, he and Pepe Gómez had waged many skirmishes, over merchandise the commissary should stock, over film scripts about Gaviotas, over whether beer should be available in the community center, whether to bring in a parabolic antenna, whether a Land Rover or a Jeep would make a better ambulance, whether the Gaviotas school should prepare students to study at a university or simply to be spontaneous self-learners.

"People have been brainwashed to think that a degree is more important than knowledge," Paolo would thunder. "They don't learn how to think. Their curiosity is blunted." He believed that Gaviotas students should be taught to do everything they needed for a new life in the *llanos:* the carpentry shop, the factory, hydroponics, the tree nursery, even the hospital. "The world has too many specialists. We need more generalists who can see all the connections and possibilities."

"And if somebody wants to become an engineer?"

"If he's raised to be creative, he will. He doesn't need a degree—look at Luis Robles. Our goal should be to give them an *educación gaviotera*—teach them that the world is one big opportunity."

"Then why haven't you been following up on opportunities to make the world one big Gaviotas? You've got a sheaf of letters from Kuala Lumpur, from Uganda, from places in the Caribbean—from China, for that matter—all wanting to start a Gaviotas of their own."

Paolo took a deep breath. "It's one thing to sell them windmills," he said. "It's another to replicate the spirit of Gaviotas somewhere else. How can we sell that? The governments of Thailand and all those other places think in terms of programs. We don't have programs. Gaviotas is a sum of random occurrences born out of chaos. Gaviotas is the Uncertainty Principle. It's a place where chance can incubate, where cooperation replaces competition."

"Then why are you and I always fighting?" Pepe asked, leaning back in his chair and shading his eyes from the sun.

Paolo stopped pacing the patio in front of the *coordinación* office. "Because you're too linear! Because you learned the traditional way of thinking in a university—a gringo university, even! Gaviotas is a non-linear phenomenon. It's evolved with absolutely no planning whatsoever."

"I've noticed."

But now Pepe Gómez was leaving, and Paolo found himself far more bereft than relieved. Their battles had never been personal; they never became enemies. When Paolo couldn't sleep in China, he went to Pepe's room and they talked all night until he finally dozed off in the chair. When Pepe's marriage crumbled, Paolo walked with him through the streets of Cali until dawn. And now, Pepe was to be Colombia's ambassador to China, an opportunity that Gaviotas couldn't deny him, even as they realized how much they would miss him.

As for Pepe, on the day in 1989 he flew the Piper out of Vichada for the last time, he cried all the way to Bogotá. At the state dinner the Chinese embassy gave before he left for Beijing, he described, speaking in English because the ambassador spoke no Spanish, how his passage through Gaviotas had changed his way of seeing and understanding. "Life is not just a linear experience."

At Gaviotas, Pepe Gómez had taught classes to second graders, assisted Marcela Salazar in surgery, and roped, branded, and vaccinated livestock with Omar Marín. He'd organized the fruit harvests, started a lending library, stocked the commissary with ice cream and pharmaceuticals, raised bees, and procured strings and instruments when he discovered great *llanero* musicians living in their midst. During one dry season, he spent nearly a month in the saddle with one of them, the *bandola* master Carlos Ceijas, driving thirsty horses from neighboring ranches to the flowing windmill tanks at Gaviotas. From Ceijas, he learned to lean from his stirrups to drink from puddles, to cook turtle stew in a land tortoise's own carapace, and to test a river for stingrays or piranhas by crossing with the weakest horse in front. Just thinking about all of it that night at the Chinese embassy reduced him to tears again.

Paolo Lugari was having enough problems keeping one Gaviotas going, let alone starting another elsewhere. Along with the disappearance of programs under the *Plan Nacional de Rehabilitación,* by the end of the decade the federal projects financed though Mario Calderón's Central Mortgage Bank, which had built thousands of solar living spaces in Bogotá and Medellín, also came to an end. The government was getting out of the business of social housing programs, and the Central Mortgage Bank now financed private construction. In 1990, a disappointed Mario Calderón had left the bank to direct a national federation of nonprofit organizations.

The United Nations Development Programme, calling Gaviotas one of its best successes, would no longer be funding new projects: The proof of success would be for Gaviotas to survive by itself. Gaviotas was in agreement, but suddenly it seemed that the world was not. After the international price of oil capsized in 1986, plunging the cost of a barrel of crude to less than half its previous value, it never returned to the heights that had prompted the initial worldwide interest in renewable energy alternatives. In Colombia, the incentive to conserve energy was further undermined by Ecopetrol's announcements of major oil and gas discoveries in several parts of the country during the late 1980s and early 1990s, coming at a rate that threatened to usurp Venezuela's position as South America's premier petroleum source.

Sales of Gaviotas solar collectors not only declined, but the market changed in a disturbing way: Gaviotas was no longer providing solar power to the people who most needed cheap energy, but more often to an eco-fashion-conscious elite who could easily afford an investment that took five years to pay for itself. Nor was the market-savvy government, as

a 50 percent partner in all Colombian oil transactions, interested in providing tax credits for solar energy. When Colombia revised its constitution in 1990, a Gaviotas initiative to insert a clause like Israel's, which
mandates that water in all buildings up to eight stories be heated with
solar energy, did not succeed.

Demand for the Gaviotas windmill had also stagnated. By now, virtually anybody in the *llanos* who could buy one already had one. The Gaviotans' hopes of finding new customers for micro-hydro turbines and
windmills were also frustrated by new government economic policies.
Colombian farmers had discovered that, under the relaxed trade policies
that George Bush's administration had enticed Colombia to adopt, they
couldn't compete with a deluge of cheap grains and other foodstuffs that
poured in from giant U.S. corporate producers. It was little consolation to
Colombia's devastated agricultural economy that the United States ultimately paid in one way for its deft dealing, as many bankrupt farmers
turned to raising one crop that no U.S. grower could: coca.

Other farmers simply gave up and sold their lands to drug barons.
Luckily, Gaviotas was spared the dilemma of whether to sell pumps and
windmills to such clients, whose immense acreage was rarely productive:
The *narco* norm was owning a few show cattle and having stables filled
with expensive *paso fino* horses. Drug dealers were even buying up Colombia's legendary three-hundred-year-old coffee plantations and ripping
out the bushes for pasture.

In 1989, the United Nations Regional Project for Overcoming Poverty
had published a three-volume set of books filled with appropriate technologies for developing societies, collected around the world by UN researchers, including Jorge Zapp. Gaviotas had accounted for more than
fifty of them. "You would think," Paolo Lugari said to Jorge, "that with all
those we should be able to make a living."

"It's not that simple, Paolo. A lot of our innovations are beautiful, but
they're beautiful failures."

The Tools

Paolo looked up sharply from the desk in his Bogotá office. Outside his window, various models of aluminum windmills twirled on bright yellow poles and metal tripods.

"You know what I mean," Zapp said. "Like the cassava grinder." It had seemed like a dream machine: The labor of breaking starch capsules of the manioc root—the staple of rural Latin America—to convert into food for her family usually took a woman ten hours each day. The pedal-powered Gaviotas mechanism, which resembled a stationary exercise bicycle, allowed her to do the job in one-tenth the time. It was a technical wonder, but no one had anticipated its inherent cultural flaws.

Among peasants, riding a bicycle was principally a masculine activity, due to a belief—similar to the one responsible for side-saddles—that female genitals could be injured. With the new grinder, therefore, processing cassava was transformed from being a job that strengthened a women's self-esteem, because she provided her family's principal food, into man's work. Women lost a basic role—or, if they operated the machine themselves, men complained that they became restless with so much extra time on their hands. Women themselves reported that relations with their children, who formerly helped wash the cassava stalks, had changed.

"Absurd as all that is," said Paolo, "I admit that we've had very few sales. But that doesn't mean—"

"I'd call the micro-turbine a failure, too."

"But that's your baby!"

"I know. It was the reason I came to Gaviotas. We produced a magnificent small hydo-turbine that technically is a success. But socially, it's a failure. A turbine isn't just a turbine. It's part of a system. There's a canal, a dam, a power line. The turbine is just one element of that system, one that's virtually always handled by the state. When there's no electricity, you call the company and complain that there's no power. Tranferring the responsibility of generating electricity to small consumers was the failure, not the apparatus. It's like remote rural water treatment plants. They don't work. They require biological and chemical expertise beyond that of the local schoolteacher. Once one breaks down, it's expected that whoever was responsible for the initial financing will fix it."

Jorge shrugged. "A micro-turbine means dams, transmission lines, and transformers—if any of those elements fails and the lights go out, unless a technician comes from Bogotá, who fixes it? We sell them at conferences to international institutions who use them for demonstrations, but meanwhile farmers keep buying diesel plants. A diesel plant is a single component. You bring it on a truck, you put it on a concrete slab, and it generates."

Paolo closed his eyes. "Anything else?"

"Sure. The biogas generator."

Lugari had heard this from Zapp before, in India. They had gone to a school in Uttar Pradesh to see the device that later became their model for the Gaviotas water-saving faucet. When students wanted to wash their hands, they pressed up on a chrome-plated knob protruding from a tap that was attached to a spring-loaded valve, and water squirted out. When they released it, it shut.

Driving back to Delhi that afternoon, Jorge had noticed people cooking over cow dung fires, and it got him to thinking. Later he made calculations. He'd concluded, he told Lugari over dinner, that the Indians extracted much more energy by directly burning dried excrement than if they first converted it to biogas—such as the Gaviotans did by mixing cow pies with water, then drawing off the methane that bubbled forth. Biogas was far less efficient, which meant a peasant using it would need more cows than if he simply dried waste from his cattle and burned it.

Paolo had immediately pointed out that, unlike in India, Mongolia, and China, South American peasants didn't cook with dung.

"True," Zapp had agreed. "In India, the word for water buffalo dung means 'resource'—it shows that you have many cattle. In Latin America, the word just means 'shit'—it's useless. But," he'd added, "neither is it part of their culture to collect fresh cow droppings every day in the corral, mix them with water, and pour the mess into a converter."

The Tools

"It's another machine that worked great, but it's a cultural failure," Jorge now reminded Paolo in his Bogotá office. "Actually," he added, "there's another problem with it in the *llanos*. Gas lends no flavor to the food, like firewood does. Without that, food loses its cultural identity." Without waiting for Paolo to protest, he concluded, "But the bottom line is that using biogas is expensive. It requires an investment in tanks, burners, stoves, et cetera, and, the strength of the flame is limited compared to what you get from firewood. A typical biogas burner generates maybe half a kilowatt of energy. In a fair-sized wood fire you can easily get up to ten kilowatts. Biogas is cleaner and resourceful, but twenty times more energy means a lot to a peasant."

"We always knew that the kitchen, with all those stainless steel pressure cookers and photovoltaic cells, was too expensive for an average *llanero* household," Lugari argued. "But it was intended to be a showcase, to show what was possible."

"I know. That's not the point."

The point was that Jorge had come to tell Paolo that he wasn't returning. The United Nations had asked him to stay on.

"It's not the same, Paolo. We've become commercial. There's nothing wrong with that. But the research spirit, the pleasure to create new ways of doing things has changed. It's now mainly the pleasure of satisfying contractors. I sought refuge in Gaviotas from the world of industrial engineering because I didn't like that world. But now we've become the industrialists."

"We've also become a community," Lugari retorted. "We have to support ourselves. We can't have research unless we earn money to pay for it."

"That's true. But how does that happen when nobody's buying? When the grants are gone? The demand for solar energy seems to have been left to future generations."

He wasn't abandoning the mission of Gaviotas, Jorge said. He would be spreading the Gaviotas knowledge and spirit around the world.

Alone, Paolo looked out on the thick, wild lawn that surrounded their Bogotá office and solar panel factory. Next to the display models of the windmills and pumps they sold, a white sign read, in both Spanish and English: "In Gaviotas, we don't cut the grass so that flowers may bloom, that birds may find food, and that soils may defend themselves against erosion." No purely commercial enterprise, Lugari mused, would ever have such a sign alongside their products. They hadn't lost sight of their goals. They just needed money to support themselves. Gaviotas had nearly 250 mouths to feed and a monthly payroll to make. And now, without grants and federally-funded contracts, they had no choice but to compete in the open marketplace that the government was touting.

Gradually, though, as money for research and development dwindled, there were fewer mouths to be fed. One by one, the engineers drifted away. Jaime Dávila's last major design was the solar clothes dryer. He had been part of Gaviotas' golden age of solar energy, but with no UN money and no new projects on the horizon, with Lugari and Zapp bickering, and with Juana recently giving birth to their first child, he had to start thinking about life beyond Gaviotas. He had an engineer brother who was trying to interest him in a gold mining operation in the Chocó. Jaime wasn't looking to strike it rich, but he needed an income. And finding a clean alternative to conventional gold extraction, which was poisoning South American rivers with mercury, was an interesting engineering challenge. Jaime stayed up late several nights, trying to design an inexpensive soil washer with the mercury contained in a closed system so it wouldn't be released to the ecosystem.

On a trip home to the coffee zone to visit his family, Alonso Gutiérrez was offered a tempting research position with a company that sold gourmet coffee to Europe. They were perfecting an advanced freeze-drying process; Alonso would have assistants and be encouraged to be innovative anywhere he saw that the factory needed improvements. While touring the facilities, he noticed all the residual coffee grounds outside the drying rooms. "What do you do with these?" he asked. Not much, was the answer. Why?

"Just thinking," Alonso replied, with a faint smile.

"Can't you talk to him?" Paolo asked Teresa Valencia.

They sat in the doorway of her office in the Gaviotas school, watching a downpour soak the courtyard. An ornamental garden of Caribbean pine seedlings planted by the children was enjoying a growth spurt. The school was the recent victim of yet another government cutback. After nearly two decades, the federal subsidy Gaviotas received for providing one of the few schools for thousands of square kilometers had ended. Beginning in the 1990s, rural schools in areas where people lived so far apart that children had to be boarded during the week now had to charge enough for tuition, books, and board to show a profit. But how could Gaviotas charge the *llaneros*, or the Guahibos who had nothing?

"Alonso loves Gaviotas," Teresa assured him. "This is where he lives, he tells me. He still has his land next to us."

"Then why's he working in Manizales?"

"Because he needs the challenge. Engineers are like artists—at least Gaviotas engineers are. For Alonso, it's a question of creativity, not loyalty. He needs that. They're giving him a shop and a research staff. He's like a kid in toyland."

The rain stopped. They rose and walked through the grove of orange, tangelo, lime, and mango trees, Teresa stretching to match Lugari's long stride. They talked about how they were going to afford textbooks. Paolo picked up a fallen mango. "We should be canning these things. Or making jelly. Something." He shook it, nearly in front of her face. "What a stupid thing to waste food."

Teresa linked her arm in his. "Take it easy," she said softly. "Everyone here has so much to do. There are limits to what people can accomplish."

Paolo nodded silently.

"Anyway, I'm staying."

He glanced at her with visible relief; along with the defections in the engineering department, nobody at Gaviotas had been paid for three months.

"This is the best place," she continued. "We'll make it. Besides," she added, "it's so much quieter now, without all those trucks banging in here with more pipes and aluminum."

So it was; Gaviotas seemed drenched in the sweet music of its thrushes, tanagers, kiskadees, and finches. For years, Lugari had pondered how to avoid the noisy, costly, chassis-cracking, energy-guzzling, dust-choking or mud-wallowing truck voyages over the forbidding *llanos* to bring supplies and export their goods. Not long ago, he had finally hit upon the remedy: a dirigible. The engineers said that they could make one themselves: A big, silent zeppelin floating across the flat savanna would be the perfect way to carry tons of freight with minimal energy. There was already an electrolyzer in the meteorological station, for making lighter-than-air hydrogen to fill the weather balloons.

But with work barely proceeding, Gaviotas was now growing silent all by itself. How could they afford to build dirigibles? Without money, how were they going to develop their on-demand clay irrigators, the solar sauna, the centrifuge toilets, the remote access pumps, and all the other prototypes they had in the queue?

Lugari had found it necessary to tell Geoffrey Halliday, who was finishing a smaller version of the solar kettle and still pursuing the ultimate solution to the solar refrigerator, that there simply wasn't a budget to continue speculative research. From now on, everything had to be profitable. And quick.

Geoffrey tried. He worked for three months on a bargain-priced solar hot-water collector, something truly affordable even for the lower classes, and came up with a prototype completely made of glass. There was no way, though, to speed up the necessary months of testing before they could be sure that the seals would hold. In the meantime, Geoffrey, too,

The Tools

was feeling that the atmosphere at Gaviotas had gone from the sheer joy of trial-and-triumph research to plain old survival, like any other architectural or engineering firm.

Once they had worked fantastically hard, only it had all seemed like play, such as when they were given two months before the Pope's arrival in Colombia in July, 1986, to build a children's pavilion in a Bogotá park. They'd flown to San Francisco to study the interactive science and technology Exploratorium, stopped off at an American Solar Energy Society exhibition in Anaheim, then raced home exploding with ideas.

Everyone had chosen a different theme and gone to work. Every three days, they met to analyze each other's projects. As usual, nobody was making drawings—a famous photograph in Gaviotas from that era shows Alonso, Jaime, and Geoffrey holding sticks, sketching plans in the sand. Most often, they just leapt straight into materials. Within a month of returning from California they'd erected a colored-steel-and-glass science pavilion at Bogotá's new Museo de los Niños and filled it with a complete solar kitchen and a techno-tour showing how plants photosynthesize, how solar collectors collect, how lasers concentrate, how photovoltaics make the sun play *cumbia* music in their radios.

Two years later, when Gaviotas was asked to build an open-air science park out west in Risaralda province, they'd decided to take a conventional high school physics book and blow it up into three dimensions. Kids would be able to learn from see-saws that pumped water and sent chrome balls whirling; from a giant wind sculpture that spun simultaneously over horizontal and vertical axes in hypnotic slow motion; from undulating steel cables that replicated light and sound waves; from huge fiberglass parabolas that let them whisper secrets over a kilometer's distance.

It was all such fun. Colombia issued a commemorative stamp in their honor. With Simón Bright—another son of British expatriates, who had taken over as architect in 1988 after Esperanza Caro left for graduate school in Japan—Geoffrey even designed a prototype *lunar* collector, which intentionally lost heat to the night air in order to cool water down to near freezing.

But now those days of euphoric experimentation had given way to a chilling new imperative. "If we have to make money like everyone else," Geoffrey asked Lugari, "then why don't we advertise like everyone else?"

Everyone asked the same question, but on this subject Lugari was immovable. "We're a foundation, not a corporation. We'd lose our non-profit designation—but much worse, we'd lose our credibility. People would think that Gaviotas technology is just one more consumer product, instead of a truly different way of living."

Luis Robles had heard enough. Some big help nonprofit status was to them: The new Colombian constitution of 1990 had just leveled the biggest blow of all, one that effectively eliminated any further chance at infusing public works with Gaviotas' vision. To control a wild proliferation of personal foundations that were simply tax-exempt fundraising schemes for politicians, the constitution now forbid government contracts with nonprofit organizations. With no more prospects of interesting work at Gaviotas, Luis accepted a job offer to design an amusement park in Bogotá.

"This is at least the third time you've quit, Luis," said Paolo. "You'll be back."

But this time Luis really didn't know. He loved the *llanos*, and had claimed a finca of his own, ninety kilometers east of Gaviotas, where he kept his trucks and motorcycle and all the other noisy, smoking machines that Paolo Lugari detested. But coca growers began invading the place, planting *ilícitos* along his *caño* when he was away, and now *la guerrilla* had taken to defending their dope plots. Luis had an invitation through Pepe Gómez to teach workshops over in China. Maybe it was time not just to get out of Gaviotas, but away from Colombia altogether.

"What do I do?" Paolo asked Mario Calderón. "Everyone's leaving." The last to go was Geoffrey Halliday; he, Simón Bright, and Jaime Dávila were starting a solar panel business and solar architectural design firm in Bogotá.

Calderón—Lugari's friend, financier, and confessor—whose bank had built so many solar public works projects and kept Gaviotas fed, was about to leave Colombia himself. In 1991 he would be the new ambassador to Greece.

Calderón's large frame was silhouetted at the window of his second-story Bogotá apartment as he gazed outside, fingering his necktie. Below, an armed guard was screening visitors to the building. Turning, he said, "Even if they go, Paolo, you have to stay. What you've done out there can't stop. An invention as brilliant as the solar kettle can change the world. The sleeve pump, too."

"I used to think that. But we're a tiny dot on the map. So easy to ignore. Or crush."

"Greek civilization also began at a small, local level. You're creating something just as revolutionary."

"Not if the rest of the world doesn't care. Gaviotas doesn't exist in isolation—no place does. Everyone in the same ecosystem, remember?"

Paolo slumped on Calderón's sofa, absently examining his hands. "We've proven that people can live in the *llanos*. In fact, Gaviotans live better than most people. Halliday and Dávila were practically in mourning when they left. Pepe, too. But we can't eat solar panels and windmills. We need the world as much as it needs us." He paused, then laughed briefly. "How arrogant of me. Apparently, the world doesn't need Gaviotas very much at all."

Calderón sat in the chair across from him. "They do. They just don't see it right now because there's so much petroleum. But with more people using more oil than ever, it won't last forever. In the meantime, you have to keep solar energy alive and incubating. Not everyone can afford an oil well: they're in just a few places. But everyone has a sunshine well. Someday they'll have to go to it."

～

ACCOMPANIED BY LEADERS OF THE VARIOUS WORK GROUPS THAT RAN Gaviotas, Paolo Lugari trudged through the woodland they had planted back in 1982, nine years earlier. Like children who seem to grow when their parents aren't watching, Sven Zethelius's *Pinus caribaea* seedlings, which Pompilio Arciniegas and his pine nursery crew had tended so carefully, had shot up past eight feet, then ten, then twenty.

"We're in a real crisis," Lugari told them. They knew that. They had worked so many months without pay that finally they'd asked to talk to him about it.

"We've got some smaller contracts in Bogotá to sell solar panels," Paolo said. "Pompilio's brother Héctor is running the plant there. There's enough money to pay everyone's back wages, and some more for the next few months at least. I can't promise you there won't be more hard times. I've got some ideas, and I'll be meeting with some people soon. But you're all free to go—you know that."

What he didn't tell them was that he had personally taken out a loan to pay their salaries. As he looked around, he didn't regret it for a second. All these *llaneros*, in their straw hats and canvas, flat-heeled *cotizas*. Carlos Sánchez, his wiry hair graying almost overnight when a brother was murdered, who kept producing vegetables in the hydroponic farm. His wife, Mariela, now running the kitchen, who somehow managed to feed everybody, even though they'd had to stop buying things like mayonnaise and ketchup. Omar Marín and his cowboys, keeping the cattle alive to give the Gaviotans a bi-weekly treat of meat. Henry Moya, amazingly, old enough to be running the electrical shop. Gladys Marchena, who'd arrived at age eleven from the mission school her parents could no longer afford and asked for a job washing dishes, now a qualified nurse who delivered babies, treated snakebites, assisted on emergency hysterectomies. Abraham Beltrán, oblivious in his bare feet to the thorny underbrush sprouting beneath the pines, seemingly capable of doing any job that Gaviotas needed doing. . . .

"What I want to ask is this: Can you continue without a coordinator for a while? I know everyone misses Pepe. But you've been doing magnificent work, and we should consider every crisis to be an opportunity. Maybe we'll learn that we don't need an administrator. Maybe we'll discover that you can make your own decisions."

The Tools

By their silence, he realized what a foolish thing he'd said. For years, they had been making their own decisions every day. No coordinator— not Luis Adelio, not Gonzalo Bernal, not Pepe Gómez—could have dreamed up the community that had spontaneously materialized here, like an orderly planetary solar system out of inchoate space dust. Cooperation at Gaviotas was symphonic, each section adding its part without overpowering the rest. There had been no symphony conductor in Gaviotas for nearly two years now since Pepe's departure, but it continued to run in harmony. No jail, judge, or police force, but no crime—the place didn't even have any locks. No church, but an understood morality.

No marriage, even: Out here, people just didn't bother. A few partners had changed over the years—Omar's companion, Míriam, used to be with one of the Landaeta brothers, who was now with someone else, but Lugari had seen the four of them eating lunch together that very day. Yet families remained intact, and children behaved. Some of the potentially doubtful cases, the ex-street kids like Juan Novoa who'd come out here to work, had adapted to Gaviotas so well that they'd refused to leave the *llanos*. Juan and Meri were now expecting a second child.

"Look, *jefe*," said Carlos Sánchez. "We don't need a coordinator to think for us. It just helps to have someone with an overall view to organize. And you're not here enough. Especially now." Paolo didn't even keep a house for himself in Gaviotas, but flopped in any empty bed or hammock if the guest house was occupied. "But we understand that. You're working for us in the city. Someone has to."

Nearly everyone—even Abraham Beltrán, grudgingly donning shoes—had been to Bogotá at one time or another, and knew that Lugari wasn't living like a king off their sweat. Despite stories over the years of various girlfriends, he had never married. He maintained a simple apartment a few blocks from the office, drove a small Toyota that belonged to Gaviotas and lived like a reasonably comfortable monk, surrounded by bookshelves. The closest thing to a valuable personal possession he owned was a treasured copy of *One Hundred Years of Solitude*, inscribed by Gabriel García Márquez to "Paolo Lugari, inventor of the world."

"We're here, *jefe*," Carlos continued. "As long as you let us stay. We've been through crises before."

Paolo smiled. "It's not up to me. This place is yours. Remember?"

They didn't remember, and he explained again that, long ago, he had claimed the land in the name of the foundation, *El Centro Las Gaviotas*. "And you're the foundation. It's all of us."

Again, silence. *Llaneros* didn't fully grasp the concept of collective ownership, Paolo already knew very well. Sometimes he wondered if the obsession to own the land under one's feet was congenital, but he remembered again that Indians like the Guahibo weren't burdened by such needs. But if this desire weren't congenital, then it was surely addictive. The *llaneros* were all exiles or the children of exiles, deprived of their landed birthright by one *violencia* or other, and they yearned for a home. Many Gaviotans had claimed some small surrounding chunk of the *llanos* as their own. The strategy that could keep them surviving, Paolo realized, was for Gaviotas to be the sun to their little satellites, the source of satisfying work and sustenance and collective ideas for their collective future.

He looked around at the pines, still shooting up like giant weeds, a veritable forest where just a few years ago there was only open savanna straight to the horizon, and far beyond. These trees were nearly all that Gaviotas had left. There must be something they were supposed to do with them.

Like a huge secret, the pines loomed over him, whispering in the wind but not telling.

The Tools

Part III ~ THE TREES

ON THE MORNING OF FEBRUARY 20, 1996, THE GALLERY FOREST ALONG Caño Urimica was so swollen with orange-cheeked parrots that at dawn it popped, emitting a huge bubble of parrot squawk that burst over the village of Gaviotas. Two whistling herons with long, elegant necks, breakfasting daintily on the *minifutbol* field in front of the school, flapped away like panicked swimmers. As they passed the new solar-powered microwave telephone tower, the rush of air from their ungainly wings set three long, dangling nests belonging to crested oropendolas swinging in the boughs of a nearby tall *gualanday* tree. Presently the oropendolas themselves appeared at the top of these fibrous slings, adding their musical waterfall to the sounds of awakening.

Soon, the first hot rays of sunlight were slicing away the thick equatorial night and steaming the dew off the moss-covered clay tiles on the roof of Gaviotas' bachelor quarters. Inside, resin tappers tumbled from their hammocks and out the doors of their rooms, milling under solar showers and, with towels slung over their bare brown shoulders, peeking out windows at the rising light. Luis Adelio Chipiaje, one of several Guahibos working in the pine resin, pulled on jeans, rubber irrigation boots, and a white tee shirt with the yellow and green Gaviotas logo. He was headed to the dining commons with his coffee cup when the plunk of an overripe *guayaba* dropping on the roof reminded him.

Finding a bamboo pole, Luis Adelio joined several of his colleagues in the glade of guava trees behind the administration office and started wacking. On Day of the Guava, no one got breakfast at Gaviotas unless they brought in at least four sweet juicy ones. *Commisary*

Where they lined up for meals in the *comedor*, the bulletin board that served as the Gaviotas news digest bore a newly inked poster. It explained the chemical composition of guavas, named the four species that grow at Gaviotas, and reminded everyone that guavas are rich in Vitamin C. Breakfast was potato soup, fried eggs, hot rolls, hot chocolate, and a portion of hard cheese with a slice of a firm, ruby-red preserve known as *dulce de guayaba*—but only a slice. While everyone else went off to work in the forest or the new resin factory or wherever, the cooks and the school children would be rendering bucketsful of fruit that represented the morning's price of admission into guava juice, guava cookies, guava jam, guava cakes and pies, guavas preserved in honeyed syrup, and more *dulce*. With luck, everyone would sample these at afternoon coffee. The previous year on Day of the Guava, that almost happened—until the fire alarm sounded.

The men and women who went to fight that blaze didn't return for two days. When no breeze stirs, a prairie fire on the tropical savanna laps at the grassland like a gentle orange surf, slowly leaving a widening blackened sheet behind it. But that day the wind was goaded by the prow of a storm pushing over the eastern horizon from Venezuela. The flames jumped twenty feet high and surged forward.

It had started in a pasture out beyond the hospital, sparked, the tower sentry believed, by a *bola de fuego:* a ball of lightning that rolled down from the sky and smoked across the savanna like an incandescent billiard ball. Infernos such as this one, fanned by trade winds that blew too consistently for the old tropical forest that once stood here to spring back, had created the savanna. Early on, the Gaviotans had scythed enough firebreaks around their compound to safely allow nature to run its course, except now they had another, new forest to save—a forest that itself had miraculously saved Gaviotas.

With moriche palm fronds, *batefuegos* made of bamboo poles tipped with rubber flaps, a five thousand-gallon pumper pulled by a tractor, and a plow clearing more firebreak swathes across the savanna, the Gaviotans attacked. Heat distortions swirled off the plains. Rogue zephyrs spun the flames in unexpected directions. For two nights they battled to keep the *incendio* from leaping across the gallery forest. At one point, surrounded by firelines, the tractor stalled. Filling his hat with water from a puddle, Carlos Sánchez ran through the flames repeatedly to douse the engine so it wouldn't explode until they could haul it to safety.

At the end, so blackened they barely knew each other, they pounded each other's backs in joy and relief. Gonzalo Bernal grabbed a *batefuego* pole. "Watch!" he yelled, splitting it across his knee. Then he took a bundle of them and did it again, but the bunch wouldn't break. "See?" he declared. "One person alone can't resist. But together, a community can. Gaviotas will never go hungry, because together we can hold back the devil himself!" Gonzalo wiped away soot and tears. "I'm so proud to be your *coordinador* again."

They headed home to a feast of stale guava delights, leaving behind the caracaras and gray hawks to gorge on rabbits and snakes racing across the naked, charred ground. Yet again Gaviotas was saved. This time, by themselves.

⌒

GONZALO AND CECILIA HAD TOLD THEMSELVES THAT THEY WERE lucky. Their daughter, Tatiana, was about to enter college. If Juan David's brain lesion had affected his mental prowess, it certainly wasn't apparent to anybody: At thirteen, he was already a terror at chess and far swifter on the computer than his parents. His condition was fairly stable, and, assured by several doctors that his impairment owed to a prenatal accident and not genetics, they now had two-year-old Federico. They were living in La Calera, a mountain enclave just north of Bogotá. Gonzalo was teaching secondary school in the city and Cecilia was a partner in a rehabilitation clinic for children. The work was good, although having to confront Bogotá every day was an assault on their souls.

Paolo Lugari called. He came to dinner. "By the way," he remarked over dessert, "Did I tell you what the *jefes del grupo* decided last week?"

News from Gaviotas was precious. "What?" they both asked.

"After three years of running the place themselves, Gaviotas has gotten so busy that they need an administrative coordinator again."

Gonzalo and Cecilia exchanged a look whose meaning was not lost on Lugari.

They had never been so serene, yet so alive and fulfilled, as when they lived in Gaviotas. Had it not been for Juan David, they'd never have left—and it was Juan David who decided the matter again. The cruelty he endured at school because of his limp and curled left arm would be unthinkable at Gaviotas, where the only friction he'd inspired among the children was over who got to babysit him next.

Juan David still remembered how the weight of his damaged limbs had lifted when friends at Gaviotas taught him to swim in the *caño*, how he'd paddled and chased minnows for hours while toucans and howler monkeys croaked overhead. Everyone there had embraced him, whereas in Bogotá, pets were his only friends. The Gaviotans lived in a way that someone like him could feel equal to anyone: They did not believe in competition.

Gaviotans gravitated to the tasks where they felt most suited, or invented their own job description. There was no personnel chart; when someone left, they shared responsibilites until another appeared who could take over. Over the years, wages had equalized, so there were no hierarchies. Salaries were above Colombia's legal minimum; everyone received free housing, food, schooling, and health care. Whoever was in charge of the sewers or the garbage was as proud as the inventor of the latest solar device, acknowledged for contributing a vital service, not treated like an untouchable.

All his life, Juan David had heard his parents compare the traffic, smog, insecurity, and infernal bureaucracy of the city to their lost Eden in the *llanos*. Gaviotas was the way life was supposed to be, and now they were asking him if he wanted to go back.

"*¡Vámonos!*" he hollered.

As the single-engine Piper, winging them back after their long exile, entered Vichada, Gonzalo and Cecilia strained at their seatbelts, barely believing what they saw out the window. Nearly a decade earlier, when their plane circled for one last look before they dejectedly retreated to Bogotá in late 1983, the surrounding *llano* had resembled a vast yellow quilt, dotted with evenly spaced green stitches at the tufts of its pillowed surface. Now those green dots had broadened until they engulfed the

plain. The Piper banked, and they gaped at a solid blanket of evergreen.
Where before had been so much nothing, now stood more than two thousand hectares˙ of thick forest.

As they taxied to a stop on the grass airstrip walled in by dark green
pines, children and adults arrived on bikes to greet them. Cecilia grabbed
Gonzalo's arm. *"Ay, no,"* she whispered.

Squeezing her hand, he winced. It had never dawned on them that
Gaviotas' mode of public transportation would set Juan David apart from
everyone else here, too. Their tenth birthday gift to him, a bicycle, had
proved a tragic blunder. After repeated falls followed by impotent rages, a
doctor judged that Juan David was incapable of riding one, which left
him even more miserable.

But two days after they arrived, as Gonzalo stood talking with Juan
Novoa outside the factory, he suddenly glanced over Juan's shoulder,
gasped, and broke into tears. Juan wheeled around to see. The ecstatic boy
with curly brown hair pedaling across the plain, leading the pack of cheering Gaviotas kids who had taught him how, was Gonzalo and Cecilia's
elder son.

Otoniel Carreño, so lanky that his knees jutted toward his chin as he pedaled, bumped across the wooden bridge over Caño Urimica, up to
Gonzalo Bernal's house in Villa Ciencia, on the northern edge of the village of Gaviotas. Dismounting, he leaned his bicycle against the trunk of
a seje palm, under a wooden sign that read *"Aquí vive una familia que
cambió una selva de cemento por un bosque de esperanza"*—Here lives a family that exchanged a jungle of cement for a forest of hope.

Gonzalo and Cecilia waved and pointed to a vacant hammock.

For a few moments, they swung quietly in the shade, soaking up some
blessed afternoon before the dinner bell rang. Cecilia, whose fringed

---

˙nearly five thousand acres

hammock was crocheted from twisted moriche fiber, had just returned from a class taught by Miguel Tello, the best Guahibo weaver at Gaviotas, and was knotting strands of the same substance into a shoulder bag. It was a class she loved so much that she even skipped her ritual afternoon volleyball game, where Juan David was currently taking her place.

Oto complimented her work. "I have something to show you," he told Gonzalo.

"Now what?"

"Something that will save us hundreds of thousands of pesos."

The next morning, Gonzalo and Otoniel rode their bicycles past the hospital, then followed a southward curve of the *caño* toward the pine nursery. An early rain had muddied the road, and their rear tires painted the backs of their hooded slickers with stripes of reddish-brown clay.

The nursery was six shining green hectares of more than a hundred raised beds, each two meters wide and 130 meters long. Together the beds held about two million seedlings. An artifical pond, fed by windmill pumps and lined with *gaviones*, provided water during the brief, dry summer. The red, aluminum-laden soil was so sandy and lacking in organic material that pine cultivation at Gaviotas was practically hydroponic. During the first three months, they gave the pine seedlings a tiny boost of potassium, magnesium, and boron: twenty grams per hundred plants. From then on, the infant trees were on their own—except for a little symbiotic help in extracting nutrients from the meager ration nature afforded them in the *llanos*. That, Oto told Gonzalo, was what he wanted to show him.

They waved to Pompilio Arciniegas and his crew, who were out weeding the beds, dressed in yellow, red, black, and green rubberized capes. In August, after four months of steady rains soaked the *llanos* and the current crop of seedlings reached thirty centimeters, each plant's roots would be pruned and coated in protective clay, and they would be transplanted out in the empty savanna. The previous year, 1995, they'd planted two thousand new hectares with 1.8 million young pines. The goal for 1996 was nearly the same. They now had seven thousand hectares planted, and hoped to maintain their pace until the Gaviotas forest reached three times that size.

Like Pompilio Arciniegas, Otoniel Carreño had been a government forester who was lent to Gaviotas for a year and then never left. When he first arrived, eight years earlier, they weren't dunking the roots in dissolved clay or pruning seedlings before transplanting, because nobody was doing that. At Gaviotas, however, people were prone to fiddle and experiment, and now he was doing nearly everything the opposite from what he'd been taught. Everybody else transported seedlings between nursery and plantation with their roots protected in black polyethylene bags, but the Gaviotans had reasoned that in the tropics, plastic bags get hot inside. Switching to clay had lowered seedling mortality below five percent—a third of what the forestry literature predicted—and saved them the expense and pollution of the plastic.

Likewise, they'd noticed that unpruned roots often got bent when transplanted, and they figured that this might slow a young tree's development. No one could be sure if this were so, but eight year-old trees in the Gaviotas forest were already taller than fifty feet.

Otoniel led Gonzalo to a bed of three-year-old seedlings, left unharvested at the nursery's southern edge during an old experiment, to show him the latest felicitous infraction of conventional forestry wisdom. It was a scattering of brown puffball mushrooms, barely more than an inch across. Underground, fungi such as these form a relationship with the roots of baby pine trees, a bond as vital to the growth of the forest as a neural synapse is to the execution of a thought. Their scientific designation is *Pizolithus tinctorius*, but Otoniel and every schoolchild in Gaviotas referred to them by the name of a natural symbiotic exchange that allowed the pines—and their community—to survive. "Those," he announced proudly, "are mycorrhiza."

"Here?" said Gonzalo. "You're kidding."

Back in 1982, Sven Zethelius had suspected that Caribbean pines would require the help of mycorrhiza to digest the *llanos* soil, and had obtained and injected dashes of dessicated fungi around the roots of the first experimental seedlings. When Otoniel and Henry Moya went to Venezuela to study commercial pine cultivation a few years later, foresters there confirmed that without a mycorrhiza fungus, their plantation would fail—and that the one they needed didn't occur naturally in the *llanos*.

While they were there, a Caracas company donated three kilos of *Pizolithus tinctorius* from the United States to Gaviotas, worth nearly two thousand dollars, enough to get their project underway. They'd learned to apply it, dosing month-old trees with water mixed with fine brown powder made from crushed mushroom caps. Soon, little white chains of mycorrhiza fungus formed on the roots, creating the biochemistry needed for them to absorb whatever nutrients were available.

Then, something unexpected occurred. The foresters who ran the pine plantations in the Venezuelan *llanos* needed to reapply the mixture repeatedly. But once trees in Gaviotas were innoculated with mycorrhiza mixture, they never seemed to require more. Each time Pompilio or Otoniel dug up a specimen, the roots were webbed with thriving, healthy fungus—so healthy, it turned out, that now, after a few years, the mushrooms had begun to reproduce in Gaviotas. As Oto and Gonzalo picked their way along the long bed of pines, they found the little brown caps popping up everywhere. "We have our own mycorrhiza bank," Otoniel said. "This wasn't supposed to happen."

"Wonderful! Any idea why?"

The biggest difference between them and the Venezuelans, Oto speculated, was that Gaviotas wasn't using herbicide to eradicate extraneous foliage that inevitably sprang up in the pine rows. As in weeding a garden, routine forestry practice requires clearing underbrush that might compete with or actually displace the cash crop. Partly to avoid chemical sprays, partly due to cost and labor, partly out of curiosity, Gaviotas hadn't bothered to eliminate the other growth in one of their earliest experimental stands of pine. Since they weren't adding fertilizer, they reasoned that the surrounding savanna grasses might contribute some nourishment to the meager, two-centimeter-thick soils. As the pines grew surprisingly fast, there seemed no need to weed subsequent plantings, even when all kinds of vines, shrubs, and woody plants began emerging in the moist, cool shade of the spreading pine boughs.

Several years later, they would realize how momentous this casual decision to let nature take its course would prove to be.

Once it had been established that Caribbean pines could thrive in the *llanos* where nothing else seemed to, the question facing Gaviotas was what to do with them. Mill lumber? Produce wood pulp? Maybe one day there would be a demand in the *llanos* for these, but so far, masses weren't streaming over the Andes into the savanna, in need of construction materials for new homes. Paper companies in Cali already produced plenty of pulpwood, and soft timber that had to be hauled sixteen hours over horrendous roads and steep mountains wouldn't be very competitive. It was Paolo Lugari who'd spotted a newspaper article that mentioned a scarcity in Europe of natural gum colophony, the resinous ooze found under the surface of pine bark. Production in traditional sources such as Portugal and Spain had fallen as labor-intensive resin collection became too expensive in the European Community, and as petroleum-based substitutes became available. Nevertheless, demand was growing for the natural stuff, especially for use in quality paints, glues, cosmetics, perfume, and medicines.

From the Venezuelans, they learned that tapping the resin of Caribbean pines was viable, but the trees needed first to mature for at least twenty years. Nevertheless, by 1990 their eight-year-old pines, still sprouting vigorously from an increasingly tangled understory, were already 20 percent taller than predicted heights for trees their age. Once again, Gaviotas set to experimenting.

They scraped away outer bark and pruned the branches two meters up the trunk of their oldest pines, as they'd been instructed. Using a Portuguese hand tool that was part hatchet, part hammer, they made incisions in the exposed bark and stapled thick plastic bags, also imported from Portugal, to the trees and let them fill with the sticky amber fluid. Every twelve days they made a new cut, slightly higher than the last, and applied a sulfurous black paste they'd purchased from the Venezuelans to keep the incision from closing. At the end of thirty-six days, their yield of golden resin was, according to the manuals, what they should be getting from trees twenty-five years old.

In Colombia alone, companies making paints and varnishes had been importing four million dollars' worth of pine resin a year. "Not any more," Lugari told a meeting of all the Gaviotans. Their Caribbean pines had turned out to be veritable nutrient pumps, machines that processed light and water into a forest product for which he had already identified a willing clientele. "Gaviotas will still be in the solar energy business," Paolo announced. "Whether we do it with solar collectors or with trees, our future is to transform sunlight into energy."

Best of all, like solar energy, the resin was renewable. Otoniel explained that it wasn't the sap they were drawing, but a fluid produced by the bark that acted like a natural insecticide, protecting the tree from wood-boring ants and other pests. They could safely tap a pine for at least eight years, working their way up the trunk on all four sides, two years to a side, then resting the tree for another eight years, then beginning again. This would mean never having to chop their forest down in order to make a living from it. And, like an extra bonus for finding a way to have their resource and profit from it too, when they heated raw resin to purify it, the residue they extracted was another marketable byproduct: clear turpentine.

Like the old days, everyone had ideas of how to make a good thing better. In the mechanics shop, Juan Novoa, Otoniel Carreño, and Carlos Sánchez devised an improved tool to make a smaller, cleaner incision that removed minimal bark. On its handle was a scale that showed a resin tapper exactly where to space the next cut. They found cheaper, locally produced plastic bags that had the added advantage of being accepted by a Bogotá recycler, who turned them into plastic pallets and black hose.

Otoniel spent weeks in the laboratory mixing a substitute for the expensive black anti-coagulant paste that was critical to the harvesting process, and whose formula was a trade secret. All they knew was that it con-

tained sulfuric acid, mixed with some organic glop thick enough to stick
to tree trunks but sufficiently fluid to use with a hand-held metal applicator that resembled a cake decorator. He tried grinding up sawdust, pine
bark, rice husks, charcoal, and coconut shells, but all of these clogged the
applicator. One day, in frustration he threw in the leftover mashed potatoes from his lunch, which, to his surprise, worked better than anything
else.

Eventually, a young bacteriologist named Luisa Fernanda Ospina
would come to Gaviotas to fulfill her requirement of a year's rural service
and, like Oto himself, never leave. Playing a hunch after hearing about
the mashed potatoes, Luisa Fernanda would analyze the imported prepa-
ration and determine that bran was the secret ingredient. Experimenting
a little further, she and Otoniel would arrive at a mixture made from
wheat bran and a fraction of the sulfuric acid that the literature recommended. This mix cost them about one percent as much as the commercial paste, left fewer acid burns on both the tree and the resin tapper's
clothing, and stimulated the resin itself to flow better than ever.

But first, Gaviotas had to find the money to put themselves in business. They needed equipment for rendering raw resin and extracting turpentine. They needed land to expand their forest, start-up capital—in
short, the sort of strategic investment and financial planning that Gaviotas, with its tradition of applied chaos and spontaneity, was not inclined
to undertake. But to survive, Paolo Lugari told his people and himself,
they had to be flexible, not rigid, even about being spontaneous. "Otherwise, we'll be frozen in time, and the times will pass us by. There's nothing
more unstable than trying to cling to stability."

The times, after all, had changed. After decades of infectious idealism
that had variously spawned the sixties, the Cuban Revolution, John F.
Kennedy's Alliance for Progress, human rights movements, and Earth
Day, civilization seemed to have finally recoiled from too much growing
awareness. Overwhelmed by complex, mounting pressures to save so
many plants, animals, and people, the world had backslid, lurching off on

a slick, new, self-indulgent technological binge and getting promptly hooked on computerized, jet-fueled supply lines capable of keeping a global marketplace well stocked.

There were two possible outcomes of this trend. One was corporate feudalism, based on an entire Third World full of serfs hacking resources from the land until supplies were exhausted. Or, there were visions like that of Gaviotas, suggesting how technology might free people more than subjugate them, and how humanity might restore to the earth what it borrows.

But admission to the global arena in these days of intercontinental trade agreements meant entering a realm where stern international lenders and monetary funds obliged governments to purge more and more social commitments from their budgets, in the process yanking many nonprofit organizations off their life-support systems. Gaviotas could no longer count on entities like the *Plan Nacional de Rehabilitación* or even the United Nations, whose goals it had once translated into tools and action.

To deal with the present devil-in-charge meant leaping right into the fire.

And so it was that in late 1992, a letter from Belisario Betancur arrived at the Inter-American Development Bank in Washington, D.C. The letter and an accompanying proposal—hand-carried by Mario Calderón, who had served there during the 1970s—were passed along to the IADB's Colombia desk. The name of the esteemed former president, considered in his country as much poet as politician, caught the attention of a young officer named Joel Korn. Betancur's letter intrigued him. Then he opened the proposal and found himself getting excited.

A few years earlier, Joel Korn had abandoned an enviable career because he wasn't excited at all. He had an MBA, nine years of seniority at Chemical Bank, and increasing responsibility with a commensurate salary, but the most memorable events of his life had nothing to do with his job. They included a year as an exchange student in Brazil, a summer on a kibbutz in Israel, and a college semester in the sunny Colombian city of Medellín. So he quit and started over at the IADB, hoping to put his expertise in finance where it might do some good in the world.

He ended up working right where he wanted to be: in the social sector, directing special funds for health, education, nutrition, women's programs, and urban development. Justifying such expenditures for Colombia, however, was becoming trickier, however, because despite the country's growing notoriety for drugs and violence, it was considered among the more economically advanced countries in Latin America.

This was no surprise to Joel—having lived in Medellín, a city whose prosperity owed far more to its fine textile industry than to inflationary drug dollars, he knew of Colombia's impressive tradition of educated technicians and thinkers. But for that reason, poorer nations, such as the Dominican Republic or Paraguay, were more likely to receive development funding than countries like Colombia that were considered to have "graduated."

But the Bank managed several international development funds inclined to help nurture good, hopeful ideas toward fruition. The biggest such fund belonged to Japan, and Korn suspected that the Japanese might be very interested in Gaviotas. He knew that he personally had never seen anything quite like the community described in the proposal. He called Bogotá and learned that the IADB's representative there hadn't either, having declined all invitations to visit because travelling to Vichada sounded too dangerous.

So Joel Korn flew to see Gaviotas for himself. Immediately, he felt like he was back on a kibbutz—except that, unlike Israel, Colombia wasn't a country whose idealism was buoyed by donations from millions of overseas religious faithful and by strategic subsidies from the U.S. government. Colombia had become practically a pariah nation, growing more isolated because of lurid drug scandals, despite its repeated, frustrated insistence that the heavy cocaine consumer nations in North America and Europe were equally to blame. Nevertheless, it was Colombia that suffered. Foreign investors were growing leery of terror and kidnapping. The advice from Washington and Brussels to throw the country's markets open to global free trade had backfired in an unexpected way: The chief beneficiaries turned out to be money-launderers, who dumped vast quantities of imported goods purchased with drug profits onto the local economy, creating havoc for legitimate business.

Colombians were dying, and Colombia's incomparable ecosystems were being ravaged. A community like Gaviotas, Korn realized, would be extraordinary anywhere. For Gaviotas to exist in the midst of its beautiful land's sustained tragedy was practically miraculous.

As Korn reviewed Gaviotas' ledgers, he saw that, in spite of surrounding physical and economic peril, Gaviotas was surviving. Through their recent crisis, they'd hung on and found niche markets for their alternative systems. Colombia's biggest hospital, Clínica San Pedro Claver in Bogotá, had contracted them to convert its water system to solar heat. Gaviotas seemingly had also been blessed by a bit of divine intervention: Several churches, convents, and orphanages were hedging against future rising energy prices by switching to Gaviotas solar technology.

In Vichada, Joel Korn was stunned by the hospital in the middle of nowhere that combined ultra-modern mechanisms with indigenous customs. The cheerful Gaviotas school charmed him. The notion of a sustainable civilization in the hitherto-neglected savanna made wonderful sense to him, as he imagined it would to the board of the Japanese fund as well.

"They're very interested in the natural environment," he told Lugari.

"Gaviotas is a completely natural phenomenon," Paolo assured him. "Millions of years ago, a group of African primates were running out of resources in the forest, so they ventured into the savannas. To defend themselves, they had to learn to stand upright in order to see predators." That place where *Homo sapiens* emerged, Lugari claimed, was practically identical to the Orinocan *llanos*. "The savannas of the tropics are the only big open spaces left today. We have to learn to live in them again."

Paolo took Joel to see their test plot in the forest. Carlos Sánchez and a four-man crew were trying out their new hand tool, ergonomically designed to perform all of the scraping, pounding, and cutting functions

necessary with minimal strain on a resin tapper's back and shoulders. Two
of the tappers present were Guahibo Indians. They had never liked to enter the Gaviotas factory, they told Korn, but liked being paid to spend all day in the cool, pleasant forest.

Paolo pointed through the pines at a doe and fawn, lapping rain water from resin catchments. "We're seeing wildlife in this forest that had nearly disappeared," he whispered. "Deer, anteaters, *chigüiros*, eagles, armadillos, but especially—" he said, indicating the tangle of vines he was disengaging from his ankle, "—all this."

All around them, interspersed among the pines, grew shrubs with crimson flowers, wispy jacarandas, paper-barked white saplings called *tuno blancos*, and wild fig vines. Lugari explained that a pair of biologists from the Universidad Nacional had begun compiling a list of dozens of species sprouting in the moist understory of the Gaviotas pine forest, where formerly there were only a few kinds of grasses. No one knew yet if these were from dormant seeds of native trees not seen on the savanna for millennia, or if birds were sowing seeds from the gallery forests here with their droppings. According to Sven Zethelius, either way the reforestation was unprecedented: Sheltered by Caribbean pine trees, a diverse, indigenous tropical forest was either regenerating or being replanted in the *llanos* with surprising speed.

"The native plants don't hurt the pines?" Joel asked.

"We think to the contrary. Sven and the biologists believe this is a much healthier forest than the plantations in Venezuela, because it's not a monoculture. Our trees grow and mature faster than theirs."

"Amazing."

"Still, we expect that one day the tropical foliage will overrun them. Sven tells us that we can harvest resin for decades until the natural forest chokes out the *Pinus caribaea.* If you help us take our agro-forestry project to a commercial level, we can keep marching across the savanna, planting more pine trees, and leaving a tropical rain forest in our wake. We can give seedlings to all our neighbors, process their resin, turn this desert into a productive land, employ campesinos and the Guahibo, and at the same time return the *llanos* to what Sven says many ecologists believe was their primeval state: an extension of the Amazon. Imagine that, Joel!"

~

IN 1979, EULISES ALBARRACÍN HAD LEFT CASANARE TERRITORY IN THE northern *llanos* because he'd heard there was work at the government agricultural station at Carimagua. This turned out to be true, but there wasn't much job security. Field hands worked short-term contracts, which were extended if they were lucky enough to be assigned to an experiment that lasted a while. Eulises' luck held out for four years. He was still trying to figure out what to do next when Pepe Gómez heard him play the harp at a *llanera* fiesta.

Back when Eulises still had his little cattle finca in Casanare, he'd played the *cuatro*, because no one in his pueblo owned a harp. They'd heard its sound only on tape players or faint radio broadcasts from Venezuela; it was like a flock of *saucelitos* all making love at once. Eulises decided he had to follow it. He heard of a master harpist who played at a tourist hotel far up on the Río Ariporo. Eulises had no vehicle: To get there by bush plane and pay for lessons meant selling a bull.

Several months and all four of his bulls later, Eulises was out of the cow business but could pass for an angel on the 32-string *arpa llanero*. He was also out of money, and couldn't afford a harp of his own until Gaviotas gave him one, along with a job raising beets and carrots in the hydroponic garden. Before Joel Korn returned to the Inter-American Development Bank in Washington, Eulises and a band of *músicos gavioteros* serenaded him with the lovely strains of *los llanos*. Abraham Beltrán played *cuatro*, and a Gaviotas cowboy named Pedro Gómez joined on *maracas*. *Bandolista* Carlos Ceijas took the melody when Eulises' fingers needed a rest. Manuel Corredor, a young Guahibo Indian and indigenous mechanical prodigy, who'd invented a wind-powered irrigator by crossbreeding a windmill and a hydraulic ram pump, provided vocals from an equally prodigious repertoire of *llanera* songs.

His verses told of the horses, hawks, locusts, snakes, corn-stealing
monkeys, *tigres*, and palm-lined rivers that defined their life on the broad
savanna. They described how passionately a man can love a woman when
the flower in her hair is the brightest color for hours in any direction.
They invoked the vast, opalescent blue bowl inverted over the equatorial
plains, which was surely the world's grandest sky, and the gratitude and
struggles of displaced settlers who followed the government's siren per-
suasions to come to a "land without people for people without land."
Last, they performed Abraham's and Manuelito's original *poemas* about
their beloved Gaviotas, odes to the *caño* and to graceful windmills and to
wonderful madmen like Luis Robles who built them.

They sang for all the foreign visitors who showed up in Korn's wake:
Venezuelans and French and Finns, experts in forestry and resin processors who did the feasibility and environmental impact studies for the
Bank, and finally for the Japanese funders themselves. They delighted
them all, but every visitor was reminded by Lugari that what they had
come to decide would matter far beyond Gaviotas.

"There are two hundred-fifty million hectares of savannas like these in
South America alone. There's Africa. The tropical Orient. Places where
there's space and sun and water. If we show the world how to plant them
in sustainable forests, we can give people productive lives and maybe absorb enough carbon dioxide to stabilize global warming in the process.
This is a gift we can give the world that's just as important as our sleeve
pumps and solar water purifiers. Everywhere else they're tearing down
rain forests. We're showing how to put them back."

August, 1994: Paolo, Gonzalo, and Pompilio convened all the Gaviotans
into the community hall. They were only one hundred-fifty now, though
if all went well during the coming month, there would be permanent
work for many more, and their numbers would grow again.

They had survived the feasibility study. Despite competition from an
understory now thick with native plants, both the quantity and quality of

their resin were actually superior to that of neighboring Venezuela, which didn't get nearly as much rain.

They'd also passed the environmental impact study, and then some, with yet another providential stroke: The Caribbean pines that grew so vigorously in these *llanos* did not naturally reproduce here. This meant that, although birds and wind might seed their plantation with native tropical species, the opposite would not occur. The riparian ecology of the gallery forests along the *caños* would not be invaded by an exotic species of pine.

Processing the raw resin would actually benefit the environment as well. A former Los Andes engineering professor, Enrique Devis, had designed a steam boiler that would burn trees and branches thinned from the forest in a two-tiered oven designed to produce nearly smokeless heat, to refine their harvest into the clear, cultured amber known as industrial-quality gum resin. Since the wood fuel came from their own renewable agro-forestry crop, the contribution of added carbon dioxide to the atmosphere would be zero. Although Gaviotas had two ten-kilowatt micro-hydro turbines, they still partly depended on a diesel plant, especially during dry months when the *caño* ran low. But now, a two-cylinder, steam-driven engine would tap the resin boiler's exhaust vapors to generate electricity, bringing Gaviotas virtually to full energy self-sufficiency.

Joel Korn called to confirm that funding was approved. Now came the hard part: meeting the schedule set by the Inter-American Development Bank. They had already dismantled all the assembly machinery in their factory to make room for the giant still to boil and purify raw resin and separate the turpentine. Although the Gaviotas water technology would now be subcontracted to workshops in the city, it saddened them to pack up equipment that, for more than a decade, had built thousands of windmills, sleeve pumps, see-saws, and ram pumps. It had been an axiom at Gaviotas that seventy percent of life on earth consists of water, and they had been bringing water to the world. But they had to make way for yet another thing the world needed: a renewable industry.

The resin factory would eventually process twenty tons of *colofonia* per day. But everything depended on getting enough new trees in the ground so that over the next decade, both production and their human population could expand. According to their contract with the Bank, they had to plant at least two thousand hectares by the end of the year—nearly a million trees. But they were way behind, because 1994 had proved the wettest year in Colombian history. According to the Gaviotas weather station, average annual rainfall in the *llanos* was 106 inches. They had already passed that mark by May.

During one day that month, six inches of rain fell in just two hours, nearly destroying the nursery. The long, banked sides of the raised beds started to collapse into the dividing furrows, and a million seedlings began to tumble. Everyone in Gaviotas, school children included, brought whatever they could find to shore up the eroding banks—boards, clay roof tiles, scrap aluminum sheets. This was an imperative emergency measure, but tractors couldn't prune and add mineral supplements with all that junk on the ground.

"Any ideas?" Pompilio had asked, and Mariano Botello, who was just a boy here when the first trees were planted, offered one. Mariano and Otoniel Carreño never slept that night. By morning they had fabricated a set of heavy rollers from two metal wheel-rims, which they'd recycled from scrap and stuffed with soil cement, still barely dry. These they had placed at either end of an axle, canting them at the same angle as the banked edges of the nursery bed, and then hitched their improvised rig to a tractor. As the tractor's disks loosened the earth alongside the beds, the new rollers came right behind, packing the soil back into place.

Men, women and children ran through the rain in front of the tractor, removing the tiles and boards as the disks came through, followed by Mariano's rollers, reconstructing and reinforcing the banks. Over the next month, all other work at Gaviotas stopped as everyone straightened and replanted a million seedlings by hand. But the rollers worked so well that eighty percent of the crop was saved and Gaviotas had a new invention to share.

Now, barely three months later, Paolo was telling them that yet another heroic stand was needed. It would be even harder this time, he admitted. They had already spent most of the year's Japanese funding installment on the nursery and on new resin processing equipment. Lugari had managed to procure another grant through a government forestry incentive program that would pay them to sow an additional 1,500 hectares of pines over three years. "But no more money comes in until we actually get all the seedlings transplanted permanently in the savanna. I can't ask you to work again for delayed pay. It's up to you to decide if you want to do this."

Henry Moya stood up. "This forest is our future. Our lungs are out there. We're breathing oxygen that Pompilio and Dr. Zethelius planted ten years ago. I want to be around in ten more years to harvest what we're planting."

Hernán Landaeta was next. He had worked in *Agua Para Todos* and the *Plan Nacional de Rehabilitación*, and would now direct the new *colofonia* factory. "We brought water to the *llanos*," said Hernán. "Now it's time to bring trees."

One by one, without any public campaign or discussion, they had even given up smoking because it presented a fire hazard to their forest—only Omar Marín still had a cigarette up in the corral at the end of the day. This had to be unprecedented in Latin America, Lugari marveled, and such commitment would surely see them through however long it took to plant a million trees.

It took twenty-four days, working twenty-four hours around the clock, never stopping. Never in Colombian history, they told each other, had an entire village worked all night like that. Especially because every night, it rained.

"Bad day for people, good day for planting," sang Pompilio, who never seemed to sleep at all. They had to finish before the rains slackened in October, because the seedlings required moisture and because rain helped mycorrhiza cling to roots after transplantation in the open savanna. The Gaviotans had three tractors pulling planters purchased in Venezuela, which they'd redesigned to accommodate the crusty local soils. Atop each planter was a hutch woven from moriche fronds to shade the fragile new pines. Inside sat a worker surrounded by boxes containing five thousand seedlings apiece, their roots coated with wet clay. As the vehicle passed along, the worker placed each baby pine in a rubberized clamp, which deposited it in a hole punched by a spiked wheel within the furrow. Behind the planters came men and women with trowels, straightening every new tree.

They divided into twelve-hour shifts, one beginning at dawn, one at dusk. At night they mounted spotlights atop the planter hutches, and the workers with trowels wore miners' lamps. By day, the schoolchildren helped; by night came women who weren't on the regular crew. Lunch was served once at noon, once at midnight. Another month went by with no salaries. No one missed work, or was even late. No one complained, although the thick mantle of clouds, gloomy as the steppes of Russia, rarely broke above their heads. The tractors stayed tuned, the meals arrived hot, and when they finished, two thousand hectares and a million trees later, they slaughtered a steer and stayed up one more night, eating *carne asada* and drinking sweet *aguardiente* and dancing in the community hall and right out the doors, onto the soccer field and under the rain, to the music of harps and *cuatros* and *bandolas,* toasting each other for never giving up.

~

APRIL, 1996: AT TEN A.M. ON Day of the Garden, Jorge Eliécer Landaeta, brother of Hernán who ran the resin factory, clicked off the scratchy radio in the government meteorological station at Gaviotas. Like Hernán, he had close-cropped black hair and solid shoulders, with a square face befitting the stoic *llanero* stock from which they sprang. He checked the supply of graph paper in various devices that charted temperature, wind, atmospheric pressure, sunlight, and relative humidity.

He noted all the gauges, and concluded that rain was imminent. Again.

Over the twenty-one years since Jorge Eliécer first arrived in Gaviotas to attend primary school, the seasons in the *llanos* noticeably had begun to blur. This year it had rained during every month, an unprecedented six inches-plus in February alone, usually the driest time of all. The rivers and *caños* were already as bloated as digesting boa constrictors. *Llaneros* blamed the rain for an epidemic that, in two years, had killed fifteen thousand cattle in Vichada. While chewing old bones to get scarce phosphorus and calcium, bovines were picking up botulism, which the excess moisture caused to bloom in the soil.

But thus far, it was a gorgeous morning in Jorge Eliécer's beloved *llanos*, where he was born and bred, and to which he composed ballads and poems. He stepped outside to enjoy it. That early, the sun was more friendly than oppressive. Lenticular clouds dangled in the blue sky like shards of polished ivory. Jorge Eliécer surveyed the yard, checking the sensors. Because of government budget cuts, they no longer sent up hydrogen weather balloons to take measurements at various altitudes—a thesis written by Geoffrey Halliday, which proposed using a windmill to generate hydrogen, was among those ideas yet to be developed at Gaviotas. Instead, Jorge Eliécer and his colleagues now took surface readings, feeding them into a photovoltaic-powered transmitter accessed by passing satellites, which beamed their data to Bogotá.

Because Gaviotas is so remote, its atmosphere is among the cleanest that remains in the world. Recently, Colombia's Institute for Environmental and Meteorological Studies had installed a device here to analyze precipitation. It consisted of a collector that opened automatically to receive a storm's first raindrops, which contain the most atmospheric contaminants. The apparatus deposited this rainwater in two bottles, one of which Jorge Eliécer sent to Bogotá, the other to the World Meteorological Organization in Geneva.

Atop a five-foot pole in a corner of the yard were two convex glass lenses, also newly arrived, balanced on either end of a plank. They enclosed radio spectrometers used for measuring two bands of ultraviolet radiation coming through the ozone layer. Jorge Eliécer was glad that this wasn't one of the days they were scheduled to take readings, which involved recording measurements every four minutes, equal to the time it took the sun to advance one degree in its arc across the equatorial sky. It was a two-person job, one technician manually focusing the devices on the sun at four-minute intervals, then yelling to a companion inside at a computer screen to record the readings. They did this from just past sunrise until sunset.

The same was occurring at three other sites in Colombia: on the Amazon, on a peak above Bogotá, and near the Caribbean coast. The reason was that the ozone layer, known to be deteriorating about three percent every twenty years, lately seemed to be thinning faster than ever, not only over the poles but everywhere, and especially over that part of the earth that received the most sunlight of all: the tropics. From data collected at the four sites over the past year, it appeared that, apart from those days when the Antarctic ozone hole widened enough to expose southern Chile and Argentina, Colombia was receiving the highest doses of ultraviolet radiation in the Americas.

For the past eight years, Jorge Eliécer's boss here was a slight, taut man named Dr. Ovidio Simbakeva, president of the World Meteorological Organization's South American Solar Radiation Working Group. Ovidio had just returned to Bogotá to analyze these findings and determine what, if any, protective measures could be taken to mitigate ultraviolet damage. What such measures might be were unclear. Humans could wear sunscreen and UV-protective sunglasses. But many plants, including pine trees and food crops such as rice, were also sensitive to ultraviolet radiation, and a forest or field couldn't be bathed in sun-block.

Jorge Eliécer had watched Ovidio grow bitter over the irony that tropical countries, which were both the greatest producers of oxygen and the least industrialized, should be the most affected. These were consequences not created by them, but by nations who invented the chloroflurocarbon refrigerants and methyl bromide fertilizers now known to attack the gauzy ozone layer that normally intercepted cosmic rays coming from space. "These are poisonous substances they've exported to us," Ovidio said. "Someday Latin America must seek redress for damages from the industrialized world."

In 1987, the industrialized world and nearly every other country had signed the Montreal Protocol, agreeing to replace ozone-destroying chemicals with benign substitutes. If the schedule were met, ozone destruction should peak by the year A.D. 2010, then gradually diminish over the next six decades. A fund was created to help developing nations, such as Colombia, pay to retrofit or replace existing freezers, refrigerators, and other equipment that used substances soon to be prohibited.

Never before had 140 countries united for the common good of all. But even as the Montreal Protocol was touted as history's most successful pact to save the planet, researchers like Ovidio Simbakeva worried that what looked so hopeful on paper had little to do with reality. The initial fund for developing countries contained only $160 million. Over the ensuing decade, another $560 million had been allocated and more was promised for the future, but Simbakeva believed that, compared to the scale of the problem, these figures were so paltry that they only meant one of two things: Either the most influential countries intended that innocent victims least able to afford to pay would be charged for the mistakes of the rich, or the Protocol would disintegrate and the ozone layer with it.

Already Russia had postponed compliance, saying it needed several extra years. Russia's environmental ministry was even again questioning the link between chloroflurocarbons and ozone loss—a hint that they might be rethinking participation in the Protocol altogether. Changing over to ozone-safe equipment, the Russians claimed, would cost at least $600 million just for their country alone. If so, how did the world expect to pay to convert China, India, all of Latin America, the Far East, and Africa?

With global market competition now exalted as the highest human pursuit, Ovidio also knew that investing in costly controls, an expense bound to blunt a poor country's competitive chances, wasn't too likely. In fact, the entrepreneurial opposite had occurred: Ozone-destroying chlorofluorocarbons now produced in Russia, India, and Mexico had reportedly surpassed Colombian cocaine as the most common illegal chemical smuggled into the United States. Over decades, these freshly produced CFCs would also find their way to the stratosphere. There they would be ripped apart by solar ultraviolet rays, liberating free chlorine atoms that, in turn, tear apart ozone molecules. As Ovidio and Jorge Eliécer took their soundings of the invisible ultraviolet menace growing over their beautiful, pure *llanos*, they knew that, despite the miracles Gaviotas had wrought here, the future might very well be out of their hands.

They didn't talk much about these things to the Gaviotans—what was there to tell them? Don't pollute, when already they didn't? Better to do what Gaviotas planned for today, *Día del Jardín:* celebrate the loveliness of life flowering all around them. Jorge Eliécer headed for his cottage near the weather station, where his *compañera* Lucy and their children were whitewashing the low patio wall around their garden. Sitting on the steps, he drank a cup of milk and inspected their landscaping efforts, the violets they'd planted in hanging baskets made of recycled PVC tubing sliced lengthwise into troughs. Then he went inside and donned a fresh blue long-sleeved shirt and a pair of dark slacks, and slipped his bare feet into a pair of flat canvas *cotizas*. As he emerged, his daughters flocked around him.

"Papá, sing to the flowers to help them grow."

"It's almost time for the judging."

"We know. You have to help us win."

They lead him to their newly-potted heliconias and orchids. "Which one?"

They chose *"Plegaria del Saucelito,"* a song about the golden-eyed thrush whose voice is so divine he surely must be addressing God. "If you want a song about a bird," Jorge Eliécer asked, "why not '*Garcita Blanca?'*—"The Little White Egret," his latest composition to be recorded on a national label. Nevertheless, the *"Saucelito"* was their favorite. As he sang, Eulises Albarracín appeared with his three-holed harp clutched against his big body, followed by various others bearing *cuatros* and *maracas*. Finding his key, they joined in. Then, with Jorge Eliécer's kids trooping behind, they headed for the dining commons, where the rest of the community was waiting for Day of the Garden to begin.

En masse, they paraded up the road toward Villa Ciencia, musicians and adults on foot, the younger children on bicycles, including five riding in the stake bed of a pedal-driven cargo bike. The children had just returned from an excursion. Alonso Gutiérrez and Teresa Valencia had taken everyone to Santa Marta, a mystical peak that rose to 19,000 feet just twenty miles from Colombia's northern Caribbean shore, to see the Lost City of the Kogui Indians, who still lived in the isolated upper mountain reaches.

As they crossed the bridge over the Caño Urimica, one of Juan Novoa's kids spotted a large crane camouflaged in a gentle eddy near one of the *gavión* pilings. A bird guide identified it as a fasciated tiger heron, previously unknown here. Like a puff of tinted smoke, a cloud of shiny blue butterflies with lilac underwings encircled it. Tiny swallows skimmed the water, cheating the fish out of insects. Here, where the gallery forest was thickest, the birds of Gaviotas emerged in rapturous display, and the children's eyes had been sharpened by recent Day of the Birds festivities. They saw vermilion and yellow-breasted tyrant flycatchers, black-crested antshrikes, a blue-crowned mot-mot with a racquet-shaped tail, a rufous-tailed xenops, bananaquits, brown-throated parakeets, a dusky-billed parrot, and a plump tinamou quail, swaying in the feathery *caño* treetops. As they continued, scaled doves and *el saucelito* himself, the little golden-eyed thrush of Jorge Eliécer's song, hopped on the road in front of the throng.

> *Esta es la dulce canción que canta mi saucelito*
> This is the sweet song my *saucelito* sings
> *para todo mi Colombia, viene con mucho cariño*
> for all Colombia, my love it brings

with hugs and with kisses for all the children
y una plegaria de paz pido para mis amigos
and a prayer of peace for all of my friends

Two houses in Villa Ciencia were garden contestants this year, but *Profesora* Teresa's wasn't among them. Tere and Alonso had just learned that they were expecting the next Gaviotan; she'd stayed in Bogotá following the excursion to Santa Marta in order to see an obstetrician, but would arrive later by plane with Paolo Lugari. Alonso Gutiérrez had to fly to Europe to consult to coffee processors in France and Germany, but he'd promised to return soon to Gaviotas to take the kids fishing.

The gardens grew in soil they mined from the *caño* and fertilized with compost and steer manure. The judging criteria were beauty, species variety, design creativity, size and placement, and the level of household participation. They began at the home of Gladys Marchena, the nurse, and Hernán Landaeta, the factory director, whose array of foliage and blossoms focused around an exquisite spreading vine of pink and white seaspray. The musicians serenaded, the judges conferred and nodded, and everyone moved on, waltzing their instruments and songs from house to house, through the aromatic extended garden that the Gaviotans had sown, redolent with birds-of-paradise, lavender, hortensia, pothos, winding fig, shrimp plants, monsteras, huge begonias, wandering Jews, and tropical flowers they'd found in the *caño* or grown from cuttings brought from western provinces by their mothers, when *La Violencia* drove them across the Andes into the *llanos*.

There were blooms with blood-red petals and violet leaves named wounded heart, and a succulent with long, wispy, trailing hairs called lady's gray tresses. Yellow, indigo, and purple orchids of all sizes had invaded feeders built each year for Day of the Birds; with the constant traffic of velvety maroon silver-beaked tanagers, these hanging tableaux, suspended amidst yellow guavas or red cashew fruit, became positively kaleidoscopic.

The Trees

Whenever the music turned to the irresistible *llanero* beat called *joropo*, the contest was forgotten as everyone spontaneously began dancing. They danced to the mechanics shop, pausing to serenade a truck driver for his birthday. In the school, the garden was like a shrine, with a Caribbean pine as its centerpiece. They wound up in the polygonal modular living quarters known as Villa Armonía, where Nancy Narváez and Héctor Eli Suárez received special accolades for their artful and surprising display of carnations.

"Where did they come from?" everyone wanted to know, and a smiling Nancy revealed that, via a letter someone had carried to Bogotá for her, she'd sent away for seeds advertised on the back of a package of cookies, and they actually arrived. She credited their survival to Héctor Eli, for protecting them from the water buffalo. Ever since Paolo Lugari had hitched the first pair to Gaviotas' garbage and recycling cart a year ago, Héctor Eli had spent many days chasing Resino, the male, and Colofonia, the female, who were quite friendly but helplessly tantalized by the smell of flowing water, which they followed wherever it led. The last time, they'd covered forty kilometers, tracing the *caño* to the Río Muco, then all the way down to the Río Rojo, where Héctor Eli found them wallowing like tapirs.

But they never got lost; the whole region knew *los búfalos de Gaviotas*, and someone always sent word when they were sighted. Now, in fact, Héctor Eli had the opposite problem—the pair's first baby, Gaviota, liked to nuzzle him with her curled black horns and follow him home, where she would be distracted by the appetizing colors in Nancy's garden. Héctor Eli had even defended the flowers by moonlight, Nancy told them, on nights when maurading water buffalo crashed the hibiscus hedges. Such valor inspired a neighbor to break out a bottle of homemade *copa de oro*: egg nog laced with *aguardiente*. The garden contest dissolved away into a kids' game of *futbolito* on Villa Armonía's mini-soccer field, everybody cheering their children and the glorious *llano* day.

〜

José Ignacio López didn't think about Gaviotas all that often anymore, except when he'd pull out pictures from the *Plan Nacional de Rehabilitación* to show to his friends. There he was in Magdalena Medio in 1986, ten years earlier, lugging cement well casings on his broad back, descending bamboo ladders to connect submersible double-action windmill pumps, meeting *la guerrilla*. Those were amazing experiences for a kid who grew up in a Bogotá squatters' colony, until chance led him to Gaviotas. There he became a mason, a carpenter, a truck driver, a solar energy technician, and, finally, assistant to Gaviotas' coordinator, Pepe Gómez. When Pepe Gómez started zipping around the country for the *Plan Nacional de Rehabilitación*, José Ignacio often went too.

With a Gaviotas emergency crew, he helped build new water lines for the survivors of the volcanic eruption that buried the town of Armero. He assembled pumps in Indian villages in the south central province of Tolima, but he stayed longest in Magdalena Medio, installing Gaviotas technology up and down the Magdalena's central river valley for nearly two years, seeing things alternately beautiful and horrible. He got out of there alive—miraculously, all the Gaviotas technicians did—and returned to Vichada.

Then Pepe Gómez was named ambassador to China. With his boss leaving, and with Gaviotas' role in the *Plan Nacional* over and work at Gaviotas declining in general, José Ignacio decided to return to Bogotá. Nearly three years later, it was time for Pepe Gómez to fold the Colombian flag and deliver it to his successor, shedding tears like he hadn't done since he departed Gaviotas. The former black sheep who had distinguished himself as an ambassador returned home. Entering the family business, he proved a wizard at managing holdings on two or three continents. He accepted a professorship in Far Eastern Studies at Bogotá's Universidad Externado and built a new solar house, designed by Geoffrey Halliday and Simón Bright.

When he learned that José Ignacio López hadn't remained at Gaviotas, Pepe Gómez hired him to be his assistant and driver. Pepe himself wasn't going out to Gaviotas anymore—his new wife didn't even want him flying planes now that they had babies, let alone traipsing out to no man's land. José Ignacio knew that on at least one occasion, Pepe and Paolo Lugari had met for breakfast in Bogotá. José Ignacio heard later that they shook hands, immediately started to argue, gradually found that they mostly agreed except for details, argued some more, and ended up embracing.

Exactly what future role Pepe might have in Gaviotas was uncertain, but hearing about it had re-opened José Ignacio's own memories, and he hauled out those Magdalena Medio pictures again. Then, in August, 1996, he found himself with some time off while Pepe was in Japan on business. Colombia's central Río Magdalena valley wasn't the safest place to spend a vacation, but it would be nice to know, a decade later, what the legacy of their labors to bring water to everybody truly meant.

His flight arrived in Barrancabermeja, an oil port on the Río Magdalena, just after sunset. The waning dusk was accompanied by a ring of natural gas flares from an Ecopetrol refinery, reflected by the oil-streaked surface of a mangrove estuary. José Ignacio checked into a waterfront hotel. He was arranging for a launch to take him downriver when sirens began to howl and the docks were suddenly awash in flashing red light. The Colombian army kept the river closed to traffic from 6:00 P.M. to 6:00 A.M., but two ambulance boats now screamed into port. The rumor was that the town of San Pablo, an hour downriver, had been taken again by *la guerrilla*. San Pablo had been Gaviotas' base of operations for nearly two years; José Ignacio was hoping to visit old friends there. He also had to pass by San Pablo on the way to villages where he'd worked farther downstream. But now he might not be going anywhere if the guerrillas and the army were engaged in pyrotechnics.

Later, the real story filtered through Barrancabermeja's hot streets. A seven-year-old boy in San Pablo had found a hand grenade. Not knowing what it was, he'd carried it home. When it detonated, he and three adults died; others reportedly were missing various limbs.

The army's grenade? *La guerrilla?* The paramilitaries? Nobody knew. The last time José Ignacio was in Barrancabermeja, the mayor had been assassinated. It was just another night in one of the hemisphere's most fertile valleys.

Or, perhaps, formerly fertile. At dawn, José Ignacio walked to the public pier to catch his chalupa and was astonished to find the big cement dock landlocked. People were strolling past it and continuing along a muddy landspit, far out into what had once been the river. At its tip, the chalupas and collective launches were anchored alongside floating bridges made of metal pallets lashed together to form provisional landings. As they cast off and entered the broad Magdalena, the boatman, a hollow-chested man in black nylon shorts named Eusebio, explained that the river was being buried. Throughout this valley, which was nearly the size of El Salvador, sedimentation was filling in the marshes and raising the river bottom.

The reason, Eusebio had heard people comment, was deforestation. For more than a decade, Magdalena Medio had lost about a hundred thousand hectares of forest per year. "In the entire country, they're saying about six hundred thousand," he added. Clearing land for cattle grazing was a big reason. Another was that *narcotraficantes*, who, by the 1990s, owned more than one-third of Colombia's arable land, kept buying up choice Magdalena bottomland to launder their relentless supply of drug dollars, and needed pastures for their obligatory *paso fino* horses. The tremendous erosion due to clear-cutting was now blamed for the collapse of fish harvests. During the 1970s, the commercial catch averaged eighty-four thousand tons a year. "Last year," the boatman said, "it was thirteen thousand."

Where the land had crumbled away, the river was wider and shallower than José Ignacio ever remembered seeing it. They passed islands of slick gray mud and red reflectors warning of submerged shoals. A black commercial dredger bore an ominous slogan: "The Future of Colombia is with Dredging." None of the bare-chested men they saw fishing from dugout canoes with seines and cast nets appeared to be having much luck.

The Trees

After an hour, José Ignacio asked if they shouldn't be nearing Boca del Rosario, the first village he hoped to visit.

Eusebio pointed to a collection of houses on the western shore, some concrete, some mud-daubed and thatched. *"Allí está."*

José Ignacio gaped. ."Where's the church?"

"El río se la llevó."

The river took it. With barely any trees left in the hills to absorb runoff, the Magdalena flooded several times a year now, scouring its banks deeply, then dumping millions of cubic meters of sediment. A villager lending a hand as José Ignacio skittered up a steep clay slope into Boca del Rosario showed him that he was actually climbing a buried rooftop. Any houses near the shore not carried off by the river were buried in silt. A nearby bulge was the former school, now seven feet underground.

José Ignacio spotted a thin, bearded man he knew, named Alberto Cruzado. "What about the wells that Gaviotas installed here?" he asked. Cruzado took him to a cement well-casing, barely protruding above the ground near the buried school. Pump handles and sleeve were missing; just the thick wooden cross-piece that once anchored them remained in place. The well was filled with mud, sticks, and banana leaves. José Ignacio shook his head, and inquired if all seven wells they helped dig here were silted.

"No," says Cruzado, "but they may as well have been."

Cruzado led him along the village's single street to another well. This one had water, but the sleeve pumps were missing. In their place was a new one-horsepower electric pump. When José Ignacio was last here, there was no electricity in this or any river village. A length of black hose led from the pump across the dirt street into a house made of weathered planks. "The water is too salty to drink. They use it to wash dishes." Most of the Gaviotas wells were just the same, he said: too brackish for human consumption. "And the hand pumps stopped working after a year." The storekeeper across the street had just purchased the electric pump, which worked on days when there was electricity.

"All the pumps needed were new gaskets," José Ignacio said. "We explained that: once a year. Didn't anyone change them? We left wrenches, a supply of gaskets, and a manual with pictures showing how to make them out of leather if you run out."

The gaskets and manual were still there, it turned out, although the wrenches had disappeared. "The water wasn't drinkable, so nobody cared," Cruzado said. "We told Gaviotas that these wells weren't deep enough. This close to the river, you have to go down eighty meters to get good water."

"But someone from the local council must have signed a release verifying that Gaviotas had fulfilled its contract. They wouldn't have signed if the well was bad."

Cruzado shrugged.

In Sitio Nuevo, a village of bamboo shacks just five minutes farther, one well had given delicious water at first, they told him, but then it turned dark and sulfurous. José Ignacio looked; it was filled with frogs. "Too foul to drink, too hard for soapsuds," an old man spat. Other wells, he said, simply overflowed whenever the river rose, and had to be plugged with dirt. No one recalled where the pumps went.

José Ignacio started back up river, appalled by its color. Ten years earlier, fishermen had told him how a few days after the volcano buried the town of Armero three hundred kilometers upstream, the river here had turned to thick gray soup and thousands of catfish had died. The water again fit that description, and local fishermen had largely retreated to the swampy inland *ciénagas* to catch enough to feed their families.

He stopped at Chingalé, another village where he'd worked. Chingalé was larger, maybe a hundred families, and wires strung between low power poles indicated that electricity had also arrived here in his absence. He found Orfa Pacheco, a woman who used to cook for his crew, and heard essentially the same story. She was angry; the people had trusted Gaviotas. She herself had claimed a set of pumps from a well gone brackish, but didn't have any plans for them; they were hanging in a mango tree in her yard. She'd also sawed off the top of the Gaviotas spherical water tank and was using it under the eaves as a rain catch.

It was barely 10:00 A.M., but already José Ignacio was getting sunburnt. He removed his cap and wiped perspiration from his forehead. "Have people gone back to drinking river water?" he asked.

It was complicated, she said. Two years ago the provincial government dug a seventy-five meter well, one kilometer inland. "But we're still waiting for pipe lines to run the water to town. The government never came back." Meanwhile, people were drinking river water. They added laundry chlorine if they had some.

"Why don't they carry buckets from the government well?"

Because there was another problem. A well that deep required an electric pump. They got electricity four years ago, but running the 220-volt pump proved to be too expensive. "And," Orfa added, "when the pump runs, it blows out everything else in town."

The vice-mayor of Chingalé came by. "This wasn't Gaviotas' fault," he told José Ignacio. He led him to a well on the outskirts of the village, now too brackish for humans, but adequate to water cattle. On it was an intact set of Gaviotas sleeve pumps. The rancher who tended them had no problem making and changing gaskets, said the vice-mayor; even the children could do it. The pumps had needed no other maintenance in ten years.

Gradually, José Ignacio pieced together what had happened. When the Gaviotans first arrived, they had realized that several sites along the river selected by the government's lottery were unsuitable: Water that was reliably pure lay far below even the reach of their sleeve pumps. José Ignacio recalled how Pepe Gómez wrote to the government, begging permission to put the equipment in villages on higher ground instead. He'd flown to Bogotá and argued, to no avail. In the end, they'd had to follow the contract and install the pumps anyway, hoping that the water would be potable at least part of the time, when the river wasn't rising.

But now he saw that even wells that had once consistently provided decent water had all gone bad. "It's a different river now," the vice-mayor told him. "It used to give life. Now it's taking it away."

He almost couldn't bear to stop at the next pueblo, Paturia, where the river-bank had vanished under an entire block of mudbrick houses, carrying away walls that once faced the water, leaving rooms exposed and naked to passing boats. "The Magdalena used to rise only in March and November," an old acquaintance told him. "Now there's May and October, too. We paddle around the streets in canoes."

But he urged José Ignacio to go to the village of Canaletal, where the Gaviotas project continued to be a success. Canaletal was where Pepe Gómez had made the film of their work. José Ignacio felt greatly relieved; Canaletal was one of his favorite places in Magdalena Medio, situated on a high bluff with firm soils and good water.

He climbed the hill into town and headed for the school. Along the way he was greeted by women shucking rice in the doorways. Canaletal had been a disease-ridden tropical backwater when he'd arrived a decade earlier. There was now a church with a tile roof and new concrete electric utility poles. At the school, a teacher named Francisco practically gave him a hero's welcome. "All the wells have worked perfectly," he assured him.

"Can I see?"

There was one behind the school, below a spreading acacia filled with cacique bird nests. The water was sweet and clear, the *profesor* told him. José Ignacio peered through the foliage. The pump mechanism was missing. "You should have come two months ago," the teacher added sadly.

José Ignacio sighed. "What happened here?"

A man had appeared with orders to remove all the sleeve pumps. Everyone protested, but the orders bore the seal of the municipal governor. Because Canaletal now had electricity, there was no reason any longer for hand pumps, they were told. The equipment would be taken to where it was needed.

"But," said the *profesor,* "often there's no electricity. Sometimes *la guerrilla* blows up the transformers. Or the ground under a tower erodes and it falls over. We bought a diesel plant, but there's not enough money to keep it going. Whenever the power went out we still used your pumps. Now we have to lower buckets. We're almost back to where we were when you first came, when we carried water a kilometer from the river."

The Trees

As he returned to his chalupa, José Ignacio noticed through the open doorways the silent television sets, fans, and blenders people had purchased when electricity arrived. His last stop was San Pablo, the raw town that was their headquarters during the *Plan*. A woman named Doris, who ran the boarding house where they'd stayed, served him a bowl of fish stew. All of the wells and pumps they installed at the school here still worked fine, she assured him, patting his hand. The same with all the surrounding inland villages. José Ignacio brightened. Where was old Lucho, who used to drive them to all those places, he asked.

"*La guerrilla lo mató.*" She had no idea why they shot him. "Everybody's dying," she said glumly. First there was the violence. Now even the river had turned against them.

Before boarding his boat, José Ignacio stood on the dock, drinking another beer as he contemplated the turgid gray water. When Gaviotas was here, everyone had talked so hopefully about a new future along this river. But now Armageddon itself seemed to be pouring down the Magdalena, leaving the earth's next desert in its wake. Or, if not *el Apocalipsis*, then another Flood. At least, when the land and waters themselves began to die, politics and ideological battles would become irrelevant. Is this what it took to cleanse the earth again? Or was the future just draining to the sea, finally to drown?

～

AFTER OSCAR GUTIÉRREZ, THE FIRST GAVIOTAS DOCTOR, LEFT THE *llanos* in 1976, he went to England for residencies in internal medicine and cardiology, followed by a research fellowship at Cornell in upstate New York. He liked Britain, but the United States disturbed him: Doctors he met there seemed more preoccupied with investments than healing. He ended up back in Cali, where his father was a noted internist, and went into practice.

He was successful, but restless. At Gaviotas, he, Paolo Lugari, and Sven Zethelius had often discussed natural medicine, a favorite interest of

Oscar's father. They'd talked of one day starting a nursery for medicinal plants at Gaviotas. He'd never forgotten, and in 1992, in his early forties, he surprised everyone by returning to Cali's Universidad del Valle for a degree in pharmacology.

He loved it. Since so many medications were derived from plants growing in the tropics, people in his department had a logical interest in medicinal plants. Oscar wrote his thesis on capsaicin, the fiery compound in chili peppers. In his medical practice, he had diabetic patients with painful skin ulcers that wouldn't heal. Learning that capsaicin was a pain treatment, he'd ground some up in his kitchen and concocted an ointment to apply topically.

It proved surprisingly effective. More than one of his patients, misunderstanding, ate the stuff rather than swabbing it on affected areas and thought surely they'd swallowed a gulp of hell. Amazingly, it worked for them, too: Ulcers that had lasted for years cleared up within a few months. Oscar theorized that capsaicin accelerated healing by promoting growth of fibroblasts, cells that help form connective tissue fibers. He wasn't sure why, but he had plenty of evidence that this was so. Some of the ulcers he'd cured were the size of small craters.

He continued using his cream on patients with ailments besides diabetes. One day, it occurred to him to test it on leprosy victims. At the Universidad del Valle's dermatological clinic, doctors were skeptical but agreed to try. This time, sores that were twenty years old began to close. They attempted a double-blind experiment, but it broke down: Patients in the control group realized that they had been given a placebo because their ointment didn't sting, and had relatives in the United States send capsaicin preparations available there in health food stores.

Oscar didn't really object: The important thing was that nearly every leprosy patient was showing extraordinary progress. He joined the faculty of the Universidad del Valle, which now had an interdisciplinary group that investigated medicinal properties of plants, involving the medical school, pharmacologists, microbiologists, biochemists, and faculty from the natural sciences. Then, in January, 1996, he got a call from a niece who was studying graphic design in London. She was coming home, but needed to work on a project for her master's degree. Did he have any ideas what she might possibly design in Colombia?

By now, Oscar Gutiérrez had concluded that if medical cures were growing on the hillsides and along tropical rivers, it was essential to preserve such places. How could people squander the very source from which life emerged? He convinced his niece to design a campaign in biodiversity conservation, with posters, pamphlets, and illustrated educational materials. He personally took her to the department of national parks in Bogotá to see which ones would be safe for her to visit.

The answer, he was appalled to learn, was none of them. The road to every major nature reserve in Colombia was currently either controlled by guerrillas or passed dangerously close to their domain. Gutiérrez was shaken: Had it come to this? His country, the greatest repository of biodiversity on the planet, unable to control its most precious heritage?

Then he thought of Gaviotas. It had been exactly twenty years since he left, two decades since he'd seen Paolo Lugari. He called the office in Bogotá. "Oscar!" Paolo rumbled over the phone. "Where are you? Come see me immediately. We have to talk!"

Lugari's beard was mostly gray now, and the top of his head glinted as he and Gutiérrez embraced. But he had the same old effervescence, and, as always, seemed to be looking for more places to put it. "Oscar," he boomed, throwing an arm again around the physician's narrow shoulders as they entered his office, "you haven't changed." Gutiérrez's niece, Lugari assured him, was welcome to visit Gaviotas for as long as she liked. "But you should go with her."

"I will. Someday soon," Oscar promised. They began to talk medicinal plants. Oscar learned that one of the hemisphere's greatest experts on tropical botany, Dr. Hernando García Barriga, the elderly author of the seminal three-volume *Flora Medicinal de Colombia*, was on the Gaviotas foundation's board of directors. "I understand you have a wonderful hos-

pital out there. Do you ever still think of a laboratory to investigate the
properties of plant—"

"Oscar. You have to go out and see for yourself. Then we can really talk."

He hadn't really planned to, but then his niece's parents absolutely forbid her to travel to Vichada because it was too dangerous. Frustrated, Oscar decided to go after all—by land, the same way he'd traveled there the first time.

He was surprised to find that a portion of the road leading out of urban sprawl of Villavicencio, the former cowtown, was now paved. He also didn't recall kilometers of barbed wire attached to white-washed concrete fence posts, enclosing a string of haciendas that stretched for hundreds of thousands of hectares, each with a life-sized statue of a Brahma bull or cow posed above the entry arch. They belonged to the biggest emerald magnate in Colombia, a man on *Forbes* magazine's billionaire list, who had been arrested on occasion for allegedly being linked to paramilitary armies accused of political assassinations and multiple murders. In each instance, he had been released without being brought to trial.

Further on, the *ranchos* were less ostentatious, but some were impressively large. Their owners, people said, were *narcotraficantes*. This was where Oscar had once watched puma bounding across the savanna after deer and boa constrictors swishing across the road. Other than birds and one forlorn anteater, resembling a giant broom looking for its handle, the main wildlife now were swarms of yellow-and-black locusts, which also extended for kilometers. The family at a maloca where he stopped for coffee near Puerto Arimena told him that the locusts had been sent by the United States to punish Colombia for growing *ilícitos*. But, they said, the insects were devouring food crops instead of eating coca leaves.

Farther still, a huge revolving radar dish now loomed above a major military base appended to the government experimental station at Carimagua. Officially, this was for controlling international air traffic headed toward Venezuela, but many people of the region believed it belonged to the U.S. Drug Enforcement Agency. So, possibly, did the guerrillas, who periodically attacked, most recently shooting down one of the army base's helicopters.

Ahead of Gutiérrez now rose a shape that was dark, green, and immense, one that he also had never seen. Twenty years earlier, Paolo had told Oscar something that seemed particularly crazy, even for Lugari. At the time they were flying over the pallid green *llanos*, laced with darker green ribbons of gallery forest along the *caños*. Savannas are usually considered transitional zones between rain forest and desert, but Lugari insisted that the *caños* were like probing fingers of jungle, feeling their way back to their former domain. "The forest can repopulate itself here, Oscar," he told him solemnly. Oscar had wondered if he was out of his mind.

But now, two decades later, arriving in a Gaviotas reminiscent of a jungle settlement with its surrounding dense woods, he experienced an eerie feeling that Lugari's premonition had come true. When they showed him the tropical forest sprouting among the pines—the latest count was 245 native species—he was convinced. How could Paolo have known?

Carlos Sánchez and Otoniel Carreño took him to a section of pines that Gaviotas had planted back in 1982. It had been thinned so that light could enter, but also to allow room for the tropical understory to grow. It was hard to imagine that this had begun as a planned woodland. It had the delectable aroma of a wild forest: cool, inviting, and lush with a mélange of species. Guitiérrez recognized ficus, laurels, scheffleras, ferns, horsetails, purple and red jacarandas, fig vines, curare, sandbox trees, pale-barked *tuno blancos,* several legumes, and an assortment of flowering specimens whose taxonomy he couldn't immediately identify, but which he thought might hold pharmacological promise.

They followed what sounded like a flock of giant woodpeckers to a section where men were hacking incisions in the pine bark for resin collection. Carlos and Otoniel explained that the resin was self-replenishing, a substance that protects tropical pines from insects. "The proof is the plague of locusts—pines are the only plants they're not eating."

The *resineros* wore Gaviotas caps, long-sleeved shirts, and rubber boots to guard against pit vipers and carnivorous ants. About sixty in all, Oto told him, were drawing resin from 250,000 trees. Many were Guahibo Indians who had been children when he was the doctor here, and Oscar was bemused to watch them zip in and out of the forest on white all-terrain bicycles adorned with the Gaviotas logo. "Where do they get them?" Carlos Sánchez explained that Gaviotas had contracted a Bogotá factory to develop a *bicicleta gaviotera* to their specifications. Gaviotans purchased them at factory cost over several months, with an interest-free loan.

"But we're starting our own bicycle factory next year. We've already got a repair shop." Carlos mounted his own bike, whose handlebars were outfitted with a tilted, hinge-topped desk—the mobile office from which he coordinated the resin gathering teams. They headed to another patch of forest where the men were collecting resin with receptacles made from old bike inner tubes; once perfected, Carlos and Otoniel said, the design would be reusable, eliminating the need for plastic bags. Next, they showed him coffee plants that Carlos had raised hydroponically and transplanted between rows of five-foot pines. The idea came from Alonso Gutiérrez, who was convinced that if coffee could grow in Brazil's savannas, it could likewise grow in Colombia's.

"We have another experimental plot in open *llano*. But we think they're going to do better here in the shade of the pines."

"Coffee needs good soil. Are you fertilizing?"

They had divided their test plants into two groups. One received mineral supplements similar to those used in the hydroponics. Others were getting cow manure. "But," said Otoniel, stooping down and picking up a handful of soft tan dirt, "we think we might be able to go with just this. Look."

He opened his hand. It was filled with the decomposing residue of pine needles, leaf-mold, and bark from various native plants. Otoniel dug down a few inches and came up with more powdery humus. "Pines are supposed to make soil too acidic. But the pH of this is far less acidic than the surrounding savanna. We're making soil here. Real organic soil. Look at all the stuff growing here." Oscar glanced around at the flourishing native undergrowth, in time to glimpse a pair of gray foxes disappear into a thicket.

"In three years, when this coffee matures," Oto told him, "we'll know if we have a new viable crop here. *Café Orgánico de Gaviotas*—think it'll sell?" He laughed, stood, and wiped his hands. "It'll be interesting to see if it's pine-scented."

They followed the water buffalo cart, which was hauling bags of resin to be rendered, back to Gaviotas. The boiler's exhaust jet wasn't yet connected to the steam-driven engine for the co-generation electrical plant, and a white cloud of water vapor billowed from behind the factory. Inside, Hernán Landaeta, wearing heavy blue coveralls, goggles, and a yellow hard-hat with the Gaviotas logo, stood on a metal staircase alongside one of several tall stainless steel cylindrical vats, sampling the current batch of turpentine. He descended, pulled off his gloves, and shook hands. Hernán took a few minutes to walk Dr. Gutiérrez through the process, showing how the raw resin was agitated in a stainless steel vat and allowed to settle. Then it was heated, filtered, decanted, and finally distilled for ninety minutes to separate out the turpentine. "And then—come watch."

They walked to where five men dressed like Hernán were gathered around a single brass spigot, the focus of all the gleaming stainless cylinders, pipes, and galvanized troughs. A thick hose was clamped over its mouth. The nozzle was inserted into a round hole in the lid of a cardboard box resting on a pallet, printed with a slogan that read: *"Producto Natural, Cosecha de un Bosque Sostenible"*—a Natural Product, Harvested from a Sustainable Forest. Hernan turned the spigot, and golden liquid poured forth. It took about a minute for the box to fill with twenty-five kilos of 400° F. resin, which cooled quickly in the air. The hose was moved from box to box; soon they began to stack up on pallets.

"The box with the hole was Henry Moya's invention," Otoniel explained. "Before, we did it the conventional way: fill an aluminum tub with resin, let it solidify, then break it with pickaxes into chunks that we'd bag in burlap sacks. With four tons of resin a day, that was a lot of chopping. They said we couldn't pour hot liquid *colofonia* directly into cardboard boxes. The truth was that nobody had ever tried. This design just won a national prize for innovative industrial packaging."

Oscar was introduced to a pleasant young woman with brown hair and soft features, dressed in a white lab coat. Bacteriologist Luisa Fernanda Ospina explained that a paint manufacturer in Medellín was buying every drop they produced, but their resin quality was high enough for a much wider range of uses. Besides paints, enamels, and varnish, natural *colofonia* was used in soap, ink, newsprint, cosmetics, perfume esters, incense, drying agents, medicines, and to rosin the bows of musical instruments. Gaviotas hoped to capture a big slice of the market in Colombia, especially since it would be at least a decade before anyone else could grow enough pines to compete with them.

He watched her pour samples into beakers for the daily quality control analysis. In her laboratory, she showed him how its light color, purity, and high melting point qualified it for the highest category of resin available. "And we're still playing with the process."

They had a drink of ice water in the factory, from a solar kettle that Juan Novoa had routed through a refrigerator, then went out into the afternoon. Oscar marveled at the changes since he was last here. "All the solar buildings, and now even a telephone in Gaviotas!"

"Also solar-powered," Luisa Fernanda said as they coasted their bikes past the Telecom microwave tower. The transformers and storage batteries were protected by a canopy of moriche palm leaves; a flock of orange-capped saffron finches hopped over the twelve photovoltaic modules, feasting on sunning insects.

They rode by the preschool playground; not only the see-saw, but the swings now also pumped water. Slowly but surely, Gaviotas was working through the backlog of pending inventions left by Luis Robles and the crew of engineers. Nearby, Juan Novoa had a prototype of what Gaviotas

The Trees

hoped would be one of their most revolutionary products: the remote source pump. Developed jointly in 1992 by Manuel Corredor, the resident Guahibo Indian mechanical prodigy, and Pedro Nel Martínez, an engineering student researching his thesis at Gaviotas, the remote source pump would allow people to draw water from a well three hundred meters away without leaving their houses. The small hand pump used double hydraulic lines: Through one, well-water drawn by a submersible double-action pump flowed to a storage tank. The other, a return line, transmitted pressure created by the weight of the stored water to greatly ease the pumping process.

They stopped to try it; it required only slightly more effort than the sleeve pump. They continued on, pausing at the school where children were painting a mural on an exterior wall with an artist-in-residence from Bogotá, who told Oscar he was thinking of remaining permanently in Gaviotas. On the patio, they watched Jorge Eliécer Landaeta teach first-graders to dance a *joropo* in rapid waltz time. At least forty different steps and routines comprise *joropo;* Jorge Eliécer held up numbered cards for the children to follow as they twirled to music coming from a portable tape player.

Luisa Fernanda introduced Dr. Gutiérrez to Juanita Eslava and Ana María Luna, two young women who shared the house next to hers. Ana María, who had short-cropped chestnut hair and smiled a lot, studied fashion design at the Universidad de Los Andes. She was researching a thesis on bio-climatic work-clothing for Gaviotas' agro-forest industry. Juanita, a violinist and soprano, was teaching voice classes and studying *llanero* music with the Gaviotans. There were music classes almost every night, she told him. "The problem is deciding which to attend."

The afternoon sun, magnified by humidity, emerged from a bank of cumulus clouds. A huge blue iguana crawled out of a cashew tree to bask in the sandy volleyball court. "I could use more water," Oscar said. One of the ubiquitous solar kettles was nearby: a flat collector and two small tanks set atop four yellow poles, connected to a stainless steel spigot attached to the trunk of a guava tree. But Luisa Fernanda said she had a better idea, and the four of them bicycled over to the commissary. As they arrived, Gonzalo Bernal rode up on a tandem bicycle with his son Juan David. "I'm buying," he said, and went for drinks. The others waited on the stoop, next to recycling bins with signs in both Spanish and Guahibo, indicating where to toss paper, aluminum, and plastic.

Gonzalo emerged with sealed plastic bags, beaded with cold sweat. Their labels read "Agua Pura Gaviotas." Each bag held three hundred cubic centimeters. As they gnawed at the corners and drank, Gonzalo explained that they were now bottling—bagging—pure water to distribute in the region, in hopes of lowering the rate of gastro-intestinal disease. "As you well know, eighty percent of diseases out here are water-related," Gonzalo said. "We figure that anything we can do to give people good water to drink will help."

"A wonderful idea," said Oscar. "Is this out of your solar kettles?"

No, Luisa Fernanda said. It came from the windmill field that formerly supplied the hospital. She analyzed the water quality there and at the solar kettles daily for bacteria and parasites, and also tested to makes certain the *caño* was safe for swimming. "The well water is excellent. The kettles work perfectly. I've seen them sterilize water even in the presence of fecal matter."

"What do you mean, 'formerly supplied the hospital?'" Oscar asked. "What's the hospital doing for water now? And when am I finally going to get to see it?"

Luisa Fernanda turned to Gonzalo. "That's what we need to show you, Oscar," Gonzalo said. "There is no hospital at Gaviotas anymore."

~

PAOLO LUGARI AND THE DIRECTOR OF THE GAVIOTAS SCHOOL, TERESA Valencia, flew through thick, ragged storm clouds, headed for Gaviotas. They were in Pepe Gómez's old Piper Dakota, now piloted by a neighbor who was dropping them off on the way to his ranch, where he had to put out salt and minerals for his cattle lest they succumb to botulism. The

Andes disappeared in a gray swirl below them; when they broke through to clear sky, they were over the *llanos*. With the early rains, the savannas were already green as a Colombian emerald. Below the plane, the road was a rust-red stripe that turned to silver in sections where it was already inundated.

Paolo was telling Tere about his recent trip to the province of Tolima in south central Colombia. Tolima straddled the Río Magdalena; west of the river valley, the land was arid and less fertile. Since before Columbus it was Pijao Indian country, and since 1991 it had also been a zone of cholera. After the first outbreak killed dozens, the Pijao petitioned the provincial government to purchase sleeve pumps from Gaviotas so they could pump deep, uncontaminated water. Now, Paolo said, there was another wave of cholera, with hundreds of cases reported. The only disease-free settlements were the ones with the Gaviotas pumps.

"The index of public health shouldn't be the number of hospital beds per capita, but the number of potable water taps," he said. "If we can revolutionize the water people drink, we can do away with most of the reasons people need hospitals."

"Not all of them," Tere reminded him. For the past month, she had been under special obstetric observation in Bogotá due to complications during her first trimester. The doctors had determined that the child she was carrying, a girl, was in no danger, and that Teresa could return home. But to be safe, they insisted that she give birth in a hospital, which meant that her daughter couldn't be born in Gaviotas.

Paolo knew and regretted this, but what could they do? Colombia had adopted a new health system for all its citizens. Everyone had to participate, either through a private health insurance corporation or through federal Social Security, which now competed with the private sector for customers. The idea was to make medicine more efficient through market competition, a concept that had caused more displeasure than satisfaction in the United States, whose managed health care provided the model for Colombia's new system. Nevertheless, the plan was seen as a boon to the poor, promising them the same level of care as everyone else.

Hospitals—now known as "health servers"—were required to staff at least four full-time staff specialists. Bones had to be set by orthopedists, births supervised by obstetricians, children's ailments treated by pediatricians. Health servers had to provide ambulance services and maintain accounting departments. Because they had to be profitable, they needed to see a minumum number of patients per month. When Gonzalo Bernal went to the provincial capital to inquire what this number was, he was told two thousand.

"How can we possibly do that in the middle of the *llanos?*" he asked an official. The answer was a shrug, followed by the suggestion that rural areas might form their own health insurance corporation, which could then contract with a local hospital. To be legal, however, a health insurance corporation needed at least 15,000 participants. Gonzalo reminded the official that only about 3,000 people lived within a four-hour radius of Gaviotas. To try to band together with other rural provinces over such huge distances was nonsense, for no other reason than how quickly it would overwhelm the region's meager telephone service.

And even if they could overcome these obstacles, Gaviotas and other rural clinics would still have fallen far short of the required numbers of patients and specialists. Not only couldn't they afford that many doctors, but it would be unconscionable to make specialists wait days for a patient suffering from their specialty to appear. Nevertheless, rural medics legally could no longer do much more than treat colds and fevers. The new law, which arguably made sense in cities, had effectively outlawed their hospital.

"We have to remain flexible and consider this an opportunity," Paolo told Teresa. In response to the sullen look she gave him in reply, he added, "Listen to what just happened:"

What just happened was that Dr. Oscar Gutiérrez had returned from Gaviotas and come straight to see him. Oscar had seen the former hospital. They showed him the ingenious devices and the beautiful maloca built for indigenous patients, such as those he himself had first brought to Gaviotas. The maloca was now storing porcelain latrines Gaviotas had purchased for a sanitation program they intended to inaugurate in surrounding communities.

They'd showed him the water factory, now installed in the former convalescence chamber next to the surgical theater. Two women wearing masks, caps, and plastic booties stood at pedal-operated sealing machines that filled plastic bags with clean Gaviotas water from a stainless steel pipe. ("Two workers," Lugari told Teresa, "can fill 1,500 bags per day.") Gaviotas' plan was not just to distribute water in the region, but to set up similar, inexpensive factories in other rural communities. Jorge Eliécer Landaeta had composed a *joropo* musical production for the children to perform around Vichada to educate people about the need to drink clean water.

When they showed Gutiérrez the adjacent hydroponic garden, he'd come to the conclusion they'd been hoping for: That if this could no longer be a hospital, it would make a superb research facility for medicinal plants.

"Gladys took him to the pharmacy so he could see the herbal remedies we're stocking, now that we can't legally prescribe antibiotics. And they showed him the neem trees."

Gaviotas had recently planted two hundred neem trees—the shrub known as the village drug store in India, because everything from its roots to its leaves are useful. Neem seeds were believed to be antibiotic; an extract from its leaves was used to combat ulcers and as an anti-inflammatory. Gaviotas school children explained to Dr. Gutiérrez that the bark was a natural insecticide, and a light coat of neem oil could keep stored apples from spoiling.

"He loved it when they told him that the littlest branches can be used as toothbrushes," Paolo said.

Oscar Gutiérrez had also said that, while heading back to his guest quarters at Gaviotas one night, it had suddenly struck him what he was doing, and what he wanted to do. He was walking alone after dark in one of the most dangerous countries in the world, yet he felt safer than in any place he'd ever been. As if to punctuate his thoughts, the art teacher's five-year-old daughter passed him on her bicycle and waved goodnight. A little girl couldn't ride her bike alone at night where he lived in Cali, or anywhere else on earth he could think of, for that matter.

After a quarter-century, Gaviotas had somehow avoided falling into the snare of *la guerrilla*, although they were all over the region. Nobody here locked their doors. That morning he had dropped some peso bills on the floor while rushing to breakfast, and returned later to find his bed made and the money neatly stacked on his pillow. As he left the dining commons, he had seen something else that amazed him: about fifty *resineros*, chatting and drinking coffee while they waited for Carlos Sánchez to assign them to their stations in the forest. Something was missing, though, and it finally occurred to him what it was: There was no cloud of cigarette smoke over their heads. It was a sight to gladden the heart of any doctor, but utterly extraordinary among the working class in Latin America—or nearly anywhere. These were the healthiest people Oscar Gutiérrez had ever known, and he'd be damned if he was going to let them down.

"So," Paolo concluded, "Oscar hopes to convince his university to make Gaviotas its official rural laboratory for research into medicinal plants."

They could employ Guahibo and other Orinocan Indians who had centuries of valuable ethnobotanical experience, Oscar had told him, and maybe even earn them royalties for their venerable knowledge. Then there was the beleaguered crop substitution program that the Colombian government, pressured by the United States, was trying to persuade coca growers to accept. The problem was that growing coca earned them fifty times more than cassava, rice, or bananas. Even if that weren't so, those crops meant financial disaster without decent roads to get them to market. Gaviotas had been asked by the government to design affordable irrigation systems for the program, but little had happened thus far to noticeably slow coca production.

"But medicinal plants can be worth five hundred dollars a gram. Some even much more. They weigh very little and can be processed on the spot, so shipping them to market is no problem," Oscar had insisted.

The Trees

"This is the one thing in the world that can compete with illegal drugs. We can save the Indians and tropical forests and stay healthy in the process. We have to find a way to do this, Paolo!"

"So meanwhile, what do we do when we need specialists?" Teresa asked, patting her swelling womb as their plane circled Gaviotas.

"What we've always done: Rely on the civil air patrol and pilots like our friend here to get us to the city on time. And pray for the best."

Tere shook her head. The hospital seemed like such a loss. But she brightened when they taxied to a stop and the plane was engulfed with overjoyed schoolchildren. "¡*Profesora Tere!* We have to tell you everything you missed!

She knelt, laughed, hugged and kissed them. "Okay, what did I miss?"

Well, for starters she missed Day of the Bicycle. A group of cross-country cyclists rode from Carimagua to Gaviotas, including Alfonso Blanco, a sociologist who once had lived here, and his wife, Luisa Fernanda, a doctor who had done her year of rural service at Gaviotas during the 1980s. That afternoon, everybody biked over mule trails to Caribey, the Guahibo village twenty kilometers away, where Luisa Fernanda, the doctor, examined a woman with leprosy. Then she and the other Luisa Fernanda, the bacteriologist, gave a talk on how to avoid diarrhea and dehydration. Their translator was Luis Adelio Chipiaje, a Guahibo *resinero* who, representing Gaviotas, had come in second this year in the Llanos Marathon. They also inaugurated their first flush latrine, installed in an outhouse made of moriche palm leaves. Then the Indians danced for them and invited them all to join.

The next day, Alfonso the sociologist had led a workshop on relationships and sexuality for all the Gaviotas teenagers. "But a lot of the rest of us snuck in," they told Teresa.

"I'm very sorry I missed that one."

"And, *Profesora,* you also just missed International Day of the Woman!"

On that day, no woman had worked. Men rose at 3:30 A.M. to stoke the cookstoves and squeeze oranges for a breakfast of juice, cheese-filled corncakes, potatoes, rice, and hot chocolate. The evening before, Carlos Ceijas took five others down to the Río Muco, where they'd fished all night to prepare a banquet of peacock bass. After the fish dinner, the children told Tere, they'd put on a pageant in the community hall for their mothers, and all the women got presents.

That afternoon, Paolo Lugari also heard about International Day of the Woman, because it had been a revelation of sorts for the men. The kitchen, Abraham and Otoniel told him, was the least Gaviotan workplace in all of Gaviotas, much more exhausting than the factory or the forest. It needed extra solar collectors so it wasn't necessary to boil so much water in the morning. The dishwashing system took forever—it was nearly noon before the breakfast crew finished, and by then the lunch team was in there, demanding clean serving trays. And why wasn't there a set of solar pressure cookers, like in the kitchen at the hospital?

"With a good resin harvest, and a successful planting season," Paolo told them, "there'll be money to make over the kitchen by next year. In fact, let's make it a priority. No reason why we can't have all the solar-heated heated water we need in there now—we've got plenty of collectors."

Something else had happened on International Day of the Woman. A group of Guahibos approached Gonzalo and asked if they could participate in the festivities. That evening, two Guahibo dances were performed at Gaviotas in full ceremonial dress: headbands, skirts of moriche and seje palm, and body paint. The dances were sung by a Guahibo priest who squatted at a fire holding feathered bamboo spears, blowing a whistle made of antelope horn. One dance paid homage to women, the other to Gaviotas, as symbolized by the yellow-billed tern the Guahibos call *acareto* in their language and the *llaneros* call *gaviota*.

The dancers were dark-skinned Indians and pale Gaviotan *llaneros*, whom the Guahibo had also dressed and painted. Their shared celebration was a small incident, unnoticed anywhere else, but unprecedented in a land where white people had once lumped Indians with other vermin that needed to be exterminated to make the *llanos* livable, and where the term *indígena* still served as a slur. It happened in a tiny village far out in what most Colombians considered a wasteland, but it was among the most hopeful events to occur in the entire country for a long time, and maybe, on some earthly or cosmic level, someone might take notice.

"We need to talk about some things the school needs," said Nubia Perilla, the art teacher. "Now." While Teresa, the school's director, took her pre-scribed afternoon rest, Nubia was representing her at a meeting of the *jefes del grupo*. Beside education, the groups included the mechanical shop, factory, kitchen, maintenance, forestry, electrical, carpentry, cattle and telecommunications (because Omar Marín was temporarily running both cows and the telephone), administration, and special projects.

This was a monthly meeting, which, by general consensus, often didn't meet because nothing much ever seemed to need discussing. No one was sure why. Gonzalo Bernal's theory was that because everyone chose the work they liked best and, once there, were actually expected to suggest improvements, people were basically content. At the very least, since such a system encouraged communication, Gaviotas had enough internal correction mechanisms to address most problems on the spot, rather than wait for a staff meeting to render a ruling.

The library, Nubia explained, was leaking and needed to be fixed be-fore the daily rains hit. She also argued that instead of moving the natural history museum into the new Gaviotas Research Center, as the old hospi-tal was now being called, it belonged in the school where the children could see it daily. After some discussion the group decided that the imme-diate priority was a new roof; the museum must wait until after the forth-coming planting season.

Someone mentioned that an oropendola nest had fallen out of the tree near the Telecom, possibly because the kids were climbing it. Any adult, they reminded each other, had the authority and duty to instruct a child at the moment he or she required it.

They discussed the new water factory. Abraham Beltran agreed to rig a better system for moving heavy crates of bagged water once the women in the factory had filled them—perhaps some kind of toboggan. As they talked, seated around a table on the patio outside the coordinator's office in the shade of a yellow allamanda tree, they sampled their product. Carlos Cañas, the bookkeeper, reported on a blindfold test in the commissary: five out of five, himself included, picked the Gaviotas water over competing bottled brands from the city. "It's sweeter." They toasted each other, laughing because the bags didn't clink, which brought up another subject: the need to educate their customers to recycle plastic bags. Jorge Eliécer, Gonzalo said, was already including a skit on environmental responsibility in the *joropo* theater that would be traveling through the region.

There were requests for a mini-basketball court for the small children and for video tapes of Olympic volleyball for their own players to study. Carlos Cañas thought they could afford these. This was a refreshing change. A year earlier there was so little money that a palm tanager nested inside of one of his big three-ringed ledgers piled on a shelf gathering dust; long before there was a need to open it, the nestlings had fledged. As they started to discuss the imminent planting season, Paolo Lugari joined them. He had a few things to talk about, he said, ideas about their proposed musical instrument factory and about a Pijao Indian women's cooperative he saw in Tolima, which processed guava candy with water from a Gaviotas sleeve pump. Maybe there could be a similar industry for women here, with guavas and mangos. "But these questions can wait. Go on."

They did, acknowledging first that everyone was quite interested in the idea of building harps and *cuatros*. And, with the resin industry gearing up and more men needed, ventures to employ more women would be necessary, lest Gaviotas become overrun with frustrated bachelors in the middle of the lonely savanna.

They proceeded to the main issue: the planting. They had to decide whether to labor around the clock, or work normal shifts and take two weeks longer, as they had done in 1995, when they planted two million more trees. Either way, Pompilio would need extra hands from other groups, such as the shops and maintenance.

This raised problems, because Abraham had a long list of work orders that must be filled, including the library roof. "You can't take all my men," he told Pompilio, so they talked about it. As they did, Paolo Lugari listened in frank admiration at how the Gaviotans arrived at decisions by discussing calmly, always looking each other in the eye. No one was intimidated, everyone was respectful. Eventually, they reached a solution and moved on. This was a characteristic, he realized, of a community where everyone had a real stake. Two years earlier, he'd watched how they handled the commissary storekeeper who admitted overcharging to finance his honeymoon: He and his wife were quietly ostracized until their debt was repaid. He kept his post, but no further socializing occurred until the matter was resolved. It was an effective, peaceful, fair, and instructive solution, one that rarely needed to be repeated.

And their work, as Paolo told everyone he met, was just as impressive as their society. Men and women without university credentials were running the country's most innovative forestry industry, annually planting more trees than the Colombian government's entire forestry program— and running a modern processing factory as well. He compared them proudly to what Jorge Zapp talked about in his latest book published by the United Nations, *Empresas Virtuales Populares* (Virtual Corporations for the People): an empowered work force, one with ownership and pride in the quality of their products, with information generated and shared collectively, not just stuck at the top in some isolated managerial priesthood.

They'd remained flexible enough to respond quickly to change and to reorganize in a world that was spinning faster than the old structures could withstand. "Gaviotas is a not a model, it's a path," he would tell people. And now the path was about to turn again. Barring unknown disaster, they were about the grow: Within three years, they would need at least five hundred people here to run the forest industry and myriad other

projects. Scientists would arrive to work at the new medicinal plants laboratory, and if profits continued as hoped from the resin, there might even
be money to bring back the engineers.

That would happen, Lugari was sure. Alonso Gutiérrez talked continually about how much he missed the *llanos*, especially since his father
was kidnapped from his coffee finca and murdered. One night, Alonso
told them that he'd even considered returning to run for governor of
Vichada. Even more amazing, all the *llaneros* took him seriously and encouraged him.

Gaviotas had just signed a contract to heat a municipal swimming
pool near Bogotá by combining solar energy and natural gas technology,
Jaime Dávila's latest specialty, and now Jaime was working with them
again. And the last time Magnus Zethelius came to visit, he confessed that
he was sick of the winters in Michigan. Now that his son was entering
college on an engineering scholarship (won, he told them, on the strength
of an essay about growing up among engineer-dreamers in the plains of
eastern Colombia), maybe it was time to . . .

"This is always your home," Lugari had told him.

"Well," Magnus replied, "I've never found anything as good as Gaviotas in the United States."

But the promise that Gaviotas had wrought, amidst the surrounding
turbulence of its nation and its times, now begged a question waiting to
be asked since its inception: How big could they get and remain Gaviotas?
What would happen when they grew so successful that more people chose
to come to the *llanos* to live? This was something Paolo had to discuss with
them. But just not now. Tomorrow.

The next day at lunch, Paolo showed Gonzalo and Cecilia what looked
like a miniature wooden canoe, carved from a branch of a local *chaparro*
tree. "Oscar Gutiérrez made this for me." He poured water into it, let it
soak a few minutes, then drank it down. "It's a tonic for my pre-diabetic

blood sugar. Since I've been doing this, I feel terrific. Oscar says we could produce these—he knows plenty of patients who can use them." He balanced it on his fingers. "Sven would have loved this."

Just before he died of emphysema a year earlier, Sven Zethelius returned with his son Magnus for his final trip to Gaviotas. It was in the middle of the torrential equatorial winter, but he'd insisted. He had hoped to live out his days here—he'd wanted to start a Gaviotas retirement community for university professors and be the first resident. That was something else they should be thinking about, Paolo realized. "Is there a truck and driver available this afternoon?" he asked Gonzalo.

"I think Carlos Zambrano is around."

"Good. He's one I should talk to anyway."

"What's the truck for?"

"I want a few of us to go out to Villa Camisa."

"Doesn't Carlos teach chess this afternoon?" Cecilia asked.

Carlos Zambrano, who'd lived in Gaviotas nearly twenty years, was the reigning *llano* chess champion. "That's Thursday," said Gonzalo.

"Can you come?"

Cecilia declined; she didn't intend to miss volleyball. That afternoon, Paolo, Gonzalo, Carlos Cañas, Otoniel Carreño, and Carlos Zambrano went out to the forest. They drove down the middle of the firebreaks, stopping the truck to watch a three-point, white-tailed stag and a beautiful tawny doe. Lugari, standing in the truckbed, gazed around with pleasure. "Promise me," he said to his friends, "that someday you'll bury me in this forest."

They drove until they found Carlos Sánchez with one of the resin crews. Done for the day, the workers were mounting their bicycles. "How'd it go?" Otoniel asked.

"Good. We're getting about nine grams of resin per tree per day."

Carlos Cañas pulled out a calculator. Their first year, they produced 107 tons of resin; this year they hoped for 500. "Will we make it?" Lugari asked.

"It means nearly fifty tons a month," Cañas said. He closed his eyes, reading figures from memory. "We might. Maybe not. But we'll be close."

"Good enough. Climb aboard," he told Carlos Sánchez. "We have to go pick out a future."

Cañas and Zambrano rode in the cab; the rest stood in the back of the three-ton stake-bed pick-up, holding onto the wooden slats as they jerked over the *llano*, batting locusts away. Lugari yelled to Zambrano to head for Villa Camisa.

Villa Camisa was two thousand hectares they'd bought years back when they could afford to do so, east of Gaviotas along the rutted slash that was the trans-Orinoquia highway. The earth here had once suffered some ancient spasm that wrinkled the flat savanna sheet, leaving land that rippled in long, low, dune-like mesas that rose above *caños* and dropped into soft green basins. Some of this textured country had been planted the year before in pines, and they drove through undulating yellow hills dotted with green rows of two-foot trees that rolled hypnotically before them as they neared the place Paolo wanted to see. At a point where the road was about to descend again, Lugari banged on the cab. "See if you can drive down there," he said, pointing toward a *morichal*, a great swathe of palms cutting across the southern edge of the bowl.

They rocked along until Carlos felt the ground get spongy. Everyone hopped out. As they did, dozens of burrowing owls popped from their holes. There was a low, fresh breeze coming from the palm glade, which traced a long, hidden *caño* that disappeared between ridges to the south. For a while, they just stood there, absorbing the loveliness of the land under their feet.

Paolo gathered them in a circle. "If the numbers hold," he said, "in eight years—that would be the year 2004—we'll have six hundred people collecting resin. Already, the new *resineros* we've hired are getting accustomed to Gaviotas and liking our way of life. They'll need to live in settlements nearby with their families, not in bachelor barracks. We'll need factories to employ their women, to produce drinking water and fruit preserves and harps, factories of things we haven't even thought of yet—but they will."

The Trees

He removed his cap and closed his eyes for a moment, inhaling the delicious breeze. "I see enclaves of maybe twenty families, little satellites surrounding Gaviotas, no more than twenty minutes away by bicycle. They draw their services from Gaviotas, but each family owns its own home and two hectares. Every house is designed by its owner, using Gaviotas ideas, assisted by a Gaviotas architect. Not necessarily someone with an architectural degree: an architect in function, not sanction. People can choose among four alternatives where they want to live: *morichal*, savanna, forest, or among these hills."

He stopped talking and looked around him. Everyone was rapt. "Mind you, none of the above is obligatory. It's up to everyone, not me. But this," he said, an arm sweeping around him, "is where I'm building my house, and I'd love you for my neighbors. We once had an idea for expanding Gaviotas, back in the seventies, but it was premature. But it's time to get started planning and have the first phase ready within five years. Back then, we called it Tropicalia. Maybe we should resurrect that, but I'm open to suggestions."

For the next hour they wandered over the landscape, visualizing what the community of the future would be like, occasionally trying out and rejecting names. They inspected the *morichal*, which was filled with bright parrots and chittering monkeys, and sprinkled with the magenta flowers of papery-barked *siete cueros* trees. The palms, standing in muck seeping up from a clear spring that they figured was just a few meters below the surface, sagged with the weight of great chains of globular brown fruit. "This is natural mineral water," Lugari declared as he dipped his finger in a puddle, "filtered through hundreds of kilometers of sand, with no cows nearby to contaminate it. This we can bottle and sell in the cities. Export it to the fancy mineral water market."

They convened again atop a hill, standing in hip-high foxtail grass. Nearby were small outcroppings of partly metamorphosed red sandstone. The breeze, Gonzalo observed, was steady enough for windmills. He pointed to the bowl below them. "That's where the soccer field goes."

"You're right," Paolo agreed. "We could put natural seating around it like a Greek amphitheater. We could have our houses on each of these little hills, following the topography, using stone from here or wood we cull from the forest to build them." Everyone else, it appeared, had been thinking along the same lines. Remote access pumps could bring water up from the *morichal*, and they could drill through the hillsides for natural cooling ducts that would enter houses from underneath. The low areas would be perfect for fruit groves, and the pines, growing only a kilometer away, would help keep the climate fresh. "It's a natural refrigerator," said Paolo. "This is the only pueblo in the world born along with a forest."

They tried out names for this new pueblo—Tropicalia, Culturalia— and then someone noted that if this was going to happen in five years, that would be 2001. "Why not call it *Odisea?*"

Immediately, they were all shouting it. "I like it," said Lugari. "Remember that the genius of the Greek empire sprang from little islands and city-states, where people speculated on science, nature, and utopia. This is an island with *los llanos* for its sea. In the future, *los llanos* can be comprised of little island communities where people live in productive harmony with nature and technology. And with each other."

For 1,800 years, archeologists believed, millions of Mayan Indians had once lived exactly this way, in loosely overlapping city-states, co-existing in natural equilibrium with the Central America jungles and with their neighbors. Paolo Lugari's mind held a comparable vision. Recently, the Inter-American Development Bank had asked them for a feasibility plan for cultivating two hundred thousand hectares of forest—more than ten times what was projected for Gaviotas. They had also been funded to design sustainable family modules involving blends of short- and long-term crops, such as cassava and rubber, that could grow in the shelter of pines, much the way the Maya designed shaded gardens that mimicked the natural succession of the surrounding rain forest.

Already their neighbors were planting thousands of free seedlings that Gaviotas had given away, and Gaviotas had promised to buy their resin when it was ready. No one knew for sure how much natural resin the market might bear, but they kept learning of new uses, such as in shoes, chewing gum, and the fine arts. And assuredly, chemists working in the new Gaviotas medicinal research center would find as-yet-undreamed-of applications for high-grade resin. There was no reason, Paolo told the Bank, why their productive, oxygen-generating woodland shouldn't march all the way across this plain and across South America's two hundred-fifty million more hectares just like it.

For that matter, a cabinet officer from Indonesia was on his way to visit them, hoping to start a Gaviotas on an Indonesian island. Maybe it was time to . . . Paolo shook himself out of his reverie and added aloud, "With new technology like the Internet, people can live anywhere and still learn anything they need. Even here."

At that moment, a cloud of locusts blew over them. Lugari snatched one out of the air. "What other people call problems we have to see as solutions. If you toast these grasshoppers, they're a source of protein." He pointed to the *tijeritas*, the fork-tailed flycatchers gorging in mid-air around them. "We'll feed them to animals—I know! We'll dig ponds and raise fish. We can hook up vacuum bags to the tractors and harvest tons of them."

A lone army troop-transport helicopter droned overhead, following the road. Glancing skyward, they saw that it was nearly dusk. As they boarded the truck, Gonzalo remembered that this was the night of the full moon. He was supposed to be joining a group that was going to ride their bicycles out into the open savanna to watch it rise.

"We won't make it back in time," said Otoniel.

"No matter," said Lugari. "The moon will rise over Gaviotas without us. We can watch it from here."

Twenty minutes later, a drunken *llanero* careened and slithered down Colombia's rain-pocked trans-Orinoquia highway, headed west on a motor scooter. At the last moment, he avoided a wreck because he fortunately heard the shouts of six men leaning against the rails of a big pickup truck that was stopped smack in the middle of the otherwise deserted road. He braked, skidded, nearly fell, but somehow gained control of his bike in time to keep from smashing into it. He peered up. The smiling

men were visibly happy, but he didn't see a bottle passing among them.
But if they weren't *ebrios,* then what were they staring at, parked in the middle of the road?

He hollered up and asked them. "Turn around!" they yelled back down.

He did, and staggered back to see what had been there all along, if only he'd thought to look: Among the few sweet consolations to *llaneros* displaced during *La Violencia* from their ancestral highland homes was the immense, gorgeous full moon that blossomed faithfully each month over the flat sweep of the equatorial savanna. This wasn't the penny-weight moon that was already shrunk to a high, wan spotlight by the time it finally cleared the lofty Andes. This was a huge, pregnant, shimmering, crimson globe, swimming in the thick belt of tropical atmosphere at the earth's midriff. This was a moon to convince lovers that it's all true, a moon to make humans believe that anything is possible. It was a moon that reminded Paolo Lugari that the Universidad de Los Andes would soon be sending them an engineer to design a dirigible to float over this *llano,* one as big as that colossal red ball out there, rising up for them to catch.

They watched until it was nearly ten degrees high, its rust-red countenance dulling to the dark orange of the prairie fire they could see licking the distant northern horizon. The silhouettes of a pair of *gaviotas* crossed the glowing embers of the lunar face, reminding them that it was time to go home.

Clapping each other on the back, they made ready to leave. They were unassuming men, at ease in the bed of a pickup truck, fewer than half of them with degrees or pedigrees sanctified by universities. Yet on that day and in that moonlight, they believed that they were doing a good and enormous thing. Surrounded by a land seen either as empty or plagued with misery, they had forged a way and a peace they believed could prosper long after the last drop of the earth's petroleum was burned away. They were so small, but their hope was great enough to brighten the planet turning beneath them, no matter how much their fellow humans seemed bent on wrecking it. Against all skeptics and odds, Gaviotas had lighted a path through a magnificent but darkened land, whose sorrows mirrored a beautiful, embattled world.

Paolo turned and took one last look. "I see the Sea of Tranquility," he said.

Carlos Sánchez squinted at the features of the limpid moon. "Where is it?"

"All around us, *amigo*. It's all around us."

Back at Gaviotas, the others had ridden their bikes out to the airstrip to see the moon rise, too. They lay on their backs in the grass, watching until red became orange, then ocher, then white, until the dark pines turned to silver as the moon soared higher. The warm night filled with the chant of doves and owls and the marvelous, descending wail of the tropical potoo. Later that night, with the full moon overhead like a crown, Juanita Eslava would enter the forest and add her own soprano voice, serenading the young trees that Gaviotas was nurturing, and the angels would answer, blessing this place.

Afterword

~

I FIRST LEARNED OF GAVIOTAS IN 1988, DURING A *NEW YORK TIMES Magazine* assignment to write a 4,500-word "portrait of Colombia." At the time, I'd been in the country for two months on a Fulbright research grant, long enough to know how daunting this would be. It would have been easy enough to serve up a bloody slice of the current cycle of narco-bombings, paramilitary assassinations, and guerrilla retaliations. But the true sorrow of *la guerra sucia*—the ongoing "dirty war"—was that Colombia was so much more than its numbing headlines, something that everybody seemed to have forgotten.

It was especially much more than the coffee and coca plantations that people in my own nation imagined. Unlike many other struggling lands relegated to that lowly caste known as the Third World, Colombia was hugely blessed, both with resources and skilled people to utilize them. Its literacy rate rivalled or surpassed that of most countries on earth, including my own, and dozens of fine Colombian universities produced brilliant scientists, engineers, writers, technicians, and business leaders. Colombia boasted seasoned industries ranging from textiles to book-binding, more than a hundred exportable crops, truly vast mineral deposits (coal, oil, and emeralds), enough fresh water to rank third in world hydro-electric potential, and possibly the planet's richest ecosystem.

This last fact intrigued me so much that I asked the director of Colombia's national parks to tell me which place best exemplified his country's astonishing biodiversity. That, he replied, would be the Serranía de la Macarena, Colombia's oldest nature preserve, the 80-mile-long geologic uplift whose forests and rivers were believed to harbor more species than any similar expanse on earth. It was just a few hours southeast of Bogotá—"But," he warned me, "you can't go there. It's too dangerous."

He explained that the jungle canopy of this incomparable world treasure concealed a major guerrilla command base, around which a growing number of coca growers were steadily replacing large swathes of this ecological Eden with a monoculture of wispy, lime-green shrubs. Of course, I had to go. The Macarena seemed the perfect symbol to portray a nation extravagantly endowed but also savagely cursed—a nation that I increasingly recognized as a microcosm of all that simultaneously plagues and holds promise in our bountiful, beleaguered world.

Through contacts arranged by a helpful Colombian correspondent for a Soviet news agency, I was able to negotiate safe conduct from the Marxist-Leninist *Fuerzas Armadas Revolucionarias de Colombia*, who occupied the Macarena. It took a day's bus ride plus two days on foot to reach their impressive bamboo encampment. After two more days of politely chatting political doctrine with rebel *comandantes*, I was led by guerrilla guides on a journey through unparalleled biological splendor, which was only interrupted by the coca fields we crossed—and by a sudden military ambush that wiped out most of a forty-man FARC detail, moments before we were to rendezvous with them. My last view of the Serranía de la Macarena was over my shoulder, running from helicopter-borne machine-gunners and squadrons of Colombian Air Force T-33 bombers that were reducing yet another chunk of paradise to smouldering ashes.

Soon after filing my report, I left for home. "Someday," said the journalist whose connections had enabled my glimpse of the Macarena's beauty and anguish, "you must return to write a hopeful environmental story." Still shaken by what I'd just witnessed, I couldn't fathom what hope I might discover in this tortured land. Then she told me about a remarkable community that, for years, had ignored surrounding strife to prosper in a most unlikely setting: the bleak eastern Colombian *llanos*. It was called Gaviotas.

I recognized the name: One day during my research I had encountered technicians whose caps bore the yellow-and-green Gaviotas logo, turning rooftops in a Bogotá slum into thriving hydroponic gardens. Years would pass before I saw them again. From 1990 to 1992, with three other journalists I produced a 23-part series for National Public Radio that documented how so-called progress was turning entire traditional cultures into endangered species, often by literally ripping the ground from under them. Set in a dozen developing countries, our series, *Vanishing Homelands,* described the threat humanity now posed to its own habitat. It ended with me gazing at Antarctica's ozone hole and speculating whether the entire planet—everyone's traditional homeland—was now at stake.

These sobering reports led to *Searching for Solutions,* a public radio series that explored possible antidotes to what currently ails the earth. Over two more years, in places such as Brazil, India, Europe, the Middle East, and our own United States, we chronicled attempts to produce enough food and energy for straining populations—and how to humanely check the growth of those populations—without sacrificing nature and culture in the process. Mostly, we discovered how complicated the solutions will be. But the most heartening program of the series turned out to be the one I brought back from, of all places, Colombia.

To get that story, I traveled for sixteen hours in February, 1994, from Bogotá to Gaviotas in a Diahatsu jeep, including delays obliged by official army roadblocks and by truckloads of armed men whose affiliation was less certain. The car and body searches proved a relief from the sensational pounding of the highway that never was. Being the dry season—the road is often impassable the rest of the year—I was so coated with powdered clay that one sergeant doubted whether my passport picture was really me.

I was accompanied by my journalist friend from Bogotá who had formerly worked for the now-defunct Soviet news agency. I was traveling to Gaviotas to see sustainable technology created by and for the Third World; the compelling interest for my companion, who had seen loved ones and journalist colleagues massacred, was Gaviotas' reputation as an island of hope amidst Colombia's ongoing tragedy. We suspected there might be a connection.

During our stay, she was moved to tears that such a peaceful refuge could exist in her nation. But the story of Gaviotas apparently also touched a profound yearning in my own First World country: To this day, I hear from people who listened to my NPR documentary, or from readers of a subsequent article I wrote for the *Los Angeles Times Magazine*, who wish they could live in Gaviotas or start their own in the United States.

I have since returned twice, once overland, and again, during August, 1996, in Pepe Gómez's old single-engine Piper Dakota, now owned by a neighboring rancher. That flight was advisable because much of the road lay submerged during that torrential time of year, and because sections of it—especially the stretch across the Andes between Bogotá and Villavicencio—were under siege by guerrillas. Since then, Colombia's political pains have not eased; nevertheless, Gaviotas continues to advance. The resin factory's boiler, fueled by culls from their own forest, has been tuned successfully to emit no visible smoke. Its co-generating two-cylinder steam engine, now installed, portends to be so efficient that the diesel plant that long augmented the ten-kilowatt micro-hydro turbines can finally be junked, making Gaviotas at last self-sufficient in energy. As a result, Gaviotas was awarded the 1997 World Prize in Zero Emissions from ZERI, the United Nations' Zero Emissions Research Initiative.

That same year, in response to a nationwide scarcity due to ever-increasing demand for that singular Colombian delicacy, edible colony ants, Gaviotas designated a portion of its savanna as a preserve for this species of six-legged wildlife.

In another, more surprising move toward complete sustainability, Gaviotas has elected to sell its cattle herd and apply new, modular techniques for raising rabbits, chickens, and fish. These systems, more efficient than husbandry technologies available back when the Peace Corps was in residence, will be run as private enterprises by Gaviotans, in what they hope will be a healthy economic mixture with their cooperative forestry and resin industry. "It also exemplifies our recognition," Paolo Lugari told me, "that too much red meat is bad for us, that too many cow pastures are bad for the environment, and that too much *hamburgerización* is bad for the world."

The world: It has come a long way since my friendship with a Colombian journalist who worked for the Soviets had her colleagues trying to convince her that I was a C.I.A. agent, and had the U.S. Embassy warning me about consorting with Communist spies. Yet the fading of the Cold War has revealed clearly that a far more incandescent and protracted battle—a potentially apocalyptic resource war—has been stealthily gathering intensity throughout the latter part of the twentieth century. Despite sustained efforts to mobilize all human wisdom and will in defense of nature and sanity, we have yet to quench the flames that consume our forests, or to dampen the greed that stokes our excesses.

Yet a place like Gaviotas bears witness to our ability to get it right, even under seemingly insurmountable circumstances. With these pages I have returned to the inspiration Gaviotas embodies to replenish my own hopes. May we all journey there, again and again, to bring its promise home and spread it afar.

~

Postscript to the 10th Anniversary Edition

THE NEWLY PLANTED PALMS, ONLY A DOZEN, WERE MAYBE FOUR FEET HIGH: a single line of green pinnate fronds spaced thirty feet apart. So far, it didn't look like much, but Paolo Lugari was positively beaming as he hopped over to inspect, the tip of his cane punching swirls of red dust from llano soil that had been broken only the day before. "How many will you plant per hectare, Oto?"

Afterword

"Just forty-three," replied Otoniel Carreño. "A hundred fewer than in a monocultured plantation. Gives the seedlings plenty of sun and space to grow—and room for company later."

"*Excelente*," boomed Paolo. "The agriculture of the future will be the art of taking advantage of light. And," he added, brandishing his aluminum cane at the impressive botanical display rising around us, "it will be a polyculture."

We were standing in the forest that had bloomed in what twenty-five years earlier had been a monotonously treeless plain. More than a decade had passed since I'd last been here. Otoniel, his moustache grayer but still looking trim in jeans and a white shirt with the Gaviotas yellow-green logo on the breast pocket, was a ruddy testament to a healthy life led outdoors. Paolo, now in his mid-sixties, seemed indefatigable as ever, although slowed somewhat after shattering several bones in his foot on a slick Bogotá street a few years earlier. But if they were aging on a normal timescale, the Gaviotas forest had assumed a pace all its own.

It was nearly half again as big as when I'd last seen it: expanded by another three thousand hectares. Most impressive, however, was how native foliage was swallowing the original pines. A riot of jacarandas, ficus, *yopos*, monkey pods, *tunos blancos*, curare, laurels, and various ferns all but concealed the neat rows of *Pinus caribaea* among them. Although a plantation, it looked far more like a wild forest. And it was: not only deer, anteaters, and capybaras lived here, but tapir were frequently spotted and even an occasional puma.

Were the pines being overwhelmed, I wondered, by competition from primordial species that had sprouted in the shelter of their understory?

"On the contrary," Otoniel replied. "The mix of plants has just made the soil better. These pines were planted in 1983. Last time you were here, we were tapping them for resin. They've kept growing—some are more than thirty meters* tall. They're so robust, they're ready to be tapped again."

Except the Gaviotas resin crews were currently miles away, harvesting liquid amber resin from mature trees I remembered as seedlings smaller than these palms. It might take years before they cycled back to this parcel, Otoniel said. Meanwhile, they were trying something new here. Using a bladed roller they'd specially designed, they had mowed and mulched a

---

*about 100 feet

swathe of native underbrush, spaded it into the soil, and planted African oil palms. They were betting that, like their astonishingly productive pines, this commercial crop—now cultivated throughout the world's tropics for cooking oil, and lately for biofuel—would grow far better among other plants that contributed natural nutrients to the soil.

It was definitely more natural than the artificially fertilized monocultures I'd recently flown over en route to Gaviotas. From the eastern skirts of the Andes, I'd seen thousands of hectares of African palm plantations filling what had been cattle pastures a decade earlier. But were non-native African palms—and, for that matter, biofuels—a good idea? Weren't tropical forests and sustenance farmland, from Indonesia to Africa to Colombia itself, being lost to exotic energy crops at a shocking rate?

"*Sí*," agreed Paolo. "There's no justification for displacing one square centimeter of native forest for biodiesel. Nor of food production. First come mouths, then motors. But that's not what we're doing here."

The difference, he said, was that virtually no trees, let alone food crops, prospered in Colombia's rain-leached eastern savannas until Gaviotans learned to cultivate *Pinus caribaea* here. When a native forest sprouted in their shade from seeds brought by winds, birds, and animals from jungles along Orinocan streams, they'd discussed trying coffee and rubber trees in the replenishing soils among the pine rows. Then in 2003, while Lugari was in Boulder to give a speech, he met University of Colorado engineers who proposed a Gaviotas biodiesel project.

They'd taken him to see a biodiesel plant that used vegetable oil and recycled restaurant grease. The technology seemed straightforward. "I'm sure we can tropicalize this," Paolo declared. Colombian land barons were already raising African palm for the rich yields of edible oils from its fruit and kernels. Why couldn't it work for fuel?

A year later, a team of Colorado volunteers arrived. In three weeks, they and the Gaviotans built what, as far as anyone involved knew, was the world's first biodiesel plant that used palm oil.

They did not build it at Gaviotas, however, but at the Bogotá factory where Gaviotas made solar collectors, windmills, and pumps. This was at a time when civil unrest in Colombia had escalated ferociously. The llanos around Gaviotas were considered too perilous for foreign visitors in a country where kidnapping had become a major fund-raising activity for both left-wing guerrillas and right-wing paramilitaries. With ransoms for North Americans sometimes exceeding a million dollars, their presence would have made defenseless Gaviotas even more vulnerable.

The eastern savannas' notoriety as a no-man's-land where lawless bands roamed was the main reason Gaviotas hadn't grown as planned since I'd last been here. Rumors abounded of civilian massacres and war taxes extorted or vehicles seized by one group or another for their respective political causes. It was difficult to know what was exaggerated and what was true. Some of the worst confirmed violence was in the oil-rich provinces of Arauca and Casanare to the north of Vichada, but the entire llano was considered dangerous.

Perhaps because Gaviotas remained famously unarmed, no one there had been harmed by the mayhem that bedeviled other parts of the country. Nevertheless, they sold the trucks that once brought their pine resin to market, and hired contract transporters who charged accordingly for the risk of traveling the treacherous road between Vichada and Bogotá.

As the new century turned, once again the ongoing tragedy of Colombia displaced huge populations: more than two million internal refugees, at the time second only to Sudan. At least 1.5 million more fled the country altogether. With human rights workers, journalists, union leaders, and even innocent TV personalities being assassinated—the last presumably because their celebrity focused attention on the perpetrators' demands—Gaviotas kept as low a profile as possible. Postponed along with the proposed satellite village of Odisea was a Gaviotas Internet site: the less visibility the better, all agreed.

Yet survival still required making a living, often a challenge when clients for Gaviotas' pine resin were ensnared by fiscal crises that deepened along with the civil disorder. "It has taken," said Paolo dryly, "a great deal of imagination."

And flexibility, a trait at which Gaviotas fortunately excelled. Hence, the biodiesel plant: a collection of 5,000-liter vats, pipes, and galvanized tanks I'd toured in Bogotá before we'd boarded a single-engine Cessna for a visit to Gaviotas. It produced high-quality vegetable diesel from palm oil they bought from local growers—an achievement which, like some other Gaviotas experiments over the years, was impressive but not necessarily profitable.

Lugari shook his head, chuckling. "When the group from Colorado came, we could get crude palm oil for $450 per ton. That was before the world discovered that hydrogenated oils are a bad idea." Suddenly, industrial food processors began snatching up palm oil—which, though highly saturated, contained no trans fats. "In the past three years, the price of edible palm oil nearly tripled. Economically, refining it into biodiesel makes no sense."

Nevertheless, as he and Otoniel were now telling me, given the disastrous costs of atmospheric carbon dioxide, renewable biodiesel from palms grown where nothing else normally grew anyway might make sense after all— especially in a world where petroleum cost more daily. As if to underscore that point, a grizzled Pompilio Arciniegas, the government forester who, I was pleased to see, had still never left Gaviotas, rode up on a motor scooter.

"I thought this was strictly bicycle country," I said, shaking hands.

"No longer possible with a tree farm this big," Pompilio replied.

They'd built several gossamer, light-weight fire lookout towers of steel lattice anchored with guy wires, which were manned continuously. But for a fire-fighting crew to respond to an alarm by bicycle in a forest this extensive would be suicidal.

"By far, Gaviotas' biggest success of the past ten years," said Paolo, "is keeping thousands of hectares of pure fuel from burning down."

Their mechanized needs went beyond fire prevention. Gaviotas had stayed alive by becoming an agro-industrial cooperative, and the industry part meant tractors, mulchers, plows, and disks as well as motor scooters. Their biodiesel factory in Bogotá could produce enough to run them all. But rather than keep buying costly crude palm oil to refine, they'd calculated that with thirty hectares of fast-growing African palms planted in the fertile soil between their pine rows, in a few years they could produce all their own. "We'll be completely self-sustaining in fuel—self-sustaining *and* non-polluting," Paolo said. "And we'll have enough oil left over for cooking."

It was an ambitious plan, and it had already spawned another even bigger. ZERI—the same international Zero Emissions Research and Initiatives foundation that had awarded Gaviotas its world clean energy award in 1997—had approached the Colombian government. In Vichada and the neighboring province of Meta alone, there were millions of empty hectares similar to the terrain around Gaviotas. Why not plant them in pines, palms, and whatever else nature added, to capture carbon dioxide and to produce clean, renewable diesel for the whole country?

The government was interested. Soon ZERI founder Gunter Pauli, who as a young man had accompanied Club of Rome founder Aurelio Peccei to Gaviotas, was being flown with his staff and key guests by Colombian Air Force officials to see what Gaviotas had done. From there, they traveled to inspect Marandúa: the same 70,000-hectare military preserve on the Río Tomo, halfway to the Venezuelan border, where former president Belisario Betancur had once dreamed of starting a Gaviotas forest writ large, to resettle thousands of displaced Colombians from the nation's overwhelmed cities and employ them in a new Colombian capital of the plains.

In a country as politically complex as Colombia, whether the dream will actually materialize this time depends on multiple factors, not the least of which is securing financing for what could be the biggest sustainability project in the world. But the very fact that the dream had not died when horrific national events overwhelmed it two decades earlier heartened me. And what Paolo Lugari took me to see next further confirmed that at Gaviotas, dreams that hang on long enough could finally come true.

"I'll be damned. You actually did it."

We were entering a tall parabolic tent, sort of a canvas Quonset hut appended to the Gaviotas resin factory. Inside, tethered by nylon ropes was the biggest silver bullet I'd ever seen. At last, the Gaviotas dirigible.

"You like it? We built it ourselves, with no technical assistance."

The zeppelin, sleek and gorgeous, was 65 feet long and 10 feet wide. It was made of mylar, polyurethane, and polyethylene, purchased with $50,000 in grants from the United Nations and the Colombian government. It was not, however, serving the purpose originally contemplated: lighter-than-air shipment of pine resin across the llanos, to save gasoline.

"We hadn't grasped the technical difficulty, nor the cost, of a dirigible big enough to carry that much freight, plus a crew." This one, operated by remote control, carried only an infrared video camera that monitored hot spots in the forest before they turned into forest fires. Aloft, it could scan 4,000 hectares at once.

The idea of deriving hydrogen from water to inflate it had also been scotched when the government meteorological station that once launched weather balloons at Gaviotas relocated, taking its electrolyzer with it. "We're using helium. Maybe some day we'll figure out how fill it with hot air by tapping factory exhaust."

We had already toured the co-generating boiler, fired by culls from the Gaviotas forest, that provided heat to process pine resin and whose vaporous exhaust spun a turbine that electrified the entire village. In the processing plant, I found Hernán Landaeta still in charge, directing a dozen men hauling pallets heaped with aromatic bags of newly harvested pine resin. He guided me over to a new Gaviotas brainchild.

It was a tubular steel column, which, Landaeta explained, functioned much like an oil refinery distillation tower. But instead of fractionating crude petroleum into different densities ranging from tar to gasoline to natural gas, it separated refined pine resin into eighteen new potential products, from natural chewing-gum base to varnish-grade colophony to pine-oil disinfectant.

These new derivatives were born of necessity. Until 2007, the Colombian paint industry had purchased nearly all of Gaviotas' annual resin harvest. Then China entered the market in typically colossal fashion: with 500,000 tons of resin from pine forests in its rural west, lately being subsidized by Beijing to develop at the breathtaking pace of its eastern provinces. Though less refined than high-grade Gaviotas colophony, the Chinese product was adequate for paint manufacture, and it sent prices plummeting.

"So we've had to diversify," Paolo said, cradling a flask of pine-oil floor cleaner in his thick fingers. "We're think of manufacturing our own brand of sugar-free gum. How does *Chicle Gaviotero* sound?

After what I saw next, it sounded possible. The former Gaviotas hospital had been transformed—though not, as they'd hoped a decade earlier, into a medicinal plants research center: The violence whipping through the Colombian llanos had deferred that project as well. But another idea discussed back then now promised to join pine resin, solar panels, windmills, and pumps as a viable way to sustain their village.

The ex-hospital had become a bottling plant for Gaviotas mineral water—whose purity, according to a sheaf of tests by an eminent Tokyo laboratory, was exceptional. The plant's young director, Andrea Beltrán, who led me through bottle purification chambers that were once maternity rooms, I remembered as Abraham Beltrán's shy pre-teen daughter. She had been to the city for school, but returned to Gaviotas as soon as she graduated.

The *maloca*, where Guahibo Indians once convalesced in hospital hammocks under a thatched roof, was missing. "We had to minimize possible sources of organic contaminants," Andrea explained.

No one had ever gotten sick from Gaviotas water, but this was a market necessity: Gaviotas Agua Natural Tropical had to follow federal sanitary production rules, because much of it was destined for restaurants. In the former surgery, a team of women glued labels onto bottles that read "Wok"—a fashionable Bogotá chain that served Asian food. More sophisticated bottling and labeling equipment was on its way. They'd just signed a contract, Lugari said, with Colombia's most famous brand: Café de Colombia's trademark coffee grower, Juan Valdez.

A national chain by that name, with outlets reminiscent of Seattle-based Starbucks but selling only Colombia's finest, would now also offer Agua Natural Tropical from Gaviotas. Paolo handed me a bottle with a logo showing the mustachioed *cafetero* with his sombrero and burro.

"Water from forty meters deep, filtered through a hundred kilometers of sand, with no agricultural chemicals anywhere near and surrounded by a forest," boasted Lugari, draining his in two swallows. "Have you ever tasted better?"

The bottle itself was yet another innovation: instead of the typical cylinder, it was a four-sided prism with two round indentations on one side matched by rounded protrusions on the opposite face. The design allowed bottles to interlock—an inspiration that came to Paolo one morning as he watched his housekeeper's son playing with Lego blocks. Besides being far easier to ship and stack on store shelves, instead of being thrown away, children were collecting them.

"They call them *Legos de los pobres*—poor people's Legos," Lugari told me. At Gaviotas they were also filling them with sand to use as bricks to build walls.

Ingenious, I admitted. But they were still plastic.

"We use recyclable polyethylene."

"But how many people actually recycle them?"

"It's part of our contract with the Juan Valdez restaurants. Every time we deliver a shipment, we take back all the empties that people don't save for their kids."

A smart plan, and the trick of turning potential trash into toys was surely charming. But plastic was still a petroleum product, one that nature had yet to learn how to digest, and sooner or later most, if not all, of these bottles would end up in waste streams that had nowhere good to flow.

"True," said Paolo. "Unless . . ."

I'd seen the flash of an idea illumine his eyes before. "Unless what?

"Unless we learn to make biodegradable plastic out of renewable palm oil."

"That's the plan?"

"The plan is to try. Look," he said, "if you drank two bottles of this water a day for twenty-five years, we calculate that the money you spend would help us regenerate nine hectares of forest that absorb 165 tons of carbon dioxide. Even if we can't make them from palm oil, their impact will clearly be compensated a thousand times by all the trees we're planting."

Possibly. It was at least clear that selling gourmet water could be a financial windfall to Gaviotas as it tried to survive and even thrive—sustainably, no less—on an increasingly precarious global stage. Happily, we were interrupted at this point by the appearance of Teresa Valencia, *la profesora*, who'd come to fetch us for lunch.

Lush gallery jungle shaded the road that led to the center of Gaviotas. Green parrots and saffron kiskadees zipped through air thick with humidity, signaling that the rains were nearing. Next to the small bridge that crossed the Caño Urimica, two Gaviotans were bathing their baby son in the shallow stream; nearby stood a pair of whistling herons, their long necks swiveling like periscopes as we passed. Somewhere high in the canopy, I could hear monkeys leaping.

Alonso Gutiérrez, Teresa told me, was still employed in the coffee industry, returning to Gaviotas as work permitted. Sometimes they met in Villavicencio, where their daughter, Natalia, was now in secondary school.

"She was just a baby—"

"I know. I wish you could see her. She's a real *gaviotera*."

"Like her mom."

A few years earlier, when Juan David Bernal's recurring health problems forced his family to return to Bogotá, Teresa seemed the logical choice to replace Gonzalo as coordinator—except, as she pointed out, there really wasn't a need for one. Everyone knew what needed to be done, and everyone did his or her job. Still, many village administrative details had fallen to her, and a new teacher had arrived from Cartagena to run the primary school. Teresa still taught; at lunch, a dozen schoolchildren flocked around her to report on the morning's art projects.

We ate fish salad made from native *cachama* that Gaviotas now raised in its own ponds. I was surprised that the vegetables weren't hydroponic: During the worst of the recent civil disorder, with the whole country's finances reeling, they'd decided to forgo the cost of hydroponic nutrients. Instead, they bought lettuce, carrots, tomatoes, and leeks from neighbors who'd learned to coax them from savanna soils fortified with kitchen ashes and manure from chicken and hogs.

It was hard to imagine Gaviotas without hydroponics, and apparently I wasn't alone. Everyone missed the ready supply of spinach, radishes, cilantro, parsley, onions, and beets, which didn't do well in local truck gardens. "We'll

bring it back, as our new products start earning," said Paolo. "We've been
researching organic hydroponics that use no artificial chemicals. If we can
make soil in our forest, why can't we make our own nutrients? It's another
technology we can share with our neighbors."

I'd learned to take any idea broached at Gaviotas seriously, no matter
how improbable. Even those that failed often led to something that worked.
On the lawn by the community center, Pompilio showed me the latest,
in response to a neighbor's request for a really cheap pump to tap shallow
groundwater for his garden. They'd sunk an eight-inch PVC pipe four meters
into the ground, and attached a lever that lifted and dropped a flap covering
the pipe's exposed end. Each time Pompilio pumped, water gurgled closer
until finally it gushed over the top. It was little more than a giant soda straw,
and worked on basically the same principle.

The population of Gaviotas, around 200, was nearly the same as when
I'd last visited, but its economy sustained more than 2,000 people in the
surrounding area, many of them indigenous Guahibos. Llaneros still brought
children to the Gaviotas school. Some had grown and stayed, others went to
the city and remained Gaviotans, sometimes working in the Bogotá factory
that produced windmills, pumps, and solar collectors, and now biodiesel.
Although a subsequent Colombian president had removed the Gaviotas
solar water heaters that ex-president Belisario Betancur installed years earlier
at his official residence—reminiscent of Ronald Reagan yanking Jimmy
Carter's solar panels from the White House roof—Lugari considered it a
hopeful portent that that among their most recent solar energy customers in
Bogotá was the U.S. Embassy.

Obligatory solar water heaters, networks of bike lanes, redoubled mass
transit, rooftop agriculture, vegetable-based plastics, urban services within
walking distance, and trees planted wherever possible: He hadn't given
up believing that existing cities could become sustainable. But the chance
to start from scratch in this big empty savanna was clearly Paolo Lugari's
passion.

"I still dream of us building Odisea," he said as we headed to the airstrip, escorted by a throng of bicycle-mounted Gaviotans. "People were scared to move way out here. Or they went to Arauca and Casanare because they thought they could make money in the oil fields. Or they just settled on the first vacant land they found—there's still so much before you reach Gaviotas. But it will happen. Today we started growing energy in our pine resin forest. If we can do that, we can grow food, too. Some rice varieties don't need irrigation. Same with cassava, corn, bananas. Even soy. We'll fertilize with residues from the biodiesel plant. And we'll nurture mycorrhizas—they can make everything grow here."

Our plane made a circle over the spreading Gaviotas forest. The pines around the verdant *morichal* at Odisea were no longer the young shrubs I'd last seen there, but tall trees. Between them, the surrounding dry yellow llano grass disappeared beneath a deep green tangle of native flora. We made a last pass over the village, dipping a wing to the waving cyclists below, then banked toward the Andes. The savanna before us seemed big as an ocean—except oceans don't burn, and this one was ablaze, dusting the sky with chalky haze.

Lugari turned to me from the copilot's seat. "Every year they burn the llano before the rains, to free potassium so that poor savanna grass can support a few scrawny cattle. Thousands of tons of CO_2 released just to put one cow on every hundred hectares."

Through the smoke, I could see a jagged orange line creeping to the edge of the big *caño* at Carimagua. I pointed to some *moriche* and *ceje* palms in flames.

"So stupid." Paolo gestured at the charred ground below. "Have you read that article I gave you?"

I had. The Colombian business magazine *Dinero* estimated that with a million hectares of African palm, Colombia could meet all its demand for diesel.

"There's at least six million hectares burning down there. There are forty million more in Colombia, empty and available for growing palms, pines, and all kinds of food. If people want animals, we can use low-impact African sheep that don't graze down to the roots like goats. If we reforest all the tropical savannas, we can soak up CO_2—and, by making fuel from palm oil, we can stop adding more."

"I thought using palm oil for biofuel is ridiculously expensive."

"At today's price, yes. But growing it in a polyculture like ours, on land that's otherwise wasted, isn't ridiculous: it's intelligent. It's a crime to tear down Africa's jungles to grow fuel. In Europe or the United States, it's absurd to sacrifice food for biodiesel from corn, sugar beets, or sunflowers. But Latin America's savannas are the most unexploited soils in the world. We could plant all year and continually harvest different crops from a healthy, biodiverse system."

The smoke thickened around us. We were nearing the Andes, but haze had swallowed the mountains and the civilization climbing their skirts. An hour earlier, I'd stood in a clean, fragrant forest that felt so vast—millions of trees not even thirty years old, yet already so high and so varied. But now Gaviotas seemed miniscule compared to the world of troubles that surrounded it. Was it truly an example to show us how to reinvent our world? Or was it just a sweet, irrelevant anomaly—an island of sanity because of its isolation, like a sage whose safeguards his wisdom in a remote cave?

The pilot taxied to a stop, then cut the engine. The predominant fragrance was once again tarmac and fumes.

Paolo sighed. "You know," he said, I've never wanted Gaviotas to be some kind of eco-doll house, or pilot project, or some toy for NGOs. I want it to show the world how to fortify an ecosystem. Sometimes I think biodiesel may be the most important chance we have. People would be planting, not exhuming energy. They'd be restoring the planet's living skin. The atmosphere's equilibrium depends on the planet's biomass. Biofuel may be the only way to keep atmospheric chemistry in balance and global warming in check."

Was he dreaming? Could we really have our engines and our world, too?

"We have to keep dreaming," Paolo answered. "If you're not dreaming, then you're asleep. The real crisis isn't a lack of resources: It's a lack of imagination."

Afterword

The flash was back in his eyes. "Just imagine," he said, a smile starting to tug at his gray beard. "Imagine if everyone on earth were required to plant at least three trees . . ."

ALAN WEISMAN
May, 2008

For ongoing information:
http://www.friendsofgaviotas.org
http://www.centrolasgaviotas.org

Acknowledgments

~

I am ever indebted to friends and colleagues who propped me up and propelled me forward: Betsy Gammons, Nancy Grey Postero, Cecilia Vaisman, and Sandy Tolan of Homelands Productions, and Pat Flynn, for years our editor at National Public Radio; Jim Schley, my patient and prescient editor at Chelsea Green; Mary McNamara, my editor and oracle at the *Los Angeles Times Magazine*, and Bret Israel, that journal's gutsy and resourceful former editor-in-chief; herpetologist Bill Lamar, my tropical counsel; Kristie Graham, Annie McGreevy, Grant Abert, and Nancy Ward, whose extraordinary generosity kept me fueled and fed; Constanza Vieira Quijano, who first showed me Gaviotas and whose loyal friendship defines for me the warmth and brilliance of her country; and Juana and Felipe Osorio, whose hospitality, humor, youth, and intelligence hold the promise for Colombia's future.

Beckie Kravetz, my wife, contributed her incisive artist's eye, imagination, and inspiration to every moment. I can never thank her enough, but I'll keep trying.

And timeless, bottomless thanks to *los gavioteros*, the Gaviotans themselves, who transported me into their astonishing, loving lives. You wrote these pages, and you continue to produce more, and more. To Jorge Zapp, for invaluable materials of his own authorship and labor. To Paolo Lugari Castrillón, for daring to imagine that the only job worth doing is making our dreams come true.

Bibliography

Avellaneda, Mario, et al. *La Macarena, Reserva Biológica de la Humanidad, Territorios en Conflicto*. Bogotá: Universidad Nacional de Colombia, 1989.

Bergquist, Charles, Ricardo Peñaranda, and Gonzalo Sánchez. *Violence in Colombia*. Wilmington: Scholarly Resources, Inc., 1992.

Berman, Daniel M., and John T. O'Connor. *Who Owns the Sun? People, Politics, and the Struggle for a Solar Economy*. White River Junction, Vermont: Chelsea Green Publishing Company, 1996.

Bernal, Gonzalo L. *La Sonrisa de Los Bosques*. Obra inédita, 1995.

Duviols, Jean-Paul, and Rubén Bareiro Saguier. *Tentación de la Utopía: Las Misiones Jesuíticas del Paraguay*. Barcelona: Tusquets/Círculo, 1991.

Hilty, Steven L., and William L. Brown. *Birds of Colombia*. Princeton, N.J.: Princeton University Press, 1986.

Johansson, Thomas B., et al. *Renewable Energy*. Washington, D.C.: Island Press, 1993.

Martín, Miguel Angel. *Del Folclor Llanero*. Bogotá: Ediciones Marsala, 1993.

Meadows, Donella H., et al. *The Limits to Growth*. New York: Universe Books, 1972.

Meadows, Donella H., Dennis L. Meadows, and Jørgen Randers. *Beyond the Limits: Confronting Global Collapse, Envisioning a Sustainable Future*. White River Junction, Vermont: Chelsea Green Publishing Company, 1992.

McNish, Thomas. *Aves del Llano*. Bogotá: Villegas Editores, 1992.

Olivares, Antonio. *Aves de la Orinoquia*. Bogotá: Universidad Nacional de Colombia/Centro Las Gaviotas, 1982.

Pauli, Gunter A. *Crusader for the Future: A Portrait of Aurelio Peccei, Founder of the Club of Rome*. New York: Pergamon Press, 1987.

Peccei, Aurelio, et al. *Development in a World of Peace: Club of Rome Bogotá Conference*. Bogotá: Club of Rome/Banco Hipotecario Central, 1984.

Philipson, W. R. *The Immaculate Forest*. New York: Philosophical Library, 1952.

Rubio Recio, J. M. *El Orinoco y Los Llanos*. Madrid: Ediciones Anaya, S.A., 1988.

Sánchez, Gonzalo, ed. *Colombia, Violencia y Democracia*. Bogotá: Universidad Nacional de Colombia/COLCIENCIAS, 1988.

Tecnologías en la Erradicación de la Pobreza, Vols. I–III. Bogotá: Programa de Las Naciones Unidas para el Desarrollo, 1989.

Thais, Luis, et al. *Development Without Poverty*. Bogotá: United Nations Development Programme, 1991.

Uribe Hurtado, Cristina. *Anfibios y Reptiles del Llano*. Bogotá: Cristina Uribe Editores, 1994.

Zapp, Jorge. *Cultivos Sin Tierra*. Bogotá: Programa de Las Naciones Unidas para el Desarrollo, 1991.

Zapp, Jorge. *Empresas Virtuales Populares*. Bogotá: Programa de Las Naciones Unidas para el Desarrollo, 1994.

Zethelius, Magnus, and Michael J. Balick. "Modern Medicine and Shamanistic Ritual: A Case of Positive Synergistic Response in the Treatment of a Snakebite." *Journal of Ethnopharmacology* (Lausanne) 5 (1982): 181–85.

ABOUT THE AUTHOR

ALAN WEISMAN'S REPORTS FROM AROUND THE WORLD HAVE APPEARED in *Harper's*, the *New York Times Magazine, The Atlantic Monthly, The Los Angeles Times Magazine, Orion, Wilson Quarterly, Vanity Fair, Audubon, Mother Jones, Discover, Condé Nast Traveler, Resurgence,* and *Best American Science Writing.* His previous books include *The World Without Us,* an international bestseller and National Book Critics Circle finalist translated into more than thirty languages; *An Echo in My Blood;* and *La Frontera: The United States Border With Mexico.*

Weisman's documentaries have aired on National Public Radio, Public Radio International, and American Public Media. A senior producer for Homelands Productions, he is also a Laureate Professor in Journalism and Latin American Studies at the University of Arizona, where he leads an annual field program in international journalism.

Among his awards are the Harry Chapin/World Hunger Year Award, a Robert F. Kennedy Citation, and Brazil's Prèmio Nacional de Jornalismo Radiofônico, shared with his Homelands Productions colleagues, and the Social Inventions Award from the London-based Global Ideas Bank for *Gaviotas.* He and his wife, sculptor Beckie Kravetz, live in western Massachusetts.

81 No Dogs
88 Windmill 93
91 Windmill pix

94

116 Solar Refrigerator, Absorbtion
134
142
152 Lunar Collector ?
161 Caño Urimica, 188 Rio Muco, Rio Rojo
178 169 Cholophony (Resin) 170 Turpentine

202 Resin Processing

204 Remote access Pump, Double Hydraulic

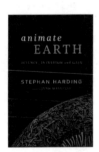
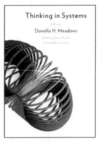
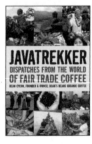